COTTON IN TANZANIA
Breaking the Jinx

Joe C. B. Kabissa, BSc, MSc, PhD
Former Head of Cotton R & D at Ilonga; Zonal Director of Research & Training, Lake Zone and Director General, Tanzania Cotton Board. Currently Executive Director, Kamal – Agro Co. Ltd.

TANZANIA EDUCATIONAL PUBLISHERS LTD

Tanzania Educational Publishers Ltd,
TEPU House,
Uganda road, Plot No. 45 Block MDA,
Tel/Fax: 028-2220833,
Email: tepultd@yahoo.com
Website: www.teputz.com
P.O. Box 1222,
Bukoba, Tanzania.

ISBN 978-9987-07-007-7

DEDICATION

I dedicate this book to members of my family: my wife, Agnes; my children, Nikusubira Kabissa, Joyce Kulembeka, Ulisaja Kabissa, Jeremiah Kabissa, Jessica Gondwe and Ceasor Kabissa; my grand children, Ambokile, Agnes, Levina, Jock, Jocelyn, Joenice and Joela; and to all cotton stakeholders in Tanzania without whose inspiration and support this book would have not come about.

Map of Cotton Areas

COTTON PRODUCING REGIONS IN TANZANIA

LIST OF CONTENTS

CHAPTER ONE

CHAPTER TWO

CHAPTER THREE

CHAPTER FOUR

LIST OF TABLES

LIST OF BOXES

ABBREVIATIONS AND ACRONYMS

AD	Agricultural Department
AE	Advanced Economies
AGOA	African Growth Opportunity Act
AMC	Agricultural Marketing Cooperatives
ASDP	Agricultural Sector Development Programme
BCU	Biharamulo Cooperative Union
BCGA	British Cotton Growers Association
BOT	Bank of Tanzania
Bt	*Bacillus thuringiensis*
CAN	Calcium Ammonium Nitrate
CBT	Cashewnut Board of Tanzania
CCM	Chama Cha Mapinduzi
CDA	Controlled Droplet Application
CF	Contract Farming
CFC	Common Fund for Commodities
C4	Countries - Benin, Burkina Faso, Mali & Chad

CDF	Cotton Development Fund
CDTF	Cotton Development Trust Fund
CIF	Cost, Insurance and Freight
C & F	Cost & Freight
CFA	Franc de la Communaute Financiere Africaine
CORECU	Coast Region Cooperative Union
CRC	Cotton Research Corporation
CRMP	Cooperative Reform & Modernization Programme
CSDS	Cotton Sector Development Strategy
CSITC	Commercial Standardization of Instrument Testing of Cotton
CTDP	Cotton and Textile Development Program
CTI	Confederation of Trade and Industries
CTF	Cotton Trust Fund
CUF	Civic United Front
DDA	Doha Development Agenda
DDT	Dichlorodiphenyltrichloroethane
DE	Developing Economies
EBA	Everything But Arms
ECGC	Empire Cotton Growing Corporation
ECGA	Eastern Cotton Growing Area
ELS	Extra Long Staple
EPZ	Export Processing Zone
ESA	Entomological Society of America
EU	European Union
EWURA	Energy, Water and Utilities Regulatory Authority
FAO	Food and Agricultural Organization

FOB	Free On Board
FOT	Free On Truck
FBG	Farmer Business Group
GCF	Gatsby Charitable Foundation
GDP	Gross Domestic Product
GEC	Genetically Engineered Cotton
GMO	Genetically Modified Organism
GOT	Government of Tanzania
GOT	Ginning Out-Turn
HPR	Host Plant Resistance
HVI	High Volume Instrument
HYV	High Yielding Variety
ICA	International Cotton Association
ICAC	International Cotton Advisory Committee
ICRAF	International Centre for Research in Agro forestry
IM	International Merchants
IMI	International Multilateral Institutions
IPM	Integrated Pest Management
ITMF	International Textile Manufacturers Federation
KACU	Kahama Cooperative Union
KNCU	Kilimanjaro Native Cooperative Union
KWK	Kolonial –Wirtschaftliches-Komitee
LC	Letter of Credit
LGA	Local Government Authority
MAFC	Ministry of Agriculture Food and Cooperatives
MC	Multinational Corporation
MCM	Ministry of Cooperatives and Marketing

MDGs	Millennium Development Goals
MMF	Man Made Fibres
NARS	National Agricultural Research Service
NEMC	National Environment Management Council
NCU	Nyanza Cooperative Union
NGO	Non-Government Organization
NIS	National Input Scheme
NCU	Nyanza Cooperative Union
NGO	Non-Government Organization
ODA	Overseas Development Administration
OECD	Organization for Economic Cooperation and Development
PBW	Pink bollworm
PP	Polypropylene
PPP	Public–Private - Partnership
PS	Primary Society
PTA	Preferential Trade Area
PSRO	Product Specific Rules of Origin
R & D	Research & Development
RCU	Regional Cooperative Union
ROO	Rules of Origin
SA	Sulphate of Ammonia
SADC	Southern African Development Community
SACCOS	Savings and Credit Cooperative Societies
SAP	Structural Adjustment Program
SHIRECU	Shinyanga Region Cooperative Union
SR	Special Rule
SSA	Sub-Saharan Africa
SSRA	Social Security Regulatory Authority

SUA	Sokoine University of Agriculture
SUMATRA	Surface and Marine Transport Regulatory Authority
TACOGA	Tanzania Cotton Growers Association
TBS	Tanzania Bureau of Standards
TCA	Tanzania Cotton Association
TCA	Tanzania Cotton Authority
TCB	Tanzania Cotton Board
TCMB	Tanzania Cotton Marketing Board
TCLSB	Tanzania Cotton Lint and Seed Board
TCRA	Tanzania Communications Regulatory Authority
TDT	Technology Development and Transfer
TGT	Tanzania Gatsby Trust
TEXMAT	Textile Manufacturers Association of Tanzania
TLSMB	Tanganyika Lint and Seed Marketing Board
TOSCI	Tanzania Official Seed Certification Institute
TPRI	Tanzania Pesticides Research Institute
ULV	Ultra Low Volume
URT	United Republic of Tanzania
USA	United States of America
VAS	Village Auction System
VETA	Vocational Education Training Authority
VFCU	Victoria Federation of Cooperative Unions
VLV	Very Low Volume
WB	World Bank
WCGA	Western Cotton Growing Area
WRS	Warehouse Receipt System
WTO	World Trade Organization

ACKNOWLEDGEMENTS

In May 2006, the former Prime Minister of the United Republic of Tanzania, Edward Lowassa, convened a series of stakeholders' meetings at the Karimjee Hall in Dar es Salaam to review the production trends of selected cash crops in Tanzania. A major recurring theme of the meetings was the need to raise the production levels of such crops. In the case of cotton, stakeholders were challenged to treble the then average yield of 750 kg of seed cotton per ha by 2015. That implied raising cotton output from a previous all-time high of 126,000 tons of lint obtained during the 2005/06 marketing season to 270,000 tons of lint by 2015.

After one brainstorming session on how to attain a production target set out for the Sengerema district of Mwanza region, I found myself engaged in a protracted debate with William Kasubi,the late Secretary General of the Tanzania Cotton Growers Association, on why cotton yields had remained quite low in Tanzania inspite of new advances in production technology. In the course of our discussion, Kasubi had unexpectedly asked me, I quote, "you have been with the cotton industry for quite a long time now, how about sharing some of your knowledge and experiences on cotton with others?" unquote. I remember to have quickly answered in the affirmative because as of that point in time I had already begun sketching some ideas relating to cotton in Tanzania. And so his remark went on to solidify the need for this book.

I had first met Kasubi in the late 1970s when he visited the Ilonga Agricultural Research Institute as part of a mission commissioned to probe on the underperformance of the cotton industry at that time. We met again between 1993 and 1999 when I was Zonal Director of Research and Training for Lake Zone and from 1999 onwards when I was the Chief Executive Officer of the Tanzania Cotton Board. Cotton development increasingly became our major issue of discussion after he had become the Secretary General of the Tanzania Cotton Growers Association. After his tragic death on 24 June 2007 I became inspired to get on with the project all the more because we had quite passionately shared some of the frustrations as well as big aspirations relating to cotton development in Tanzania.

My special thanks go to my wife Agnes who quite strongly supported my initiative to write about cotton in Tanzania. As a one time cotton farmer herself she had witnessed first hand some of the challenges of growing cotton as well as some of the negative impacts of market liberalization. Thus, we quite often discussed and argued about cotton development in general. When I joined TCB, Agnes became quite bemused by the politics surrounding cotton. Perhaps more importantly, Agnes greatly helped to keep me calm when the going became quite tough and for putting my family together when I was out and about in the interests of the cotton industry.

Several people critically read and commented on earlier drafts of this book. Their comments and criticisms went on to greatly improve this book. I am very grateful to Raphael Mlolwa who was Chairman of TCB between 1999 and 2005 for his encouragement and critical comments on the manuscript. Marco Mtunga who took over from me as Chief Executive Officer of TCB in mid-2010 gave valuable and constructive comments on the manuscript.

I am indebted to Professor Graham Matthews for being an inspiration in my entomological career and for greatly improving the chapter on the red bollworm. I also wish to thank Laurent Cockcroft of the Gatsby Charitable Foundation for his moral support and especially for critically reading my manuscript and advising on several issues that went on to significantly improve on the outlook of the book. Dr. Colin

Poulton of the University of London School of Oriental and African Studies also critically read the manuscript and gave extremely valuable comments and editorial support.

Throughout this book I have quoted quite extensively cotton data originating from both the International Cotton Advisory Committee and TCB. I am very grateful to both institutions for making such data easily accessible to me. At the ICAC I also wish to offer my special thanks to Drs. Terry Townsend and Rafiq Chaudhry both of whom greatly inspired me to partake in panel discussions of the ICAC and to present papers during the technical sessions of its plenary meetings as well as at the World Cotton Research Conferences.

Finally, I am most grateful to the Government of Tanzania for granting me the opportunity to serve the nation during the different periods of my association with the agricultural sector; as research entomologist between 1975 and 1993, as Zonal Director of Research and Training for Lake Zone between 1993 and 1999 and finally as the Chief Executive Officer of the Tanzania Cotton Board between 1999 and 2010. During those periods I had the unique opportunity of working with a series of people whose ideas in one way or the other greatly helped to shape my own on cotton development.

Dar es Salaam   *Joe Cheguevara Barry Kabissa*
                                   22nd April, 2013

THE MEANING OF JINX

"Breaking the Jinx" is a subtitle of this book. As used in this book, the word "jinx" implies some kind of bad luck, spell or curse that had kind of befallen the cotton industry during the 20th century when cotton output in Tanzania failed to reach 100,000 tons of lint in spite of the enormous production potential that exists. And so when output finally went beyond 100,000 tons on three occasions during the first decade of the 21st century, most stakeholders sighed with relief hoping that the jinx had finally been broken. In this book an attempt is made to show how the jinx got broken.

A STATEMENT FROM THE FORMER CHAIRMAN OF TANZANIA COTTON BOARD

This book, is a very powerful description of Tanzanian cotton. Written in a matter of fact - way, against the background of the global and historical overviews, the book is an allegory of Tanzanian cotton and a true testimony of the behind the scenes actions and strategies in the development of the crop over more than a century. The account is hard to fault, having been written by an iconic professional in the Tanzania cotton industry; having literally grown in the cotton industry, spanning for a period of more than 30 years, first as a distinctive cotton researcher who steadfastly rose and ultimately attained the highest position of Chief Executive Officer and Director General of Tanzania Cotton Board (1999-2010).

- Raphael Nkuli Mlolwa, Chairman, Tanzania Cotton Board (2005-2009), a Senior Economist and former Advisor to President Benjamin Mkapa.

PREFACE

The international market for cotton represents a major opportunity for the small farmers of Tanzania and other African countries. Since the crop was introduced South of the Sahara in the late nineteenth century, its potential has remained high but has seldom been fulfilled. Today, African cotton producers struggle to maintain a share of world markets for cotton lint, and find it even harder to carve out a niche for textiles manufactured from home grown cotton.

This book tells the story of cotton in Tanzania, which illustrates both the potential of the crop and the factors which have held it back. It does not neglect the fact that Tanzania's largest ever cotton crop of 376,000 tons of seed cotton was achieved in 2005/06 or that government and farmers initiatives over time have been serious and have had some success. However, Joe Kabissa shows that whether in terms of 'Research and Development', the adoption of improved cultivation techniques or the institutional structure of both the cotton and textile sectors, there has been a consistent pattern of underperformance, acknowledged at different times by all the major players.

There has been a consistent demand for Africa's cotton. In the colonial period in Tanzania first the Germans and later the British were keen to see cotton lint supplied to their textile factories. Both governments applied varying degrees of compulsion or persuasion to the small farmers of the Lake Zone and the Coast to ensure an expansion of the crop. In the British period (1918-61) this was re-inforced by major investment in developing varieties of cotton with pest resistance which was partly successful and set the scene for the description of the crop as 'white gold' in the 1950s and 1960s, a time when the world price was high. However, average yields seldom rose above about 250kg per acre, a figure which is current today. Total production has been much more closely related to the area under cultivation than to rises and falls in yield. The element of compulsion which characterised the attitude of the colonial authorities to the crop has continued to characterise aspects of government policy in the fifty years since independence. This period has seen an acute politicisation of the crop as MPs have promoted supposedly vote winning strategies, often with negative consequences.

As a former cotton research scientist at Ilonga as well as a Director of Research and Training at Ukiriguru; both of which are Tanzania's key cotton research stations, Dr Kabissa is able to show that the research establishment had considerable success in combating diseases, bollworms and sucking pests and in particular the jassids. Varieties have been released over time which have enabled farmers to combat these major threats and, after early failures, have enabled cotton to be a competitor with other food and cash crops such as maize, oil seeds and rice. However, a bank of varieties with yet higher potential has only been partially realised and the case for the adoption of genetically modified cotton has not yet been resolved, whilst other countries such as South Africa and Burkina Faso have pressed ahead.

But, it is in its enquiry into the institutional issues surrounding the crop that this book is particularly rich. As the economics of the crop became more attractive in the 1950s small farmers in the Lake Zone and elsewhere considered themselves to be exploited by the Asian traders who at that time controlled the crop. In response, the Victoria Federation of Co-operatives, led by the future government Minister Paul Bomani, came to dominate buying and processing, feeding in to a marketing Board which priced and exported the crop. This was perhaps the high point of cotton in Tanzania from an organisational point of view. Kabissa shows how later institutional arrangements, ranging from a slate of regional co-operatives, to a Cotton Board which was never properly resourced to an input financing system which was radically changed every few years, have served farmers badly. But he reserves his real fire for the misconceived and badly executed 'liberalisation' programme effectively imposed by international donors from the early 1990s onwards. He shows how the current situation with nearly seventy nine registered ginneries (of which forty actually operate), unruly and unregulated processes at buying posts and the related adulteration of the crop have caused Tanzania not only to lose the premium for good quality lint which it once enjoyed, but actually to achieve a discount on the world market price on grounds of inadequate quality. This aspect of the story represents a lost opportunity for farmers where the efforts of 'donors' and local politicians have proved a toxic mix. The story of liberalisation and the lack of co-ordination within the textile manufacturing sector is no more rewarding and the pressure to add value to the crop within the country has yet to yield substantive results. Nonetheless Kabissa shows that there are important strategic changes afoot, notably in the development of 'contract farming' which may build a stronger relationship of mutual reliance between farmers and ginners.

The search for a stable smallholder cropping systems in Africa, combining food security with cash income, remains as acute an issue as ever. It is tempting to see the way forward in terms of larger scale agriculture. But with well over half of Africa's population still relying on agriculture for survival and income, the role which specific crops can play, needs constant examination. This book is an excellent contribution and is an exemplar of the continuing need for historical and technical analysis as well as imaginative thinking in relation to future strategies.

- Laurence Cockcroft, a former Senior Economist and Consultant to FAO, World Bank and Governments of Tanzania and Zambia. Currently a Trustee of the Tanzania Gatsby Trust and the Kilimo Trust.

THE STRUCTURE OF THE BOOK

This book examines the general performance of the Tanzanian cotton industry and, in particular, how the reforms carried out between the mid-1980s and early 1990s went on to shape its prospects for the 21st century.

The book has 13 chapters plus a bibliography and a segment about the author.

Chapter 1 examines the historical contribution of agriculture to the GDP: its rise and fall. It also shows the rise and fall of cotton production, quality and its contribution to the welfare of farmers. It also examines the reforms of the commercial sub-sector that were adopted.

Chapter 2 gives an overview of the global market situation for cotton highlighting some of the major recent developments as well as challenges which the global cotton economy is facing and which Tanzania must similarly grapple with through trade.

Chapter 3 gives an account of the Tanzanian cotton economy from a historical perspective highlighting how it has tended to be influenced by policy and institutional changes.

Chapter 4 examines the contribution of R & D to the development of the cotton industry in the country highlighting the need for further work in the wake of emerging challenges especially after market reforms.

Chapter 5 summarizes the current status of the debate on a quarantine pest a called the red bollworm highlighting both the pros and cons of lifting the prevailing ban on cotton cultivation in the southern and southern highland regions of Tanzania.

Chapter 6 outlines the main features of cotton production in Tanzania and discusses in some depth how the industry sought to deal with the challenges that emerged after crop marketing liberalization in a bid to reverse the decline in production, productivity and profitability.

Chapter 7 discusses some aspects of cotton selling and buying under a liberalized marketing environment and in particular how market participants individually and collectively responded to the challenges arising as a result of the decline in annual cotton output during the period between 1994/05 and 1999/00 as well as the short and long-term implications of their selling and buying activities for the industry as a whole.

Chapter 8 gives an overview of the ginning industry highlighting the implications of a rapid shift from roller to saw ginning and how a mismatch between the demand for seed cotton and its supply coupled with unregulated ginnery construction brought about the demise of ginnery zones and hence the mix up of the varieties which they had sought to protect. The chapter also outlines how ginners sought to deal with the challenges relating to ginning in general and the disposal of their lint cotton.

Chapter 9 outlines the status of one of Tanzania's largest manufacturing sectors, namely, the textiles and apparel industries and some of the factors that have contributed to its continued limited utilization of Tanzanian lint. In this chapter, some of the initiatives being taken to make it viable and competitive again are discussed.

Chapter 10 gives a profile of some of the major cotton stakeholders as well as the challenges and constraints they are currently face under a liberalized and competitive market setting. It also describes how the institutionalization of stakeholder meetings went on to ease quite considerably some of the challenges facing the industry.

Chapter 11 discusses the extent to which both economic and technical issues on cotton development have become increasingly politicized. The chapter goes on to point out that the potential dangers of politics getting into a collision course with science can be likened to the saying that "whether elephants fight or make love it is the grass that suffers".

Chapter 12 examines the future of cotton in Tanzania by pointing out what needs to be done if it is to capitalize on its comparative advantage in cotton.

Chapter 13 contains policy recommendations. The latter are listed under each chapter. It is an important chapter to read. It is mainly intended for policy and law makers and cotton stakeholders'.

The bibliography shows the literature which the author read in the course of writing this book.

Chapter **1**

INTRODUCTION

'"If we are serious about reducing poverty, we must deal with agriculture, because 70% of the world's poor people live in rural areas and depend directly or indirectly on agriculture".

Francois Bourguignon, 2008.

"History shows very few examples of countries that have successfully reduced poverty through agriculture alone, but almost none have achieved it without first increasing agricultural productivity"

David Bradley, 2008.

1.1 The declining contribution of agriculture to the GDP
Agriculture has since independence been the most dominant feature of the Tanzanian economy. To date the agricultural sector still supports the livelihoods of 70% or more of the Tanzanian population as well as contributing 30% of the country's exports and providing over 65% of the raw materials used by the domestic industries on an annual basis. A major distinguishing feature of the Tanzanian export portfolio has been its continued dependence on primary commodities such as coffee, cotton, tobacco, cashew, tea and sisal as the major sources of its foreign exchange earnings. Recently, the position of primary commodity exports relative to non-traditional exports has changed quite significantly. In spite of their increased output, their proportion of total commodity exports has been on the decline and by 2009 they accounted for just 15% as opposed to nearly 70% in the case of non-traditional exports.

Table 1: Value of Goods Exports: 2006 – 2009 (US $ Millions)

Commodity Export	2006	2007	2008	2009
Traditional/Primary Exports	267.1	319.7	418.4	470.8
Non-Traditional Exports	1,476.2	1,704.5	2,270.6	2,163.2
• Minerals	836.8	848.7	995.5	1,114.8
• Others	639.2	855.8	1,275.1	1,048.2
Unrecorded Trade	174.3	202.4	347.8	462.3
TOTAL	1,917.6	2,226.6	3,036.0	3,096.3

Source: **2010 Economic Survey Data**

Nonetheless, while the agricultural sector would seem to be receding into oblivion, this has not yet been reflected by the Tanzanian economy becoming less dependent on exports of primary products and instead, becoming increasingly dependent on manufactures and services. The attainment of such a structural transformation of the economy has so far not materialized undoubtedly because the performance of the agricultural sector in general and the commodity subsector in particular has been far below the expected levels in terms of investments, productivity and efficiency.

1.2 Post-colonial agricultural policies

After independence and especially for the period between the mid-1960s and late 1970s, the post-colonial administration sought to boost agricultural production and productivity in an attempt to improve farmers' incomes, stabilize food prices and to generate the surpluses needed to support agro-processing. To achieve such objectives the government initiated a programme of compulsory villagization and adopted policies of import-substitution industrialization. The latter was being seen as a viable policy package to help the country achieve structural transformation and lessen its dependence on primary products. Such approaches coupled

2

with the dissolution of cooperative unions in 1976 as voluntary and independent institutions and their replacement by crop marketing parastatals ran into trouble and eventually precipitating extensive state involvement in the economy. The latter started to stagnate and the situation became further aggravated by the high oil prices in 1973-74 and 1979-80 that brought about a global economic crisis. The latter went on to impact negatively on commodity prices and thence a significant decline in the demand for agricultural exports during that period. The stagnation and eventual decline in agricultural output during that period was also due to sectoral, trade and macroeconomic policies being largely biased against the agricultural sector as a whole.

In an attempt to revamp its ailing economy the Tanzanian government embarked on a structural adjustment program (SAP) starting from the mid-1980s and coming to a head by the early 1990s. With regard to agriculture, the reforms were being undertaken on the belief that agricultural exports were constrained by the high taxation of agriculture needed to promote import-substitution industrialization. Thus apart from reducing the overvalued exchange rates, the reforms sought to open up the domestic and export markets by introducing competition in marketing, removing government intervention in commodity prices and reducing explicit and implicit taxes among other changes.

As can be seen the major objective of the reform programme was to reduce and eventually eliminate the biases against agriculture on anticipation that price incentives arising out of competitive markets would motivate farmers to increase both production and productivity and eventually overall agricultural output of the major food and cash crops. Under the reform programme special emphasis was directed at the agricultural sector for the major reason that a 1% growth in agriculture produces a 1.5% growth across the economy and GDP growth in agriculture produces more than twice the impact on reducing poverty as growth in other sectors.

3

By 2008, nearly thirteen years after the liberalization of the economy, the contribution of the agricultural sector to GDP had dropped to 26.5% from 49% and 57% in 1995 and 1960 respectively. Some policy and development analysts quickly interpreted such drastic drop in Tanzania's agricultural GDP as largely being in line with "the declining share paradox" which postulates for a gradual decline in the agriculture's share of GDP with economic development as has been the case in many countries that have followed the agricultural path during their economic development. A corollary to such an assertion in the case of Tanzania would be that after a period of market reforms its economy had finally started to take off culminating in agriculture increasingly giving way to the emergence of manufacturing and service sectors in the country.

The pundits must have ostensibly reasoned out that with tourism, mining and fishing becoming quite important in recent years, Tanzania had finally become positioned to exploit such comparative advantages outside the agriculture sector. While simple logic would lend credence to such deduction the fact still remains though that agriculture is still by far the largest employer for nearly 70% of the labour force. So, while the role of other sectors in the economy may have indeed increased over time, the rather dramatic decline in the contribution of agriculture to GDP was primarily due to the commodity subsector not living up to the expectations of the reforms. Such a conclusion can best be illustrated by the status of cotton both before and after the reforms.

Throughout the 20th century, annual cotton output in Tanzania remained below 96,372 tons of lint obtained during the 1992/93 season. Such an output, the highest during the entire twentieth century, was obtained just one season prior to the liberalization of commodity marketing in 1994. After liberalization, annual cotton output went into decline reaching a low of 35, 476 tons of lint by 1999/00. As a result, cotton's contribution to agricultural GDP similarly declined from 24.6% prior to the reforms in 1992/93 to just 6% by 1999/00.

1.3 Tanzanian cotton is not "White Gold" any more
On another front, Tanzanian lint that had for many years been referred to as "white gold" went on to increasingly lose such reputation. Inadequate protection against insect damage, the stoppage of sorting of seed cotton prior to its sale and adulteration of seed cotton resulted in lint quality declining as well. Similarly, due to increased mix up of existing cotton varieties brought about by indiscriminate buying of seed cotton across designated breeding cum variety zones, there also emerged the issue of increased within bale variability of Tanzanian lint. Such outcomes were largely due to modalities for effective and efficient maintenance of high quality standards for both seed cotton and lint quality becoming very difficult to implement due to a mismatch between the supply and demand for seed cotton at that point in time.

Consequently, Tanzanian lint became increasingly sold on discounted rates and it no longer attracted the premiums that used to be associated with it prior to the reforms. Ginners cum exporters were therefore unlikely to significantly pass onto the farmers the kind of remunerative prices that were anticipated prior to the reforms.

The experience with the international financial institutions (IFIs) which inspired reforms of the commodity subsector in Sub Saharan Africa (SSA) in general and in Anglophone Africa in particular, has generally been one of mixed flavour. So, while market liberalization brought about an influx of private capital, management and marketing expertise; increased promptness in the payment for crops purchased from farmers as well as farmers getting a rising share of the export or free on board price (FOB) due to the advent of a competitive market, the emergence of challenges associated with the supply of seasonal inputs on credit to farmers under a competitive market setting went on to impact rather negatively on production, productivity, quality and hence profitability.

In the wake of declining production, productivity, quality and hence profitability from cotton after the reforms the challenge to the government and indeed the industry as a whole became how to halt the decline and bring the industry back to the growth path. It had become quite obvious that with the withdrawal of the government and of its support after the reforms the new competitive market setting that had substituted the single channel system had not yet positioned itself to manage the issues relating to input credit supply as well as extension services and the upkeep of lint quality. Thus, in spite of all the efforts being taken to have Tanzania integrated into the globalization process under the financial and macroeconomic guidance of the IFIs, cotton farming in the country was likely to remain largely inefficient and low-tech. To circumvent the situation, the slogan by the late Julius Nyerere whereby he urged all Tanzanians "to run while they are walking" soon became turned into one requiring them "to fly while they are walking" if the cotton industry was to indeed make up for lost time and opportunities.

1. 4 First centenary of cotton farming in Tanzania
In 2006 the cotton industry witnessed the first centenary of cotton farming in Tanzania ever since the Germans commercialized it in 1906 and the realization of the biggest cotton harvest of 126, 229 tons of lint for the first time in cotton production history. Such a milestone which elevated Tanzania to fourth position amongst the 36 cotton producing countries in SSA was of significant importance in at least two aspects: that cotton in Tanzania is not jinxed and perhaps more importantly, that the country has the potential to significantly raise annual cotton output even further.

In a report on "Cotton Production Prospects in the next Decade" published in 1995, the World Bank (WB) and

Common Fund for Commodities CFC) had pointed out that issues relating to technical, institutional and policy aspects of cotton production, processing and trade tend to hold the key to the future of cotton development the world-over. In 2009, fourteen years later, another report on the Organization and Performance of Cotton Sectors in Africa also by the WB, confirmed yet again that in spite of the much touted market reforms, cotton sectors in SSA continue to face the same old challenges for which there is still no single common formula of solving them.

That there is indeed no unique policy prescription that fits the diversity of the agricultural sectors in the developing world was summed quite succinctly by Roberto Zagha who, in the aftermath of the Washington Consensus, reiterated that *''----perhaps the lesson of lessons of the 1990s, is that we need to get away from formulae and realize that economic policies need to address binding constraints to growth at the right time, in the right manner, and in the right sequence, instead of any constraint, at any time. This requires recognizing country specificities, and more economic, institutional and social analysis and rigor than a formula-based approach to policy-making''* end of quote.

Chapter **2**

COTTON: A GLOBAL OVERVIEW

2.1 Species of cultivated cotton

The word "cotton" refers to the four species in the genus *Gossypium*, namely, *Gossypium hirsutum L., Gossypium barbadence L. Gossypium arboreum L.,* and *Gossypium herbaceum* L. that have, over the years, become independently domesticated as important sources of the textile fibre. Nevertheless, the bulk of the cotton that is annually produced on a commercial basis throughout the world belongs to just two species; *G. hirsutum* (also popularly referred to as Upland cotton) which accounts for well over 90% of the total world cultivated area annually) and *G. barbadence* (also commonly referred to as either Pima or Extra Long Staple Cotton (or just simply; ELS cotton). To date, India is the only country in the world where all the four species of cotton are grown commercially on an annual basis.

2.2 The cotton value chain supports millions of livelihoods

Although cotton is grown primarily for the production of the fibre needed by the textile and apparel industries, the by-products of its seeds, namely, oil, meal and cake tend to contribute quite significantly to the overall value of the crop to growers, ginners and feed manufacturers. It is estimated that the cotton value chain when considered in the totality of its textile and vegetable oil markets, supports the livelihoods of nearly one billion people globally or roughly 15% of the global population.

In Sub-Saharan Africa, the role of cotton in poverty alleviation and attainment of the millennium development goals (MDG) goals, cannot be over-emphasized given the fact that over 10 million people are estimated to depend on it for cash, employment, foreign exchange earnings as well as food security. Finally, through taxation and redistribution cotton, similarly contributes quite immensely to the provision of other critical services such as health and education to rural societies in most cotton producing countries of SSA.

Perhaps due to its huge political and socioeconomic importance in many societies cotton has quite often tended to be referred to as "White Gold". Just how and why cotton became likened to "white gold" is not clear because on the jeweler's market the so-called "white gold" is quite simply a mixture of regular gold and at least one of the white metals; either nickel or palladium, with a whitish hue. "White gold" is reportedly more expensive than pure gold by up to 15% and so for cotton per se to be likened to white gold would tend to reinforce the popular view that the importance of cotton transcends that of regular gold – which is indeed precious but of far limited availability to the masses.

On a worldwide basis, the bulk of the cotton crop produced annually comes from small holders living mainly in Asia, Africa and South America. Small holders account for up to 80% of the total annual crop produced globally in spite of using limited capital that is entirely derived from the sales of their farms where they tend to grow both food and cash crops. The remaining 20% of the global cotton crop is produced by medium to large-scale farmers under highly mechanized conditions in the United States of America, Australia and Brazil. In Greece, production is equally mechanized but on much smaller farms. In Africa cotton is grown in about 36 countries under predominantly rain-fed conditions with the exception of Egypt, Sudan and South Africa where it is grown under varying levels of irrigation.

Table No. 2: **Africa's leading cotton producing countries**

	1992/93	1999/00	2004/05	2005/06	2008/09
1	Egypt 291,000	Egypt 230,000	Mali 260,000	Egypt 292,000	Egypt 222,000
2	Mali 114,000	Mali 217,000	B. Faso 204,000	B. Faso 264,000	B. Faso 150,000
3	Tanzania 96,000	Ivory Coast 157,000	Egypt 198,000	Mali 240,000	Tanzania 123,000
4	Sudan 90,000	Benin 123,000	Benin 142,000	Benin 171,000	Benin 113,000
5	Ivory Coast 87,000	B.Faso 119,000	Zimbabwe 130,000	Ivory Coast 139,000	Mali 101,000
6	Benin 75,000	Zimbabwe 115,000	Tanzania 114,000	Tanzania 126,000	Zimbabwe 92,000
7	B. Faso 69,000	Cameroon 79,000	Cameroon 100,000	Cameroon 124,000	Nigeria 69,000
8	Chad 68,000	Togo 78,000	Nigeria 75,000	Nigeria 95,000	Ivory Coast 50,000
9	Cameroon 47,000	Nigeria 65,000	Ivory Coast 73,000	Chad 84,000	Chad 84,000
10	Togo 42,000	Chad 64,000	Sudan 69,000	Sudan 83,000	Cameroon 46,000

Source: **International Cotton Advisory Committee (ICAC).**

Cotton is one of the few major commodities traded internationally which is produced, processed and marketed to a great extent by both developing economies (DE) and advanced economies (AE). The other crops such as coffee, cocoa and tea which are also referred to as 'breakfast commodities' tend to be produced by the DE, the majority of which are located in the tropics. It is, therefore, interesting to note that while competition between DE and AE is by and large merely confined to the processing segment of the value chain in the case of breakfast commodities; competition is a regular feature of the entire value chain in the case of cotton.

Furthermore, the production of and trade in cotton is subject to government intervention largely by way of production/export subsidies as well as border protection policies. Subsidies in general and export subsidies in particular, have the unique tendency of encouraging surplus cotton production which is then sold on the world market at subsidized prices thus further depressing world cotton prices which are already on a downward trend. In the case of border protection policies being imposed in AE, DE have become unable to diversify their export portfolio for agricultural products beyond exports of primary products.

As a result of such distortions huge disparities have tended to emerge in relation to the profitability of cotton production, processing and trade between DE and AE. It is therefore not hard to see why issues relating to cotton trade have increasingly become a major agenda within the circles of the World Trade Organization (WTO).

2.3 Global cotton output has been on the rise

During the twentieth century, the global cotton economy witnessed some unprecedented developments. Thus, between 1960/61 and 2004/05 average, lint yields per ha and total annual output more than doubled from 313 to 639 kg/ha and from 10.2 to 21.8 million tons of lint respectively. However, the annual output of man-made fibres (MMF) more than doubled just between 1986 and 2005 from 19,145 to 45,442 million tons. Increased output of cotton has largely been due to factors such as: the expansion of the area under cotton in Brazil, China and India; intensified use of inputs, especially fertilizers and irrigation water and perhaps most importantly, the advent of genetically engineered cotton (GEC) or more popularly, genetically modified organisms (GMO) or the so-called biotech cotton.

Adoption of genetically modified cotton has greatly revolutionalized the production of cotton by contributing significantly to the overall reduction in the risks and costs normally associated

11

with herbicide and insecticide use on cotton. Consequently the area under such cotton rose from zero during the 1996/97 marketing season when it was first commercialized, to 47% of the total global area under cotton by 2008/09. As a result of its increased adoption worldwide and particularly in the USA, China, India, Australia, Brazil, Argentina, Colombia, Mexico, Greece, South Africa and lately Burkina Faso the proportions of genetically modified cotton in global output and exports had reached 52% and 51% by 2009 respectively. With Egypt, Kenya and Uganda currently involved in the testing of biotech cotton, further spread of such cotton especially in SSA is being foreseen in a few years to come.

The rather rapid increase in global cotton output in recent years has also been due to the continuing decline in the real prices for cotton over time and especially after crop marketing liberalization. Due to chronic shortages of the foreign exchange earnings needed to pay for imports and debt servicing, DE have, in the wake of declining global prices for cotton and adverse effects brought about by crop marketing liberalization been compelled to produce more and more cotton for sale to the world market, regardless of price in a desperate hope that sheer quantity will make up for falling prices. Thus DE have literally had to "run fast in order to remain in the same place" by producing more and more cotton for export.

In SSA average cotton lint yields have more or less stagnated in spite of recent advances in cotton production technology. In 2007 for example, the average lint yield of 393 kg per ha for SSA was less than a half of the global average of 790 kg in that year largely due to limited use of yield enhancing and optimizing technologies such as high yielding varieties (HYV), fertilizers, irrigation and integrated pest management (IPM). The recent liberalization of cotton marketing in SSA also contributed to the stagnation of yields in part due to the collapse of input credit arrangements that were associated with the single marketing system and rising input costs. Such developments have helped make it increasingly very difficult for Africa's resource poor farmers to optimize average cotton yields.

2.4 Cotton production has become concentrated in few countries

Another recent development within the global cotton economy has been the fact that cotton production has increasingly become concentrated in just a few countries such as China, India, USA and Pakistan all of which are all located in the northern hemisphere. During the 2007/08 marketing season the "big four" accounted for nearly 73% of total global cotton output. Similarly, a group of another "big four", namely, the USA, India, Uzbekistan and CFA Zone exported nearly 70% of all the cotton lint traded in 2007/08 with the USA alone exporting over 40% of the total volume. The amount of cotton lint that is traded internationally amounts to about 30% of total global cotton output.

During the 2006/07 marketing season, the emergence of India as the second largest producing and exporting country after China and the USA respectively sent shock waves to smaller cotton exporting countries, particularly in Africa. Due to its closer proximity to the major cotton importing countries of China, Pakistan, Bangladesh and Eastern Asia, India has now become a major decisive factor on how Africa in general and Tanzania in particular can compete in the Asian cotton export market. The latter has since 2005 become the major destination for the bulk of cotton traded internationally and this being in line with the geographical shift in international yarn and fabric production from Europe following the removal of the multi-fibre agreement (MFA) in 2005. During the 2006/07 season China together with Turkey, Bangladesh, Pakistan and Indonesia collectively accounted for nearly 51% of all the cotton being processed into textiles and apparel with China itself accounting for about 40% of all the cotton consumed in the world.

2.5 In SSA commodity dependency persists

Another major development trend within the cotton economy has been with regard to commodity dependence becoming increasingly entrenched in SSA. To date cotton accounts for up to 20% of GDP and 33% of total exports in some countries of SSA. Such commodity dependence has tended to be underscored by the extreme vulnerability of SSA countries to economic shocks that have tended to characterize an increasingly globalized economy. The Asian Financial Crisis of 1998 culminated in a dramatic decline in lint exports from SSA to the Far East that has since become the global textile engine. The resulting major decline in global prices for lint in 1998 and 1999 had quite far reaching implications on the economies of SSA whose lint exports are largely destined for the Far East.

Cotton exporting countries in SSA also suffered significant financial losses during the 2008/09 global economic and financial crisis when the price for cotton on the Cotlook A Index fell from 84 USA cents per pound by mid-September 2008 to just 57 cents per pound by December 31st. The fall in cotton prices was correlated with a significant drop in the demands for raw cotton by the leading textile and apparel manufacturing countries located in the Far East following the closure of their major retail markets in the USA and Europe. The drop in the demand for cotton was an outcome of a severe credit crunch coming in the wake of the collapse of financial institutions based there. Both crises created very severe strains to the economies of most cotton dependent countries in SSA as farmers, ginners, textile manufacturers and the government went on to incur significant financial losses.

2.6 Cotton production and trade are distorted by government policies

The global cotton economy has similarly witnessed an increased distortion of cotton trade due to governments intervening in the cotton market by way of domestic and border policies. A market distortion is broadly understood to be the use of government authority to stifle competition, enhance market position, subsidize favoured activities, raise barriers to entry, control or distort prices, mandate behaviours, or impede the free flow of information. To date, both cotton production and trade have become increasingly distorted by government policies through subsidies to both as well as by tariffs on cotton, textile and clothing imports. During the 2001/02 marketing season more than 20% of world cotton producer earnings came from government support to the sector. Subsidies in general and export subsidies in particular have the effect of encouraging surplus cotton production which is then sold on the world market at subsidized prices, thus further depressing world cotton prices which are already on a downward trend.

Ironically, some members of the Organization for Economic Cooperation and Development (OECD) while purporting to offer aid to African countries in order to help them fight poverty, have quite often been engaging in unfair agricultural support and trade policies that tend to make it very difficult for Africa to maximize the benefits of trade in agricultural commodities for which they have an overwhelming comparative advantage. It is a truism that when SSA and DE elsewhere were urged to liberalize and undertake major macroeconomic reforms at the inspiration of IFIs and OECD countries, they complied in good faith but have since then become both disappointed and disillusioned by what they now see as a case of double standards akin to what some preachers tend to tell members of their congregations, namely, "follow what I say but not what I do". Such hypocrisy has become a major raw deal for DEs, because apart from eroding their export potential, it condemns them to the continued export of primary products.

The task of dealing with all trade related disputes in general and those with special relevance to cotton is one of the regular agenda at the WTO. Ever since it was formed in 1995, one of the major tasks of the WTO has been trying to conclude the negotiations initiated in Doha in November 2001 on the need to reduce trade distorting farm support, slash tariffs on farm goods and eliminate agricultural-export subsidies and cut industrial tariffs all of which affect cotton quite significantly. Cotton producing countries, particularly from SSA, have further been actively demanding under WTO for trade rules relating to agriculture to be structured in a manner which is compatible with their development and poverty reduction objectives because agriculture is the sector that holds considerable prospects for trade and development. Regrettably, because the WTO is a democratic organization that works by consensus but without formal procedures to get there, it often faces immense difficulties in trying to promote free trade on a win-win basis.

2.7 Real revenue from cotton per ha in dollar terms has declined over time

Finally, the global cotton economy has witnessed a continuing decline in the real average revenue earned per ha of land cropped to cotton over time. To put this into some perspective, records from the ICAC show that while the price of cotton; cost insurance and freight (CIF) Europe reached a high of 94.10 cents per pound during the 1980/81 season, such dropped to 82.90 and 57.20 cents per pound respectively ten and twenty years later during the 1990/91 and 2000/01 marketing seasons. Such trend has obviously been of great concern to the DE where average yields have generally stagnated in spite of recent gains in productivity and especially because the real average cotton revenue per ha. in dollars terms has actually declined over the years when adjusted for inflation.

In AE factors such as new technological advances and especially the wider adoption of GMO and IPM coupled with increased irrigation have progressively resulted in a significant reduction not only in average production costs per ha for cotton but also the risks that are quite often associated with it. Consequently, both average yields and acreage under cotton have risen quite considerably in such countries culminating in dramatic increases in the supply of cotton to the global market. Unfortunately, supply has not been increasing in tandem with the global demand for cotton and as a result cotton prices have tended to become depressed. During the past two decades the global per capita consumption of cotton worldwide stagnated at around 3.5 kg as compared to 16 kg in the case of the USA where institutions such as Cotton Incorporated have been greatly instrumental in promoting cotton and, hence, boosting the overall demand for cotton there.

The continuing decline in global cotton prices over time has not only been due to the supply of cotton being way out of balance with demand but also due to an ever - growing competition from MMF. Due to recent technological advances, the demand for the cotton fibre has been on the decline due to increasing customer preference for the MMFs to the cotton fibre. MMF have recently been able to compete quite successfully against cotton because of their strength, durability and most importantly by delivering clothing with enhanced performance and aesthetics at consistent quality and at a price much lower than that for cotton.

The old notion of consumers' liking for the "feel of cotton" in preference to that of MMFs has recently become challenged by new attributes which are making MMF essential components in apparel incorporating thermal regulatory properties, protective properties (such as flame retardance) and water absorption properties (without the feeling of wetness). For example, as a result of popular consumer demand, the present trend is towards increasingly biodegradable, eco-conscious and recycled synthetic products. These and other rather cotton-specific features would seem to have been the major reasons behind the decline in cotton's share of the global market from 75% to 37% between 1945 and 2005.

To date, cotton and polyester are respectively the largest players in the global textile market with each accounting for well over 30 percent of total fibre usage. The relative importance of cotton and polyester as respectively the leading natural and synthetic fibres would seem to derive from the fact that each one of them is endowed with rather unique characteristics. Thus, while cotton is a renewable resource and tends to be liked for its wearing comfort, natural appearance and moisture absorbency qualities; polyester is on the other hand 100% synthetic but recyclable. Moreover, polyester is noticeably more stain resistant than cotton; it can be washed in cold water and dries up quite quickly; and it does not lose its shape like cotton and, hence, tends to have a much longer wearing life span than cotton.

Nevertheless, in the quest for increased production of either polyester or cotton, issues relating to the environment as well as type and cost of raw materials being used to produce them as well as the overall cost of production, are increasingly coming into consideration. Thus, while cotton as a biological material tends to be quite variable in its fibre characteristics; an attribute which tends to somewhat undermine its ability to meet the demands of spinners for certain characteristics, such as strength and uniformity. Similarly, its high requirement for pesticides and irrigation water during production has recently become a major bone of contention in the debate on environmental sustainability. In the case of polyester its relatively high requirement for energy, wood and oil tends to greatly conflict with the increasingly topical agenda on environmental sustainability in spite of its generally lesser requirement for water than cotton during the production process. The extent to which each of these fibres complies with such demands and concerns may well be the future determinants as to which fibre to use or not.

Table No. 3. **A comparison of the main end-uses between cotton and polyester**

Fibre	Apparel use	Household use	Home furnishings	Carpets	Technical use
Cotton	66%	13%	14%	Nil	7%
Polyester	52%	7%	11%	2%	28%

Source: **CMAI - Global Fibres & Feedstock's Report-March 5, 2002 issue No. 007**

In a nutshell, it can be seen that the profitability of cotton as an internationally traded commodity has become inextricably linked to a rapidly changing horizon involving technology as it affects production and processing as well as the extent to which nations are willing to reform global trading rules.

Chapter **3**

COTTON IN TANZANIA: A HISTORICAL OVERVIEW

3.1 Cotton: An introduced crop

It is widely acknowledged that cotton farming in the country was introduced by the German colonial administration during the latter part of the 19th century. One of the primary motives of colonialism was quite obviously, economic gain and one of the ways by which colonialists sought to benefit their economies was to use the colonies as sources of cheaply produced raw materials for their industries. Up until 1860 the textile manufacturing industries in Britain, Germany, France, Belgium and Portugal had been sourcing for their cotton from the southern states of United States where it was being produced relatively cheaply using slave labour.

However, with the start of the American civil war in 1861, the flow of raw cotton into the British Lancashire textile industry and continental Europe as a whole ceased. During the war, the southern states had apparently stopped the export of the famous "King Cotton" in order to force England, which was until then the largest importer of cotton, to either recognize the Confederate States or to join the war along their side.

3.2 Cotton farming did not start off smoothly

To cover for the shortfall in cotton supplies during the so called "cotton famine" period between 1861 and 1865, the British government and other colonial powers were compelled to source for it from elsewhere and their colonies in Africa became an obvious choice to look for. India, which was until then the world's second largest supplier of cotton after the USA, could not be relied upon on due to fibre quality considerations and for being too adulterated for their use. Germany which at that point in time had the second

20

largest textile and apparel in Europe after Britain, sought to source for cheaply produced cotton for its industry by introducing cotton farming in Tanganyika and its other colonies. That became the task of a business company called Kolonial-Wirtschaftliches-Komitee (KWK). The latter was formed in 1896 to specifically spearhead agricultural development in Africa. The actual commercialization of cotton production in Tanganyika by KWK is said to have begun around 1906 although production data is only available for the period starting from the 1920s.

In the quest to deliver big volumes of cheaply grown cotton to their metropolitan textile industries quickly, the challenge became how best to achieve such an objective when cotton was a newly introduced crop. Initially, KWK opted for the production of cotton as an estate crop with farmers being paid for their hired labour. Unfortunately, such an approach is said to have failed and the Germans blamed the failure on Africans whom they assumed to be apathetic and chronically lazy by nature.

In their bid to get things right, the Germans in Tanganyika just like other colonialists in Ivory Coast, Central Africa, Belgian Congo and Mozambique decided to use coercion, intimidation and other mechanisms of social control quite prominently. Moreover, they also wanted cotton to be grown as an estate crop just like rubber, sugar cane and tea. Literature is replete with information on how farmers reacted both passively and actively to all forms of forceful cultivation of cotton. The so-called "Maji Maji" rebellion against German rule in 1905 was precipitated at least in part by the deprivation associated with the coercive cultivation of cotton. The latter was deployed as a strategy to boost cotton production and hence maximize hard currency earnings. Such strategy was also adopted after independence as farmers in all cotton growing areas became pressured to allocate a minimum of one acre of their arable land to cash crop production and another acre or more for food crop production as well.

Policies of compulsory cultivation of designated cash crops, including cotton, persisted up until the early 1980s. In the Eastern Cotton Growing Area (ECGA), in particular, forced cultivation of cotton after independence was similarly resisted albeit more passively. Thus, farmers in parts of Coast and Morogoro regions deliberately boiled the cotton seeds distributed for planting and then blamed the failure of such seed to germinate on both the extension service and the cotton board for allegedly passing on to them poor quality seed. Since then, there has tended to emerge amongst the majority of cotton farmers a perceived notion that as "a regulated crop," cotton is a *de facto* "government crop" ostensibly due to frequent state intervention in activities relating to its cultivation, marketing and processing totally unlike most other crops particularly the food crops.

3.3 Cotton farming faces a myriad of constraints

In retrospect, the attempts by the German colonial government to have cotton production increased through either forceful cultivation or by designating it as an estate crop failed for several other factors as well. It would seem plausible to assume that as a newly introduced crop, cotton cultivation did not take off quite smoothly due to factors such as the lack of knowledge on how best it should be grown for economic yields; the lack of suitable varieties given the diversity in agro-ecological conditions; cotton's bigger demand for care and labour relative to other crops among other factors. Such factors may have probably come into play resulting in its initial rejection by the indigenous people. The issue of cotton's high demand for labour would seem to have been the most logical reason for the failure to mainstream cotton as an estate crop given the practical difficulties associated with the organizing and managing the labour needed during the different periods of the cropping cycle and the cost implications involved.

To date, the numerous resource-poor smallholders who grow cotton still face a series of major production and marketing

22

challenges which tend to limit not only its attractiveness to more growers but also its profitability relative to other crops. Cotton, unlike most other so-called cash crops has a very high demand for labour particularly during sowing, weeding, spraying and harvesting. Due to the difficulties associated with organizing and paying for such labour, cotton farms have tended to be small and managed on a family basis unless farming is both mechanized and high tech.

Furthermore, cotton unlike most other cash crops has a much higher requirement for purchased inputs such as herbicides, fertilizers and insecticides and so its cost of production tends to be higher. In the past most of the seasonal inputs were provided to farmers either on credit or subsidized terms. After liberalization the scenario changed quite drastically following the removal of the single marketing system, abolition of subsidies and devaluation of the local currency. Consequently cotton farming has become an occupation largely left to farmers in areas where it is the default cash crop.

3.4 The relevancy of cotton R & D

After the 1st World War and the hand-over of Tanganyika to the British government, the task of promoting cotton production in Tanganyika and throughout the British Empire was handed to the British Cotton Growers Association (BCGA). The mission of the BCGA was primarily to guarantee the Lancashire based textile industries a steady supply of raw cotton from British colonies. To achieve that goal the BCGA became engaged in distributing seed for planting, guaranteeing the price of cotton to farmers, assisting in arranging transport for cotton, establishing ginneries in some parts of Africa, financing the research needed to make cotton farming profitable. Unfortunately, the BCGA could not live up to its mission and became blamed for pushing for increased cotton output without paying attention to the incentives needed to motivate Africans to adopt cotton production as well as increase its output in designated areas. To redress the situation the British government in 1921 replaced the BCGA by the Empire Cotton Growing Corporation (ECGC). The latter became charged with the task of extending and promoting cotton production in the country and most other Anglophone countries of Africa, India, West Indies and Australia. To that end the ECGC went on to promote cotton R &D as the basis for further cotton development in general by establishing a series of research stations in Nigeria, Rhodesia, Tanganyika, South Africa, Sudan and Uganda. The cotton R & D stations worked very closely with the Shirley Institute in England in an attempt to enhance the ginning characteristics of African cotton.

In Tanganyika, cotton research programmes were initiated by the ECGC at Ukiriguru in the Western Cotton Growing Area (WCGA) and at Ilonga in the ECGA in the 1930s and 1949 respectively. The major objective of cotton research at the two stations was to provide solutions to the major factors constraining the commercialization of cotton in their respective cotton growing areas. At both stations the primary task was how to improve the yield of cotton lint without the loss of quality and if possible, to improve quality concurrently. Nevertheless, initial research emphasis was put on plant breeding on the premise that yield advances arising from improved varieties quite often tend to reach the farmers without any sizeable extension effort as is the case with changes in production technology.

The impact of cotton R & D initiatives on increased commercialization of cotton started to be seen in the WCGA with effect from the late 1940s. Prior to 1940 the expansion of cotton production in both the WCGA and ECGA was largely being held back by the lack of suitable varieties which due to their extreme susceptibility to a minute leaf sucking pest commonly referred to as jassids, *Jacobiasca* spp (previously

24

referred to as *Empoasca fascialis* (Jacobi)] could not give economic yields. Furthermore the varieties were also very susceptible to two extremely devastating diseases namely; bacterial blight or more commonly "black arm" and wilting caused by a fungus called *Fusarium* sp. Such combination of insect and disease problems had made the commercialization of cotton growing in both the ECGA and WCGA almost impossible. Through conventional breeding methods Ilonga and Ukiriguru contributed quite greatly to the resolution of such problems by releasing cotton varieties that were resistant to the jassids as well as the fungal and bacterial diseases. Such technological breakthrough went on to constitute one of the most significant scientific contributions by research to cotton growing in the country.

One of the major outcomes of the release by Ukiriguru and Ilonga of varieties that combined high yielding ability, high ginning out-turn, suitable fibre characteristics and resistance to the jassids as well as the prevailing diseases, was that cotton output in the country between the late 1940s and late 1960s, increased more than sevenfold from 4,230 to 29,322 tons of lint. Other factors that contributed to the dramatic increase in cotton output during that period included: the dramatic expansion of the area under cotton cultivation, particularly in the areas that had previously been infested by tsetse; the very significant increases in producer prices from 12 to 52 cents per pound between 1943 and 1960 and by the advent of new marketing developments that guaranteed farmers an easy disposal of their crop.

3.5 The rise of agricultural marketing cooperatives
The purchasing and domestic marketing of cotton in the country up until the early 1950s had been under the private hands of mainly citizens of Asian origin. In spite of cooperatives having been in existence in the Lake Province of Tanganyika as early as the 1930s, it was not until 1953 when their

societies were allowed to buy seed cotton and by the late 1960s they had taken control of primary marketing, ginning and a significant proportion of the seed crushing industry. The take-over of domestic marketing of cotton by primary societies and cooperative unions from private ownership was apparently necessitated by farmers' resentment with their middlemen's marketing facilities and services such as: low prices, unfair determination of weights and grades of cotton brought for sale among other malpractices. The issue of malpractices perpetrated by the Asian middlemen had become of extreme concern to cotton farmers and the tension that arose out of it nearly developed into a major political and racial feud.

Interestingly, the use of agents in cotton buying and the malpractices that this practice often entails still remains the hallmark of cotton trading both locally and internationally. Nevertheless, while cheating on weights and measures is neither restricted nor unique just to cotton what is of great significance to cotton history is the fact that during the early 1950s, farmers dealt with the malpractice in a more resolute manner by opting to form the very first Agricultural Marketing Cooperatives (AMCs). The latter decided to put in place their own weighing facilities that allowed them to compete head on with those operated by Asians at the official buying posts.

The initiative of forming the AMCs to counter buying malpractices by a few unscrupulous Asians were championed by the late Paul Bomani who steered them to a union under the powerful Victoria Federation of Cooperative Union (VFCU) which was formed in 1952. Prior to 1967 the cooperative hierarchy had a three tier structure with the primary societies buying seed cotton from farmers, the unions transporting the cotton from the societies to the ginneries and supervising the societies, and the Federation of Unions coordinating the unions.

3.6 The launching of the Tanganyika Lint and Seed Marketing Board

With the issues of seasonal input supply, primary marketing and ginning firmly under the ambit of VFCU, the colonial government established the Tanganyika Lint and Seed Marketing Board (TLSMB) in 1952. TLSMB became charged with tasks of marketing lint both abroad and overseas on behalf of the cooperatives; overseeing quality control and setting up minimum quality standards for cotton being exported from Tanganyika. It also undertook, on behalf of the government, the task of stabilizing farm-gate prices through price fixing. In a nutshell, the formation of the TLSMB helped bring about an important central control of cotton marketing in the WCGA.

The formation of TLSMB marked the start of an era during which the use of parastatal bodies became a regular feature of government control over the major segments of its economy. Within the agricultural sector in particular, the parastatal marketing model conferred among other things, extensive statutory powers to such marketing boards with regard to the control of commodity marketing. Thus they also became used as instruments for appropriating resources from agriculture. They were able to achieve that by simply setting producer prices below world market prices during price fixing and the use of overvalued exchange rates. The surplus revenue thus generated was then used to subsidize industrialization and keep food prices in the urban areas at low level. Similarly, the subsidized provision of inputs was used by the state to justify low prices for seed cotton offered by the marketing board relative to the world price and other crops.

After independence, a rapid rise in the number of new cotton cooperatives became widely associated with allegations of mismanagement and corruption. A probe conducted by a Presidential Committee of Enquiry appointed in 1966 found out that cooperatives were increasingly being faced with problems such as a shortage of appropriate as well as skilled manpower; an uninformed membership; lack of democracy at the union level and for being susceptible to political interference. Calls were therefore made for the overhaul of the cooperative movement and in particular of VFCU.

3.7 The advent of the Arusha Declaration and Compulsory Villagization

Recommendations to overhaul the cooperative movement came at about the same time when the government was launching the "Arusha Declaration" in 1967. In a nutshell, the latter sought to transform the economy of the country using "self-reliance" as its driving principle and "Ujamaa Villages" as its basic units of production needed for rural development and socialist transformation. With the launching of the Arusha Declaration and Ujamaa Villages, the status of independent cooperative institutions at the Primary Society (PS) level changed once and for all as they became replaced by newly established so-called "Ujamaa Villages". The former PS became registered as multipurpose village cooperatives for commercial-cum-political-cum administrative activities at village level during the process of villagization in the early 1970s.

Although the villagization programme had aimed at modernizing the agricultural sector and making social services more accessible to the majority of rural dwellers, its use of forceful means to bring rural communities to designated "new villages" was widely associated with disruptions in agricultural production through increased walking times to crop fields; competition between households for both agricultural and grazing land among other inconveniences to the rural population. Similarly, villagization entailed a replacement of member controlled agricultural marketing societies by multi-purpose, village government controlled and compulsory membership organizations. Finally, during the villagization process, coercive measures were quite often invoked in order to ensure that every household complied with the need for every member of the rural population to grow cotton in addition to their food crops.

3.8 The reform of cooperative unions

Many of the unprecedented changes cited above brought about a rapid build-up of disincentives among producers. As a result the villagization process coupled with the dismantling of cooperatives as voluntary and independent organizations went on to greatly contribute to the decline in annual cotton output from a peak of 75,373 tons of lint during the 1966/67 season to 42,170 tons during the 1975/76 marketing season. In reaction to the turn of events, the government announced on 14th May 1976 the formal abolition of primary cooperatives as well the cooperative unions and their marketing functions respectively taken over by communal villages and parastatal crop authorities. As a consequence of such changes, the former TLSMB became changed to the Tanzania Cotton Authority (TCA). The latter became charged with the tasks of organizing production, buying, grading and ginning of seed cotton as well as the export of lint cotton; tasks which were previously being shared between the cooperatives and TLSMB.

Under the new set up, TCA bought the cotton crop directly from farmers unlike the cooperative unions that bought it through primary cooperatives. Furthermore, TCA continued with the task of evening out cotton market price fluctuations by offering farmers some kind of insurance against price falls by fixing prices and applying them pan-territorially and pan-seasonally. It may be recalled that the formation of TCA after the abolition of cooperatives occurred at a time when the economy was slowly drifting into a severe economic crisis. With agricultural output on the decline, the tasks assumed by TCA became even harder to fulfill because of the effects of a second oil shock in 1979; the war against Uganda; a growing debt crisis and deteriorating terms of trade for exports during the late 1970s and early 1980s. To arrest the deteriorating situation, the government reinstated the AMCs in 1984 as Regional Cooperative Unions (RCUs) under a new legislation after having lost their property, trained and experienced manpower and general working morale.

Unfortunately, the newly reconstituted cooperatives were in fact cooperatives just by name because they significantly differed from the previous ones that had existed prior to 1976 in several important aspects. First, they had lost their identity as true independent cooperatives as a result of all villages automatically becoming multi-purpose primary cooperatives. Secondly, membership to the cooperatives had become automatic. Thirdly, they had come into being without any share capital and hence they were wholly financed by grants and loans from the government and donors. Fourthly, their management was being put in place by government rather than by the members themselves. Fifthly, the government rather than the market was responsible for fixing the purchasing and selling prices for seed cotton and lint. Finally and perhaps most importantly, the AMCs had become part and parcel of the structure of Chama Cha Mapinduzi (CCM) mass organization and hence had lost the requisite political neutrality. In a nutshell, by 1986 the once powerful agricultural marketing cooperatives had in a sense become *de facto* public service institutions with TCMB rather than TCA acting as their statutory agent for the sale of lint both abroad and overseas.

3.9 The case for market reforms
In spite of the dramatic institutional and policy changes announced in 1984, the RCUs and TCMB could not manage to bring about a turn-around in the performance of the cotton industry as reflected by cotton output merely fluctuating below 54,000 tons of lint by 1990. Due to high administrative and coordination costs, free rider problems, factionalism and political interference, regional cooperatives unions failed to live up to expectations. Similarly, as a result of a growing

financial insolvency occasioned by bad management, corruption and politicization within the marketing parastatals, inefficiencies and inequities reigned within the cotton industry.

At farm level the persistent low profitability of cotton farming due to substandard margins brought about by both explicit and implicit taxation, had resulted in stagnation of yields. Put more bluntly, just like the errors committed by BCGA in the early 1900s, the government through the cooperatives and marketing parastatals had agitated for increased cotton output while deliberately underestimating the prices at which cotton would appeal to smallholders. Inevitably cotton farmers ended up getting a raw deal. As a result, the relevance of both the RCUs and marketing boards in cotton development became seriously questioned and in particular with regard to the large fiscal burden which they were placing on the government.

To eliminate the distortions that were previously associated with the single channel marketing dominated by the marketing parastatals and cooperative unions, the need to liberalize commodity marketing became quite pressing. Liberalization has been defined as "the move to market-determined prices from what was previously a regulated regime" and with regard to cotton that meant reducing government involvement in marketing and production; increasing the participation of the private sector in such actions and reducing distortions in commodity prices. Crop marketing liberalization was thus being seen as the inevitable approach to stimulating increased cotton output by putting in place both the incentives and an enabling environment needed to motivate farmers to increase output as well as to attract members of the private sector to participate fully not only in the processing and marketing of cotton but also in its production as well.

However, in spite of the benefits which liberalization was anticipated to bring to the commodity market, there still existed at that point in time, some deep skepticism and even fear about it. The major concern was with regard to the fear of replacing a public monopoly, namely the cooperatives' monopoly in cotton business, by a private monopoly, namely, private enterprise and most likely the return of Asian domination of cotton marketing as was the case prior to the 1950s. Such feelings would seem to have been reinforced by the feeling that unlike public monopolies, private ones do not seem to have a human face. The other and perhaps even more important concern about liberalization was the perceived fear of the state losing its grip on strategic commodities like cotton as well as the institutions purportedly servicing the interests of smallholder farmers on behalf of government.

To avert an impending collapse of the cotton industry at a time when the government was contemplating for its restructuring, the Netherlands Government between 1982 and 1992 came up with a bilateral aid programme in the form of an emergency operation in order to sustain the industry. The programme was implemented in three phases and dwelt quite specifically with the overall improvement of the transport system for the cotton industry in the WCGA coupled with the rehabilitation of existing ginneries and the construction of three entirely new ginneries at Manawa, Bulamba and Mwanhuzi in Misungwi, Bunda and Meatu districts respectively.

The work by the Netherlands Government was followed up starting in 1993 by a restructuring and privatization program for the entire industry as discussed earlier. The market reform program to which the government had finally acquiesced to entailed the scaling down of its involvement in direct productive and commercial functions; opening up domestic and export markets to competition and putting in place public and private institutions that support free market activities.

Such reforms were undertaken within the larger framework of the Structural Adjustment Programme and macroeconomic reforms. One of the consequences of such reforms was the formation of the Tanzania Cotton Lint and Seed Board (TCLSB) after the amendment in 1993 of the 1984 statute that had empowered TCMB not only to undertake the marketing of lint on behalf of RCUs but also to partake in regulatory functions. TCLSB became empowered to increasingly take up regulatory and promotion functions. Commercial functions were to be undertaken only in special circumstances after authorization and approval by government.

3.10 Liberalization did not live up to the expected results
When crop marketing liberalization took effect in 1994, private sector participation in the cotton industry broadened significantly as reflected by the number of cotton buyers cum ginners rising to 30 by 1999. Due to a rather uncontrolled entry of cotton buyers into the cotton market problems relating to the provision of seasonal inputs to farmers as well as the financing of cotton R & D started to emerge. Like-wise, the monitoring and enforcement of quality control as well as the dissemination of market information also became increasingly problematic.

Such unforeseen events occurred largely because the liberalization agenda had not quite defined ahead of time how such services would be provided under a competitive market setting without the involvement of the state and at a time when TCLSB as an arm of government was under restructuring. It was therefore not entirely surprising that in the aftermath of liberalization between 1994 and 1999 cotton output declined steadily instead of rising as previously anticipated.

In order to deal with a rapidly deteriorating market situation, one of the major priorities for the government became how to coordinate the activities and interests of all major stakeholders as well as the modalities for their engagement with government through TCLSB. The latter took up the initial task of facilitating cotton buyers cum ginners to form an association that would serve to unite them as well as help provide a platform for lobbying with government on their interests and concerns. To that end the Tanzania Cotton Association (TCA) was formed in 1997.

Similarly, in order to provide for the financing of some of the critical services such as the provision and delivery of seasonal inputs, the financing of cotton R & D and general promotion of the cotton industry which were deemed essential for the general wellbeing of the industry; the ministry of agriculture through TCLSB and TCA jointly resolved to form the Cotton Development Fund (CDF) in 1999. CDF became increasingly involved in financing: the procurement and subsequent distribution of seasonal inputs to farmers; cotton R & D; the dissemination of market and extension related information as well as general promotion of the cotton industry. Later CDF became transformed into the Cotton Development Trust Fund which by mutual consensus between all stakeholders became stakeholder rather than government controlled and managed.

3.11 The need for a cotton sector development strategy
In the course of the implementation of the market reforms, it had become apparent that if the issues relating to the overall development of the cotton industry were to be undertaken in a more systematic and sustainable way, a sub-sector development strategy was essential. To that end in 1998 the Tanzanian Government in collaboration with the European Union (EU) and the Netherlands Government embarked on the formulation of the Cotton Sub-sector Development Strategy (CSDS-1). The latter specifically sought to raise cotton output to 700, 000 bales of lint by 2006/07 by solving some of the existing challenges facing the industry as well as those that had arisen after the reforms.

By the start of the new millennium it had become quite clear to most stakeholders that while the parastatal model of government intervention in the cotton market had its problems, liberalization too had failed to stimulate increased cotton output. Further reforms of the subsector were thus necessary especially with regard to the need to delineate the roles and functions of the different stakeholders and how to strengthen and finance them on a sustainable basis.

One significant outcome of that process was the passage of the Cotton Industry Act No. 2 of 2001 which apart from providing for the formation of an entirely new statutory body called Tanzania Cotton Board (TCB) it also redefined its functions to be entirely regulatory and promotional in nature. TCB became no longer encumbered by the legacies of both TCMB and TCLSB that by and large were instrumental for the near demise of the cotton industry. The new statute empowers TCB on behalf of the government to fully undertake and coordinate all activities pertaining to the overall development of the cotton industry perhaps more meaningfully than at any other time in the past.

In 2006, two more significant events occurred within the commodity subsector; first, the government resolved to take-over the financing of all the regulatory functions of the commodity boards; and two, it sought to disengage the commodity boards from the direct management of their respective commodity development funds. Thus, in the case of the Cotton Development Fund (CDF), it became transformed into the Cotton Development Trust Fund (CDTF) by mutual stakeholder consensus.

The crucial point to note here was that, unlike its progenitors like Cotton Trust Fund (CTF) which was basically an interim committee formed by cotton stakeholders to facilitate financing for R & D or CDF which was formed as part of the Cotton Industry Act No. 2 of 2001, CDTF was borne out of a mutual tripartite agreement between the Tanzania Cotton association (TCA), the Tanzania Cotton Growers Association (TACOGA) and the Government; as an industry-wide vehicle for spearheading the financing needs of cotton development in the country. CDTF as an independent and legally registered entity on its own right has the mandate and powers of mobilizing resources for cotton development not only from its key stakeholders but also from any other source both from outside and inside the cotton industry.

Nevertheless, in spite of a long period of frequent institutional and policy changes and nearly two decades of market reforms, agriculture in general and the cotton industry in particular continue to be plagued by the same challenges of low production, low productivity and low profitability which were associated with the cooperative and parastatal marketing board era. Thus, if Tanzania is to fully exploit its comparative advantages in cotton, redefining the role of the state was a useful first step. The next step must, therefore, be to facilitate the market and the institutions associated with it to work both efficiently and effectively.

Chapter **4**

COTTON RESEARCH AND DEVELOPMENT IN TANZANIA

4.1 Cotton farming was introduced on wrong assumptions

One assumption made by the colonial administration prior to the commercialization of cotton farming in Tanganyika was that cotton would flourish in the tropics just as successfully as had been the case in the southern states of the USA. In the latter, a sub-tropical environment coupled with fertile soils and cheap slave labour had made cotton farming a major success culminating in cotton being referred to as "King Cotton".

However, after the BCGA had failed to deliver large volumes of the much needed cotton both rapidly and cheaply from any of the Anglophone countries as anticipated, the British government realized that cotton farming in the tropics was totally unlike cotton farming in subtropical areas. In the tropics farming under smallholder conditions tended to be a much more difficult undertaking due to other constraining factors such as low soil fertility due to leaching and erosion; more variable rainfall; a bigger diversity of pests and weeds among other factors. Their failure to anticipate such problems was probably one of the reasons for the buildup of some tension between them and the indigenous people during the early stages of cotton farming.

Having understood the complex interplay of factors that affect average yields the British government decided to reconsider its approaches on how to raise cotton output in Anglophone Africa. Thus in 1921 the BCGA was replaced by the ECGC whose mandate was to carry out research that would resolve some of the more practical aspects of cotton production such as improving the practices and techniques of production and protecting the crop. To that end cotton research programs were initiated at Ilonga and Ukiriguru in 1949 and 1932 respectively. Their outputs went on to significantly increase cotton output in both the ECGA and WCGA.

After independence the work begun on cotton R & D by the ECGC in Anglophone Africa was taken over by the Cotton Research Corporation (CRC) until 1974 when its tenure came to an end. However, in Tanzania and a few other Anglophone countries the CRC continued with cotton R & D until 1976 when it finally closed shop. To deal with the complex of constraints and challenges associated with cotton farming, the CRC tended to adopt a multidisciplinary approach involving all research disciplines namely; breeding, agronomy, soil science, pathology, entomology and fibre testing technology. At Ukiriguru where a big team of scientists often worked together, the senior cotton breeder acted as the team leader as well as the coordinator for the cotton research programme in the country.

The continuity of cotton R & D work initiated by the ECGC and subsequently carried out by the CRC until 1976 was often subject to periodic disruption due to frequent staff changes involving the expatriates as well as uncertain financing arrangements during the era of economic reforms. Thus, between 1976 and 1982 the Overseas Development Administration (ODA) in the United Kingdom agreed to have some of the ex-CRC staff to continue working on cotton R & D under a short-term technical and financial assistance programme. Since then the World Bank (WB) also came in and posted its staff at Ukiriguru until 1985 after which the National Agricultural Research Service (NARS) took over and became entirely responsible for managing all cotton related R & D work at both Ukiriguru and Ilonga using Tanzanian research scientists.

Up until 1992 the financing of cotton R & D in the country

was largely the responsibility of the government and the cotton industry. The latter, under the existing single channel marketing system, channeled funds for the recurrent budget directly to both Ilonga and Ukiriguru through the existing cotton marketing parastatal bodies. The industry was also responsible for financing all work relating to the production and multiplication of foundation seed at Nkanziga, Lubaga and Mwanhala in the WCGA and at Muhenda, Mazizi and Mwada farms in the ECGA. Payments in relation to staff salaries as well as for the repair and maintenance of infrastructure and station overheads were being met by the central government. Such neat and elaborate financing arrangements remained in force until 1992 after which they became disrupted by changes associated with the liberalization of cotton marketing and the restructuring of TCLSB.

The financing of cotton R & D by the industry resumed in 1995 after the formation of the Cotton Trust Fund (CTF) by the industry at the instigation of the government. In 1999 the work being done by CTF was handed over to the newly formed Cotton Development Fund (CDF). A steering committee was formed by the cotton industry and the agricultural ministry to oversee the activities of the fund with TCLSB as the secretariat. In 2001 CDF became formally incorporated under the Tanzania Cotton Industry Act No. 2 of 2001 and went on to perform four major functions, namely; financing cotton R & D; financing the procurement and distribution of seasonal inputs to farmers; financing the dissemination of market and extension related information and working to promote the industry as a whole. By mutual agreement cotton stakeholders resolved in 2006 to have CDF replaced by the Cotton Development Trust Fund (CDTF) with the Tanzania Cotton Growers Association (TACOGA), the Tanzania Cotton Association (TCA) and TCB on behalf of the government as its main trustees.

4.2 Cotton R & D agenda

Cotton is produced worldwide but especially in the tropical and sub-tropical regions under a range of environments and hence farming systems. Thus, its performance in terms of seed cotton and lint yields as well as fibre characteristics has tended to vary in relation to both levels of management and input use. Similarly, its stakeholders tend to exhibit varying and quite often conflicting objectives and demands all along the seed to garment value chain. Thus, farmers for example, tend to seek for maximum seed cotton or lint yield per unit area whereas the ginners and spinners tend to respectively demand for varieties with a high ginning out-turn in the order of 40% or more and for lint delivered to their mills to be of acceptable fibre length, micronaire and strength in order to meet the demands of a rapidly changing spinning technology.

To deal with such often interrelated factors, R & D institutions have quite often become compelled to undertake their research in ways that are client-oriented, demand-led and multidisciplinary in nature and hence the involvement of diverse disciplines such as plant breeding, agronomy, crop protection, post harvest processing and socioeconomics. In Tanzania the overarching objective of cotton R & D has continued to be the need to improve the productivity of cotton farms and inputs. In both the ECGA and WCGA the increased production, productivity and profitability of cotton has often tended to be constrained by the lack of varieties with high yield potential as well as high ginning out-turn (GOT) values and requisite fibre characteristics; declining soil fertility particularly in the WCGA and some parts of the ECGA; unacceptably high levels of yield losses due disease infection and damage by insect pests; severe weed competition; excessive vegetative plant growth and increasing competition from food crops.

In the tropics, the realization of economic yields quite often

40

requires substantial use of external inputs such as improved seeds and especially fertilizers and insecticides. In SSA in particular, markets for such inputs and the credit needed for inputs quite frequently fail for smallholders and they are almost never accessible for farmers who are not organized in some form of a society, association or even a cooperative union. It has probably been for these and other factors that in spite of more than sixty years of cotton R & D in Tanzania coupled with the release of packages of best recommended farming practices, the majority of cotton farmers are still unable to achieve average seed cotton yields higher than 400 to 750 kg/ha and 700 to 1000 kg/ha for the WCGA and ECGA respectively. On research stations current commercial varieties tend to give seed cotton yields that are 3 to 4 times higher than farmers' yields. One of the major challenges facing cotton R & D stations has therefore been how to help bridge the existing gap between on-station and on-farm seed cotton yields.

One major difference between cotton farming in the ECGA and the WCGA is that while climatic and soil conditions tend to be far more favourable for cotton growing in the ECGA than in the WCGA, such conditions also tend to favour rapid weed growth and the quick build-up of insect pest populations. As a result the cost of producing a kg of seed cotton also tends to be higher in the ECGA than in the WCGA largely due to higher labour costs for weeding, spraying against pests, harvesting and uprooting of cotton stalks after harvests as well as higher input costs particularly for pest control.

In spite of the differences in production costs between the ECGA and the WCGA, average seed cotton yields as well as production costs per kg of cotton in Tanzania are by far much lower when compared to cotton grown in the majority of the Francophone countries where input use including the use, of inorganic fertilizers and better farming practices, tend to be better emphasized. In the remainder of this chapter I examine some of the areas where further research would help farmers to bridge the yield gap between on-station and on-farm yields.

Table No. 4: **Comparative costs of producing cotton in the ECGA and WCGA**

Farm operation	ECGA	WCGA
Pre-sowing • Land rent	30.00	30.00
• Ploughing	40.00	12.00
• Other	8.00	-
Sub-total	**78.00**	**42.00**
Sowing • Seed	2.40	2.40
• Fertilizer	0.00	7.60
• Herbicides	0.00	0.00
• Other	12.00	12.00
Sub-total	**14.40**	**22.00**
Growing • Thinning	8.00	6.00
• Weeding and hoeing	60.00	36.00
• Herbicides	0.00	0.00
• Fertilizers	0.00	0.00
• Insecticides	24.00	16.20
Sub-total	**92.00**	**58.20**
Harvesting • Hand picking	78.80	32.00
• Uprooting/buring of stalks	40.00	20.00
Sub-total	118.80	52.00
Grand-total	**302.40**	**174.20**

Source: **Survey of the Cost of Production of Raw Cotton; ICAC 2008 data**

4.3 Adjusting cotton farming to variable rainfall

Average cotton yields in Tanzania are quite low by world standards. This has in part been due to smallholders still being stuck to the use of poor husbandry practices and being unable to optimize the use of seasonal inputs in general and fertilizers and pesticides in particular. Perhaps more importantly, they have tended to be constantly under the mercy of variable weather when raising their crop. The issue of rainfall and in particular, the timing of its onset as well as its distribution over time has become extremely critical in recent years. In both the WCGA and ECGA cotton growing is entirely dependent on rainfall. Consequently the sowing of cotton is often timed to fit in with the existing the local rainfall pattern.

Thus, in the case of the WCGA as well as in some parts of the ECGA particularly in the regions of Manyara, Iringa and Mbeya, where the rainfall regime tends to be weakly bimodal, the optimal planting time often falls between mid-November and the end of December, during the so called short rains. The latter have tended to last until the end of January after which a short dry spell sets in. The latter may be either short-lived or fairly prolonged before the onset of the so-called long rains starts quite often between March and April. Cotton sown during the November-December window is often ready for harvest by the end of April onwards coinciding with the tailing off of the long rains. In the ECGA the sowing of cotton in areas other than Manyara, Iringa and Mbeya is often timed to coincide with the start of the long rains from February onwards.

Over the years, however, the sowing of cotton in many parts of Shinyanga and Mara regions in the WCGA has tended to be increasingly delayed beyond December to as late as January because of recent changes in the timing of the onset of both short and long rains. Similarly, in most parts of the ECGA the overall rainfall distribution pattern has increasingly become unpredictable lately. Such delays in the planting of cotton have tended to affect not only cotton yields but also the quality of its fibre because the commercial varieties currently in place were bred to flower over a relatively long period of time which, unfortunately, has recently become shorter due to erratic rainfall.

How to optimize cotton yields and quality under the "new" rainfall regime has recently emerged to be one challenge which R & D institutions have to deal with rather urgently because current sowing dates for cotton in the ECGA and WCGA that were recommended more than fifty years ago no longer hold water these days. In the WCGA for example, while cotton areas in the districts of Kibondo, Geita and Bukombe tend to get their rains as early September and October, areas in the cotton growing districts of Mara region tend to plant cotton as late as January and February: a period considered rather too late for cotton sowing during a "normal" cropping calendar.

The major implication of the change in the timing of the onset of rains in both the WCGA and ECGA would seem to be that the continued use of late maturing cotton varieties no longer makes sense under present circumstances. In trying to fit cotton varieties into the present uncertain rainfall regime, one option would be to introduce the use of early maturing short duration varieties. The National Research Council of South Africa had already initiated work along such line by the first decade of the 21st century. The strategy on early maturing short duration varieties has so far worked quite well in the case of some cereal crops most notably maize and most grain legumes such as pigeon peas, green gram and cowpeas. Several varieties belonging to these crops have been successfully bred to fit with either the short or long rains in low, medium and high attitude production areas.

As Tanzania contemplates to transform its agriculture from the present peasant form to one that is increasingly commercial in outlook, cotton R & D must seek to provide production options that address the potential needs of such kind of farming. Thus, while cotton farming is currently entirely rain-fed; the prospects for irrigated cotton production have so far not been investigated. This kind of thinking has not been pursued for the main reason that irrigation is primarily for some designated important food crops notably rice or high value crops such as cut flowers and onions. It is perhaps high time that cotton as a strategic crop for Tanzania gets mainstreamed in the plans and programs for irrigated agriculture.

During the colonial period some work on irrigated cotton farming was initiated at Mbarari where varieties bred at Ilonga were tested and gave reasonably high yields under irrigation. In the WCGA a big irrigation scheme was started by the TCA at Bugwema. However, due to some operational problems it had to be stopped. To date we have absolutely no idea just how the present commercial cotton varieties would perform if they were to be subjected to either supplementary irrigation or totally irrigated conditions. Data to this effect is necessary as Tanzania contemplates on making a paradigm shift to intensified farming because even if the smallholders may not be able to afford the higher costs of irrigated farming, those wishing to invest in higher end cotton farming should by no means feel limited to do so by an existing paucity of such data.

4.4 Converting from broadcasting to line planting

One of the major paradoxes of cotton farming in Tanzania in general and in Shinyanga and parts of Tabora and Mwanza regions in particular, has been the reluctance by most farmers to have cotton grown in rows. The recommended best practice in the WCGA stipulates that seeds should be sown on holes that are 0.30 to 0.45 m apart on rows that are spaced 0.90 m from each other depending on soil fertility and overall growing conditions. Under normal growing conditions farmers using such spacing specifications are capable of attaining plant populations to the tune of 45,000 plants per ha in most parts of the WCGA.

Nevertheless, the majority of farmers in the WCGA and

particularly in the regions cited above, prefer to broadcast their seeds rather than sow them in rows. The common practice in such areas is for farmers to broadcast the seeds onto a totally uncultivated cotton field. Such an operation is quite often done after the first rains and then followed by an ox-driven ploughing operation which then buries the seeds under. Because most of the seeds tend to be buried too deeply during the ploughing operation they tend to rot, thus leaving only a relatively small proportion of them managing to germinate and to emerge successfully above ground. Therefore, it is not hard to see why in the WCGA the twin problem of low plant population and low average yields per ha has tended to persist over time.

Reasons for farmers' preference for broadcasting to dibbling of seed during planting are not well known. There is anecdotal evidence though that the tendency to broadcast seed during planting arose out of farmer's inability to hasten the sowing of seed over the large tracks of land given the difficulties associated with handling fuzzy seeds and the need to optimize labour requirements. Thus, broadcasting seems to be the "norm," for example in Shinyanga and parts of Tabora and Mwanza regions where average farm size tends to be quite big at times and where the use of ox-ploughing is relatively common. On the other hand, broadcasting is relatively uncommon in Mara region; Chato district of Kagera region; parts of Shinyanga (Bukombe and Kahama districts), Kigoma and Singida regions as well as certain parts of Mwanza region (Sengerema, Geita and Ukerewe) where either family farms are relatively small or located on hilly terrain.

The dislike for row cropping may have also been inadvertently promoted by existing agricultural policies such as those purporting to keep the price of cottonseed as low as possible as a strategy for promoting increased cotton production. Prior to crop marketing liberalization, up to 30,000 tons of seed were being dished to farmers at token prices of up to

100 shillings per kg as an inducement for them to grow more cotton. However, after policy and market reforms total annual seed requirements for the country declined to between 15,000 and 18,000 tons in spite of the area under cultivation remaining roughly the same, namely, between 350,000 and 500,000 ha. Such drop in the amount of seeds used was largely due to the price of seed being raised up to 250 shillings per kg during the 2007/08 cropping season. Thus by purely adjusting the seed price to reflect market trends farmers became compelled to become more careful in their use of planting seed.

Partly as a result of such market development and a renewed push for adoption of row cropping, more farmers are slowly converting to row cropping even in the districts of Bariadi, Maswa, Meatu and Igunga where broadcasting is quite rampant. One obvious way of speeding up the switch to row cropping would be to replace the use of fuzzy seeds by those without fuzz which are best known as delinted seeds. Tanzania is one of a handful of countries in the world which are still using fuzzy seed for planting and which together with Ethiopia and Iran are the only three countries in the world where farmers still broadcast seed during planting.

In other countries the use of delinted rather than fuzzy seeds has tended to provide the surest way of eliminating immature and unhealthy seeds prior to sowing among other advantages such as killing surface pathogens; ensuring an easy flow of seeds during planting by a mechanical planter; speeding up moisture absorption by seed as well as economizing on both the amount of seed and dressing chemicals per unit area to be planted and hence reducing the cost of production as well.

In contemplating for the introduction of delinted seed in the country, one of the major considerations to think about would be the price to be offered for the amount of delinted seed needed to plant one ha. In Zimbabwe, the unit price for acid delinted and machine or brush delinted seeds during the 2008/09 cropping season was in the order of 0.95 and 0.90 USA dollars per kg which in equivalent Tanzanian shillings was considerably higher than the heavily subsidized price of 250 shillings per kg for the fuzzy seeds used in the country.

Nevertheless, such increment in the cost of delinted seed may be more than offset by factors such as; significant reduction in the overall amount of seed used per ha; the minimization of abuse and misuse of seed during planting; enhanced prospects for wider adoption of row planting as well as opening up possibilities for the mechanization of both planting and weeding in cotton. In the final analysis, the switch to row cropping will most probably signify the end to perhaps the most important huddle in the achievement of optimum seed cotton yields, namely, low plant populations coupled with the un-enlightened intercropping of cotton with other crops.

4.5 Facilitating cotton to coexist with competing crops
In almost all cotton growing areas farmers tend to grow both cotton and food crops on their farms in order to balance their needs for cash and food security. As a matter of priority, food crops tend to be sown first and the cash crops, of which cotton is the most important cash crop in both the ECGA and WCGA, as soon as possible afterwards. In the ECGA in general and Ulanga district in particular, the tendency was until the late 1990s to relay intercrop maize with cotton. In the WCGA, the trend has continued to be to intercrop the two crops i.e. growing maize and cotton simultaneously on the same field. Intercropping helps farmers to achieve several objectives almost simultaneously, for example economizing on labour e.g. by making one weeding operation serve two crops; providing him/her with a balance between a food crop and a cash crop and for spreading the risk of potential crop loss.

In spite of its advantages, any form of intercropping involving

48

cotton has since the colonial period been completely banned in Tanzania. It would appear that the need to have cotton grown as a sole crop arose from the need by government to have reasonable control, through its extension service, on critical operations such as planting, weeding, spraying for pest control, harvesting and uprooting after harvest; and to minimize the effects which maize and cotton tend to exert over each other in relation to attacks by *H. armigera*. The concern then would seem to be that rather than helping to optimize cotton yields, intercropping has instead tended to depress cotton yields.

So what has been the scientific basis for the ban? Maswa is one district where some of the adverse effects of the un-enlightened intercropping of cotton with maize tend to manifest themselves. Midway through the growing season, cotton plants may not be easily singled out of the crop mixture in part due to being fewer in number as well as being shaded by the taller and faster growing maize crop. It is only after maize has been harvested and the straws stashed here and there that cotton plants become visible again. In Maswa district where the two crops tend to be sown at the same time, the cotton crop tends to suffer from effects of shading because the maize varieties commonly used are the long maturing ones whose maturity period is in excess of 100 days. Thus, cotton plants are quite often etiolated and with few bolls on them due to shedding. These factors coupled with low average cotton plant populations per ha tend to further depress cotton yields.

Apart from yield losses in cotton due to competitive effects exerted by maize, intercropping has also tended to depress average cotton yields by exacerbating pest attack on cotton in two different ways. First, as a result of the crops being haphazardly intercropped, farmers are unable to correctly apply insecticide sprays on their cotton at critical times for the control of its major pest called *H. armigera* or more commonly, the American bollworm. As a result, its attack on cotton tends to be aggravated further. The other way by which maize affects cotton yields is rather indirect, namely, by influencing the build of populations of *H. armigera* before and during the growing season. *H. armigera* is a pest of both maize and cotton and which attacks both crops during the flowering period.

Attack by *H. armigera* on cotton starts at flowering and is initiated by populations that had been breeding on maize and other host plants growing prior to cotton or simultaneously with cotton. So although *H. armigera* is a pest of both, cotton and maize, its status on cotton tends to be significantly influenced by events on maize and other host plants flowering prior to cotton. Thus, in a choice situation where the flowering of maize coincides with that for cotton, maize tends to be preferred to cotton and so it may play a diversionary role by acting as a trap crop thereby diverting populations of *H. armigera* and hence its damage away from cotton onto maize where its damage is of no economic consequence.

On the other hand, maize sown prior to cotton occasionally exerts the so-called nursery crop effect by sustaining early season breeding of populations of *H. armigera* on maize which then later move onto cotton at a susceptible stage with devastating effects on yield as most farmers do not adequately spray their cotton anyway. Thus, depending on the prevailing weather and crop growing conditions, maize is capable of either exacerbating its damage on cotton either through the nursery crop effect or by ameliorating such damage on cotton by diverting bollworm damage away from cotton through the trap crop effect. In the WCGA a season characterized by good rains and a successful maize harvest quite often tends to be one characterized with severe attacks from *H. armigera* owing to its successful earlier breeding on such maize and other alternate host plants and vice versa.

In the Ulanga district of Morogoro region, a practice

50

commonly referred to as relay intercropping has for many years helped cotton to coexist with maize which it often competes for both land and labour. In that district, maize sown at the start of the short rains in either October or November tends to be relay intercropped with cotton sown at the start of the long rains in February or thereabout at a time when the maize crop is well past physiological maturity. To minimize shading effects on cotton farmers tend to cut off the tassels and all the leaves thus leaving behind only the maize stems with their cobs. Thus, relay intercropping facilitates the farmers to meet their needs for both food and cash on the same piece of land.

Nevertheless, by facilitating the cultivation of maize to occur prior to cotton the weakly bimodal rainfall regime in the ECGA allows maize to act as major source of populations of *H. armigera* which later on move onto cotton at the start of flowering with devastating effects on yield. There are a series of other alternate host plants growing in the ECGA which grow and flower prior to cotton during the short rains and which by neatly fitting in the annual feeding cycle of this pest, tend to contribute along with maize to early season build up of this pest. This phenomenon may very well be one of the reasons why *H. armigera* is more devastating on cotton in the ECGA than in WCGA because cotton is quite often sown after maize and most other food crops and in essence it becomes the sink of *H. armigera* moths emerging from such crops. On the other hand relay intercropping is often not feasible in the WCGA where the planting dates for maize and cotton tend to coincide or overlap.

During the era of the ECGC, the enlightened intercropping of cotton with other crops with which it often competes for land, labour and other resources was once suggested as a strategy for ensuring their mutual coexistence. Apart from the relay intercropping of maize with cotton as currently practiced in some parts of the ECGA, the other option proposed by R & D involved the intercropping of cotton with short duration cultivars of cowpeas. The latter, like cotton is also extremely beloved of insect pests. However, because most smallholders do not as a rule spray against cowpea pests, one suggested approach for achieving protection on cowpea was to intercrop it with cotton so that it would benefit from protection from pesticides applied on cotton but not on cowpeas.

The strategy entailed planting cowpeas in rows that alternated with those of cotton and confining the insecticide sprays to cotton only by using a controlled droplet application (CDA) sprayer called the "Electrodyne". Such a strategy helped to optimize cowpea yields as well as improve the returns to the smallholders who adopted the cotton-cowpeas intercropping package. In other countries, cotton tends to be intercropped with other crops and in particular alfalfa, sesame, sorghum or even wheat in ways that are largely designed to optimize pest control on cotton.

The debate on the cotton and maize intercropping has raged on for ages partly because cotton R & D institutions have found it quite difficult to carry out meaningful research under prevailing smallholder conditions to be able to come up with an operational recommendation on how it can be implemented without significantly affecting cotton yields and quality. Work done on station at Ilonga in late 1980s revealed that arriving at a consensus on best practices for intercropping cotton with maize was complicated by at least three factors; an unpredictable rainfall regime season after season which went on to affect growth of both maize and cotton; variable shading effects on cotton as a result of using either short and full season maize varieties and potential difficulties associated with the optimization of control of H. armigera and other economic pests of cotton. Naturally, for lack of a recommendation on how to correctly intercrop cotton with other crops in general and maize in particular, farmers have continued to intercrop these crops in defiance of the ban and in spite of the negative effects on cotton yields. This issue has also become increasingly politicized in recent years as will be discussed later on.

4.6 The need to conserve soil fertility in the short and long term

Cotton farming in both the ECGA and the WCGA is undertaken under a range of growing conditions and soil types with varying levels of fertility. Cotton in many parts of the Mara, Mwanza and Kagera regions of the WCGA is grown on hill sand soils commonly referred to as *Luseni* which are inherently low in fertility and whose nutrient status and water holding capacity falls off quite rapidly. Rapidly rising human population and declining land for pasture in these regions has meant that most of the available arable land has to be cropped rather continually with little chance for either rotation or fallowing. Use of fertilizer would thus help stabilize average cotton yields that have been declining over time.

Apart from *Luseni* there are two other soil types in the WCGA namely; *Kikungu* and *Ibushi* where fertilization is a must for optimal cotton yields due to prevailing low levels of nutrients in these soils. In the three soils, a basal application of phosphorus and potassium during planting coupled with a top dressing of nitrogen at the start of flowering has been shown time and again to increase seed cotton yields quite significantly. In the remaining two soil types that are prevalent in the WCGA, namely; *Mbuga* and *Itogoro*, fertilization is only seldom required because of high natural fertility and the fact that very little cotton is grown in areas with these soil types. The major paradox of cotton growing in the WCGA is that in spite of fertilizers being highly recommended for the realization of economic yields in areas with *Luseni, Ibushi* and *Kikungu* soil types, to date none of the cotton farmers hardly ever uses them at all.

Limited use of fertilizers on cotton existed even during the single channel marketing system when input credit arrangements existed. At that time fertilizer meant for cotton was quite often diverted to other crops such as maize and tomatoes. The reason is obvious; cotton can more easily be grown as a low-input-low-output crop than either maize or tomatoes both of which are regarded as very high value crops in the WCGA. Farmer's reluctance to use fertilizers on their cotton tended to be erroneously blamed on some perceived fear that the use of inorganic fertilizers adversely affects soil structure and increases soil acidity. The truth of the matter would seem to be that because most farmers are unable to grow their cotton as per R & D recommendations for optimal yields, their current yield levels cannot allow them to break even.

Thus, unless and until average cotton yields per ha rise substantially through improved crop husbandry, the use of inorganic fertilizers on cotton will continue to be uneconomic. In the meantime, the demand for inorganic fertilizers will continue to be for crops such as tomatoes in the WCGA or maize in the southern and southern highland regions of Tanzania the average yields of which are quite high. This is currently not the case at the moment for cotton. In the WCGA the vast majority of cotton farmers are also livestock keepers. Thus, it would be expected that they would use their farmyard manure on their cotton crops. However, this has hardly been the case and it was perhaps for this reason that coercive measures were often taken during both the colonial and post independence eras as a strategy to promote the use of farmyard manure on cotton. There is plentiful anecdotal evidence to the effect that in spite of the unpopularity such unorthodox methods, they often tended to result in spectacular increases in annual cotton output. To date the use of farmyard manure on cotton has continued to be an on and off affair in spite of its proven advantages in soil fertility enhancement.

Like the case for inorganic fertilizers, farmers' reluctance to use farmyard manure is not without reason. Socioeconomic research undertaken by Ukiriguru in several parts of the WCGA has revealed that the use of farmyard manure to fertilize cotton fields tends to contradict with farmers' use of the same raw material as a source of energy. In the greater part of the WCGA, increased population growth and an unrelenting demand for firewood as a domestic source of energy for cooking has resulted in increased use of use of cattle droppings for energy generation rather than for the fertilization of either cotton or other crops. Farmers are also reportedly reluctant to use farmyard manure for fear it aggravates weed problems on their fields. Such fears which are apparently based on some local beliefs and taboos tend to be corroborated by both empirical and anecdotal evidence which show that, over time, increased use of farmyard tends to be correlated with increased incidence of new weed species on cotton farms.

To reconcile the needs for energy and soil fertility enhancement, Ukiriguru and the International Centre for Research on Agro-Forestry (ICRAF) tried to examine the use of some leguminous crops which have the potential of being used either in rotation with cotton or just as cover crops. To date, *Luceana* spp has shown considerable promise in both regards and also as a valuable source of cattle feed and firewood for the farmers. Regarding farmers' reluctance to use farmyard manure because of its bulkiness and lower content of nitrogen content relative to the inorganic fertilizers, researchers have recently released a recommendation that prescribes for the dual use of farmyard manure combined with inorganic fertilizers.

The subject of fertilizer use on cotton has been far less controversial in the ECGA than in the WCGA. In the ECGA attempts to use inorganic fertilizers during the early 1970s and 1980s often resulted in increased vegetative growth in cotton. Such growth tended to predispose the crop to severe outbreaks of both sucking and leaf feeding arthropods. As a result the use of fertilizer on cotton became discouraged and since then the recommendation has been that no fertilizer at all should be used on cotton in the ECGA. In this area where insect pest attack and weed competition tend to be more severe than in the WCGA, researchers reasoned out that applications of fertilizers in general and nitrogenous ones in particular would be counterproductive. Such feeling was further supported by the fear that because most smallholders are unable to spray their cotton the recommended number of times for control of pests, they would stand to lose their crop to the insects.

To date, forty plus years later, the need for a re-examination of fertilizer needs for cotton in the ECGA cannot be over-emphasized. On-going work on conservation agriculture under the Cotton and Textile Development Programme has revealed two very interesting aspects on soil fertility. Most interestingly, while most efforts by government are aimed at boosting fertilizer use with nitrogenous fertilizers being prioritized, soil tests undertaken under ongoing work on conservation agriculture on cotton has revealed that while most of the soils in the ECGA and WCGA are greatly deficient in both potassium and phosphorus, those of the WCGA are also highly deficient in nitrogen.

Thus, any expansion of fertilizer use on cotton in both the ECGA and WCGA must go hand in hand with soil testing. Work on conservation agriculture has also helped to bring up alternate strategies for dealing with the soil fertility issue. Because the use of inorganic fertilizers is inherently expensive as reflected by the majority of smallholders failing to use them to any appreciable extent, cheaper and more sustainable approaches to sourcing for nitrogen should be sought. One of the options under consideration involves the use of *Desmodium* spp which apart from serving as a perennial forage legume, its ability to fix atmospheric nitrogen and to repel maize stem borer moths from maize offers tremendous opportunities for adjusting cotton, maize and soil fertility interactions at field level.

4.7 Promotion of need based management of insects, weeds and diseases

Insects, weeds and diseases collectively limit attempts aimed at increasing production, productivity and profitability of cotton in both the ECGA and WCGA. In the ECGA, crop losses due to insect attack and weed competition have tended to be higher than in the WCGA ostensibly due to better growing conditions for cotton, weeds and other plant species that act as alternative hosts for cotton's major arthropod pests. In the ECGA, cotton succumbs to yield losses of up to 50 and 100% due to damage and competition by arthropod pests and weed competition respectively. In the WCGA, destruction caused by diseases in general and *Fusarium* wilt and bacterial blight in particular has tended to be far more serious than damage by either the insects or weeds. *Fusarium* wilt tends to be particularly associated with the less fertile sandy soils occurring near the shores of Lake Victoria where it apparently occurs in association with the notorious root knot nematode. On the other hand, bacterial blight is often more serious on cotton grown in the southern parts of the WCGA where black cotton soils tend to dominate.

In the ECGA, as well as the WCGA, *H. armigera* is by far the most important pest followed by *Earias* spp and *Pectinophora gossypiella;* the spiny and pink bollworms respectively. By feeding on cotton flower buds, flowers and bolls, the larvae of these insects tend to affect cotton yield directly. Cotton is also attacked by a series of sucking insects; such as the jassids, lygus and aphids notably *Aphis gossypii* which feed by sucking the leaves and young bolls and late season pests such as stainer bugs viz. *Dysdercus* spp and *Calidea* spp. The cotton aphid together with the stainer and *Calidea* bugs which feed on seeds in open bolls jointly affect lint quality through honeydew contamination and staining respectively.

The jassid; *Jacobiasca* spp, previously known as *Empoasca facialis* (Jacobi) was responsible for completely limiting the introduction and expansion of cotton growing in all areas of the country during the early 1940s. This pest has now been relegated to the status of a minor pest, thanks to breeding programmes, which have since the 1950s been rigorously and routinely selecting for hairiness in all cotton varieties, a character which confers plants with resistance to the jassids by preventing them from feeding properly and hence failing to reproduce adequately on cotton. Breeding for jassid resistance has been one of the major hallmarks of cotton R & D institutions success stories in cotton history.

To optimize average cotton yields in the face of attack by pests and diseases R & D stations have been advising the smallholders to adopt cultural methods such as the timely planting of cotton; appropriate crop management; end of season destruction of crop residues and observance of the closed season. Such practices tend to assure a healthy and vigorous crop as well as minimizing the build-up of pest populations during the season and their carry over to the next one. In an attempt to mitigate the severity of bollworm attacks on cotton, breeders sought to select for varieties with an indeterminate growth habit. The latter confers cotton plants with high compensatory growth which allows them to produce numerous flower buds over a relatively long period of time so that in the event of an early bollworm attack the cotton plant literally shares them with the bollworm and still retains the capacity to continue flowering and producing a top-crop if and when growing conditions allow that to happen.

Use of such varieties has proven very useful to the smallholders who for lack of cash to buy pesticides tend to spray their crops just a couple of times and quite often delay the start of spraying. Experiments conducted at Ilonga between 2004 and 2007 clearly demonstrated that under sprayed and unsprayed conditions, a variety with an indeterminate growth habit performed in such a way that its yields under the two contrasting conditions differed by up to 70% depending on the level of bollworm attack and growing conditions. Owing to its indeterminate growth-habit, the cotton plant is able to replace, by new growth, leaves that have been destroyed by chewing insects, and flower buds or young bolls that have been shed following insect injury.

Nevertheless, conventional breeding methods have so far not yet managed to come up with a tactic that suppresses bollworms on cotton as effectively as is currently the case with leaf hairiness against jassids. Thus, to further lessen the yield gap between sprayed and unsprayed cotton, the use of varieties with high compensatory growth has had to be integrated with the use of other tactics including insecticides.

Use of insecticides on cotton has tended to be complicated by a multiplicity of factors. In the first place, cotton is attacked by a range of pests throughout its life cycle and therefore knowing which ones to control and when to do so has often proven quite critical. Secondly, because no single pesticide is equally effective against all categories of pests, the use of mixtures of pesticides has tended to be quite common. Thirdly, because of continuous new growth by the plant and possibilities of pesticides being washed off from the plants by rainfall, the issue on spray timing and which formulation to use is important. Fourthly, because of the propensity by the cotton plant to shed some of its fruiting points depending on need and growing conditions, spraying becomes superfluous at times; and finally, because cotton pests tend to be associated with their own kinds which behave as parasitoids, predators and parasites there is the challenge on how to use them as part of an overall management programme.

Pesticides in general and dichlorodiphenyltrichloroethane (DDT) mixed with benzene hexachloride (BHC) in dust form in particular were first used on cotton during the early 1950s for simultaneous control of bollworms and sucking pests. The use of dusts was subsequently replaced by water and oil-based sprays following the introduction of DDT formulated as either a wettable powder or as oil based ultra low volume (ULV) formulation by 1975. Over the years the use of DDT became increasingly mixed with other insecticides most notably the organophosphates in order to broaden the range of pests to be controlled to include most of the sucking pests as well.

Pesticide use on cotton reached one million litres of both water and oil based insecticides per annum by the early 1990s. Such increase was partly facilitated by an institutional arrangement that allowed farmers to get seasonal inputs on credit and at subsidized prices. As a result cotton farmers in the ECGA and WCGA were able to spray their cotton up to eight and six times per season respectively. Spray frequency in the ECGA was eight times in a season made at weekly intervals in the case of conventional low volume (CLV) applications or six times at ten day intervals for ULV spraying.

In the WCGA, the start of spraying was quite often delayed until the tenth week after sowing and spraying frequency was reduced to just six applications at fourteen day intervals. Differences in the timing and frequency of pesticide sprays was due to pest pressure in the ECGA being far more serious than in the WCGA. However, due to frequent scarcities of water during the spraying period, a switch from CLV spraying to ultra low volume (ULV) spraying had to be made in the case of the WCGA and by early 1970s DDT and endosulfan had become the first insecticides to be used on cotton there as special oil based formulations in preference to CLV spraying.

By 1985 the status of pesticide use on cotton changed quite drastically following the exit of DDT and endosulfan from the cotton market. Globally, there had been growing environmental concerns on the continued use of DDT due to its long persistence in ecosystems and in the case of endosulfan it had become implicated with the poisoning of fish in Lake

Victoria. The introduction of synthetic pyrethroids in the early 1980s resulted in very significant reductions in pesticide application rates per ha from between 625 and 1000 g/ha in the case of endosulfan and DDT respectively to below 100 grams per ha in the case of most synthetic pyrethroids.

The advent of synthetic pyrethroids and their use at extremely low dosage rates was boosted by the introduction of newer and considerably more efficient pesticide application methods. Thus with the launching of ULV spraying in the early 1970s followed by electrostatic and very low volume (VLV) spraying in late 1980s, it became possible to apply one pesticide in four different ways depending on the demands for sophistication, cost-effectiveness and type of pest to be controlled. Consequently, the time needed to spray a hectare declined considerably from 120 minutes in case of CLV spraying to 45, 45 and 30 minutes in case of VLV, Electrodyne and ULV spraying methods respectively largely by increasing spray runs (swaths) from 0.9, 1.8, 2.7 to 4.5 m/second respectively.

The broadening of insecticide choices, formulations as well as application methods was instrumental for enhancing the flexibility needed by cotton farmers in dealing with different pest situations. Unfortunately, because most of the pesticides that are currently in use are synthetic pyrethroids or their mixtures with a limited number of organophosphate products, there are risks of pesticide resistance developing among designated pests. That, this has so far not happened may be attributed to the fact that pesticide use declined considerably after crop marketing liberalization and thus any selection pressure against designated pest populations being inconsequential, among other reasons.

The use of more effective pesticides at minimal dosage rates was further boosted by the development and introduction of techniques that improve the timing of pesticide applications on cotton resulting in fewer but more effective sprays being applied. By 1989, it had become evident that if farmers timed their sprays on cotton on the basis of some damage or pest density threshold, rather than spraying by calendar the number of calendar based sprays on cotton could be considerably reduced from 6 ULV sprays in both the ECGA and WCGA to between just 2 and 3 sprays in an entire season without significantly reducing seed cotton yields. In other words, it was not the number of sprays per se that mattered for effective pest control and optimization of seed cotton yields, but rather on how well timed such sprays were made in relation to the critical periods of pest incidence and damage.

By mid-1990s farmers in both the WCGA and ECGA had become introduced to a regular practice of monitoring for pests on their cotton fields particularly during the flowering period when bollworms tend to be most active before deciding whether to spray their fields or not. The switch from prophylactic to threshold based spraying on cotton was received by most farmers with much enthusiasm particularly after crop marketing liberalization and macroeconomic reforms because it allowed them to economize on pesticide use at a time when the prices of pesticides had escalated tremendously following the removal of input credit; abolition of input subsidies and devaluation of the shilling. Regrettably further uptake of threshold based spraying on cotton slowly waned for lack of sustained institutional support.

One positive outcome of the push for adoption and promotion of need based spraying for cotton was that because farmers were being compelled to check for pests as well as damage, they soon started to know first- hand the identity of both the individual pests or their "enemies" as well as the beneficial ones or their "friends". Such understanding was instrumental in enhancing and promoting not only farmers' awareness but also their desire to improve pest control on cotton by integrating pesticide use with other methods of control including biological means in an IPM based system. Farmers are already aware of some of the existing control tactics, such as the early sowing of cotton, in order to minimize effects of stainer attack; the adoption of area-wide end-of season uprooting and burning of cotton remnants after harvest for control of stainer bugs, pink bollworms and diseases such as bacterial blight and Fusarium wilt; and host plant resistance (HPR).

Farmers who had been introduced to scouting and threshold based spraying on cotton for bollworm control had become aware of the diverse complex of natural enemies associated with the major pests; a complex of lady bird beetles, lace wing and syrphid larvae that prey on the cotton aphid, *A. gossypii;* ants and wasps that prey on *H. armigera* larvae as well as several assassin bugs that prey on stainer bugs, *Dysdercus* spp among several other natural enemies. Their knowledge and appreciation of biological control is therefore not to be doubted. Apart from a few studies on the biological control of *H. armigera* and a few other pests, knowledge on many of the parasitoids and a range of generalist predators that are commonly being found to be associated with cotton remains quite limited. The lack of information on the biology and ecology of such natural enemies tends to limit the capacity on how their effectiveness on cotton can be maximized at field level.

In the case of some generalist predators such as ants, lace wings and lady bird beetles which have the propensity to prey on both bollworms and other pests, the case for more research on them is quite compelling given their adaptation to survive in annual, multi-pest and seasonally disrupted agro-ecosystems such as cotton. Cotton urgently requires an overall strategy that will seek to mitigate the insect pest problem on cotton at less cost and in a more sustainable manner than present single tactic approaches premised on insecticide use. The use of indeterminate varieties coupled with threshold spraying offers some scope for optimizing insecticide use in ways that may help enhance the contribution of natural control mechanisms.

IPM, by its nature, is a knowledge intensive system for insect management and therefore its full adoption under smallholder conditions is quite clearly something for the future. Nevertheless, one option that offers almost immediate advantages would be the adoption of technologies that come in pre-packaged form e.g. in the seed for immediate use by farmers such as the use of biotech or transgenic or GMO cotton. In the ECGA where increased cotton output is largely constrained by the need to deal with the twin problem of weeds and insect pests, the introduction of cultivars with stacked genes would probably offer the opportunity of dealing with both weeds and bollworms concurrently. Such intervention, if carried out may very well hold the key to the possible expansion and increased profitability of cotton farming in the ECGA which is by all accounts a sleeping cotton producing giant.

Unfortunately, the pace of its adoption in Tanzania has been much slower than expected ostensibly due to the need for the finalization of compliances to some basic legal, regulatory and policy requirements at the local and international levels. A stage does seem to have been reached where Tanzanian varieties may now be amenable for transformation and subsequent tests as provided by the requisite evaluation protocols. This stage may be circumvented given the fact that the newly introduced privatized seed multiplication and distribution system for cotton also allows for materials say from Zimbabwe and other countries to be eligible for testing in Tanzania as well.

Weeds and weed competition constitute quite a major limiting factor to increased cotton production in both the ECGA and WCGA. Yield losses of up to 100% due to weed competition are not uncommon in the ECGA where up to four manual weeding operations may be necessary during the season depending on rainfall and general growing conditions. Some of the commonest and most obnoxious weeds in cotton field in both the ECGA and WCGA include nut sage, *Cyperus* spp; *Commelina benghalensis; Panicum maximum; Cynodon dactylon; Bidens pilosa; Amaranthus* spp; *Ipomea* spp*; Boerhavia diffusa and Digitaria* spp; among others. In the WCGA, in particular, *Rynchelytrum ripens, Lactuca taraxacifolia and Heteotropum zaylanicum* may be quite important.

All over the country, smallholders tend to manually remove such weeds from cotton fields using the traditional hand hoe. In the WCGA Ukiriguru tried to introduce the use of ox-driven ploughs for both land preparation and inter-row cultivation of cotton. There has been limited uptake of the so-called oxen-driven weeding implements simply because most of the cotton in the WCGA is not planted in rows. Use of herbicides in general and pre-emergence herbicides, in particular, for weed control has been approved and recommended by R & D stations. Nevertheless, attempts to promote their use on smallholder cotton proved futile on socioeconomic grounds and because of problems associated with the need to have cotton fields properly ploughed, harrowed and then seeded prior to application of the pre-emergence herbicide; things which most smallholder farmers are unable to do.

Thus smallholders can hope to benefit from herbicide use if cotton R & D stations can come up with recommendations on post-emergence herbicides that can be sprayed directly on to cotton after its emergence from soil. Again biotech cotton offers this possibility. In the past use of pre-emergence herbicides was quite a regular feature of cotton cultivation on the large cottonseed multiplication farms under the defunct Tanzania Cotton Authority. To date herbicides are no longer used at all and hence mechanical cultivation by hand hoe or animal drawn equipment continues to be the norm. Such scenario would change quite drastically in the event of transgenic cotton varieties possessing stacked genes for dual control of weeds and bollworms becoming adopted and commercialized in Tanzania.

Apart from being affected by insect damage and competition from weeds, cotton in Tanzania also succumbs to a series of fungal and bacterial diseases. First challenge relates to the need for cotton R & D to be demand-led. However, unlike insect pests which are very many and whose seasonal activity and damage on cotton differs tremendously between the ECGA and WCGA, there are only a few diseases of major economic importance on cotton in Tanzania. In both the ECGA and WCGA the bacterial disease commonly referred to as bacterial blight or black arm; *Xanthomonous campestris pv malvacearum* (Smith) Dye occurs rather sporadically.

The other disease commonly referred to as *Fusarium* wilt, *Fusarium oxsporum* Schlet, *F. vasinfectum* (Atk) occurs only in the WCGA in the regions of Mara, Mwanza and Kagera of the WCGA near the shores of Lake Victoria. It often occurs in association with the root knot nematodes, Melodogyne incognita (Kofoid and White) in soils that are predominantly sandy. Until recently the occurrence of the disease was fairly restricted to the regions cited above. However in the aftermath of crop marketing liberalization the disease has increasingly been reported in some areas of Shinyanga region in the districts of Maswa and Meatu which had previously been considered as *Fusarium* wilt free. The increased spread of the disease into new areas is now being solely attributed to the collapse of the former variety zones after market reforms and the inevitable movement of infected seed between the two previous variety zones one of which was considered to be free of this disease.

The recent sighting of *Fusarium* in new areas that were previously known to be free from it would seem to reiterate the need to continue with breeding for resistance in order to ensure that all varieties destined to be grown in the WCGA are resistant to both *Fusarium* wilt and bacterial blight. Apart from these two diseases, there are other less important diseases that occur sporadically on cotton. One of these is

Ramularia sp which occurs in both ECGA and WCGA. It occurs widely during extremely wet seasons and so it can be quite helpful in defoliating the crop prior to harvest.

Another lesser common disease is *Velticillium* wilt. It has so far only been seen to occur in parts of the ECGA in the districts of Kilosa and Handeni. Although it has so far not been reported elsewhere in the country, it is well worth monitoring for its incidence on a regular basis. Over the years, the two major diseases, namely, *Fusarium* and bacterial blight, have tended to be managed mainly through breeding for resistance and all varieties that are currently in use are resistant to both diseases. Nonetheless, to further limit outbreaks of bacterial blight, which can be quite damaging during some particularly wet seasons, the seed commonly used for planting must, as a rule, be coated with a designated bactericide cum fungicide prior to distribution for planting.

There are currently two products recommended for cotton seed dressing namely, Cuprous oxide (as Nordox SD 45) used specifically for control of bacterial blight and damping off of cotton and Bronopol (2-bromo-2-nitropropane-1, 3-diol) which acts as a bactericide cum fungicide. In other countries, notably Zimbabwe seed dressing materials are used in combination with insecticides for dual control of seedling diseases and some early pests of cotton. The relevance of this for Tanzania has to be studied and in particular the economics of continued use of seed dressing chemicals either singly or in combination with insecticides.

4.8 Capacity building to deal with emerging challenges

Cotton R & D has over the years been striving to achieve increased cotton production, productivity and quality. It has sought to do so by breeding for varieties with high lint yield, superior fibre qualities and for resistance to insect pests, particularly, the jassids and diseases such as *Fusarium* wilt and bacterial blight; developing appropriate agronomic practices for optimized performance of newly released varieties; establishing best practices for soil fertility management as well as developing appropriate strategies and tactics for economic weed and insect pest control.

In spite of the disruptions brought about by SAP and challenges arising in the aftermath of crop marketing liberalization, cotton R & D stations have, during the past decade and a half, managed to contribute to the development of the industry by releasing a new variety designated MKOMBOZI (ALAI 90) for use all over the ECGA in place of the outmoded IL 85. The new variety gives higher yields and has better fibre characteristics than its predecessor. Similarly, a recommendation package for the intercropping of cotton with short season cowpeas was released to help boost the output of both crops. In 1999 the first sighting of the red bollworm, *Diparopsis castanea,* on commercially grown cotton in Tanzania was made in the district of Chunya and went on to form the basis for the imposition of a quarantine ban on cotton growing for the entire Mbeya region.

In the WCGA, the cotton R & D station has recently released two new varieties; UK08 and UKM08 whose GOTs, fibre strength and micronaire values are far superior to those of UK91, their predecessor which has been in use all over the WCGA since 2005/06 in place of UK 77 and UK 82 which had become mixed up in the aftermath of crop marketing liberalization. On soil fertility, the use of sulphate of ammonia (SA) has now been replaced with that of either calcium ammonium nitrate (CAN) or urea in a bid to minimize the acidifying effect of SA on soil. To boost the content of nitrogen in farmyard manure, a recipe has been provided which explains on how it should be admixed with either CAN or urea. Finally in both the ECGA and WCGA researchers have periodically been releasing recommendations on new insecticides and applicators with the intention of availing to smallholders the information and tools needed for cost-effective control of pests on their crop.

To date, cotton R & D stations are hard pressed to face up to a series of challenges. The first challenge relates to the need for cotton R & D to be demand-led. In the ECGA the issue on how to make cotton growing a viable proposition and in particular how to reduce the high cost of production relative to food crops remains critical. This may well boil down to finding sustainable solutions to the twin problems of weed competition and damage by insect pests. For many years, the cotton industry has generously supported cotton R & D. There is now an ever growing demand of value for money and indeed tax payers now feel that they should not be paying for scientific research that is neither commercially useful nor theoretically outstanding. No doubt R & D attention should now turn to research agenda that addresses new areas such as biotechnology, nanotechnology and global warming.

That brings us to the second major challenge namely, the need for R & D to increasingly advise government on how to have biotechnology mainstreamed in agricultural development. African countries have been procrastinating on the subject of biotechnology and except for South Africa, Egypt and Burkina Faso and lately Kenya, Uganda and Zimbabwe most other countries including Tanzania have until recently been non-committal to adoption of GEC or GMO cotton. This has partly been due to the fact that issues relating to GMOs or GEC are also being addressed in the political arena. The dangers arising out of illegal GMOs cotton crossing into Tanzania through the back door are quite real given the fact that most of its neighbours are already at different stages of development towards the full adoption of GMO cotton. Tanzania as the leading producer of cotton in Anglophone SSA stands to benefit from GEC and should now move on to starting a fully fledged program on GEC lest it become compelled like Brazil, Colombia and India to hurriedly formalize its adoption due circumstances beyond its control.

Finally, agricultural research in general and cotton R & D in particular is increasingly being called upon to provide answers to old as well as emerging problems such as the need to arrest the continuing decline in soil fertility; increasing environmental degradation; how to deal with new pests in the wake of increased use of pesticides as well as how to deal with the red bollworm problem in the southern and southern highland regions of Tanzania. The last point is critical because agricultural research findings quite often tend to provide a basis for better-informed policy dialogue and public policy and private sector discussions on issues crucial to the future of the agricultural sector. The case of the red bollworm is quite clearly one point in mind in view of its broader ramifications on the future development of the cotton industry not only in Tanzania but throughout the East African region as a whole.

Chapter 5

THE SAGA OF THE RED BOLLWORM
IN TANZANIA

5.1 Cotton and the insect problem

It has quite often been said that cotton is beloved of insects. On a worldwide basis there is perhaps no other crop that suffers from trepidations of insect pests more than cotton. With over 1326 insects and mite species reportedly associated with cotton it is not surprising that cotton has led all other crops worldwide in terms of annual pesticide utilization. In the tropics in general and sub-Saharan Africa in particular pest control is recognized as being by far the most costly operation in cotton production and dealing with pests under smallholder conditions poses immense challenges to the farmer, his family and the institutions that work with him.

Although cotton is quite often associated with a big diversity of pests, by far the most damaging ones are the various species of moths whose larvae feed on flower buds, flowers and bolls and which, therefore, affect yield directly. Such pests which are collectively referred to as bollworms include: the American bollworm, *Helicoverpa armigera* (Hubner); the spiny bollworm, *Earias* spp, the pink bollworm, *Pectinophora gossypiella* (Saunders) and red bollworms, *Diparopsis castanea* (Hamps); *Diparopsis watersi* (Roths) and *Diparopsis tephragramma*. Nonetheless, while the first three species of bollworms are relatively quite easy to manage through the use of a combination of tactics such as insecticide use, biological control and observance of the closed season, the red bollworms on the other hand are relatively more difficult to control than the other bollworms, as the larvae feed inside the bolls and are thus less exposed to insecticide sprays.

The ECGC that had come to Africa to produce cotton for the Lancashire textile industries found it so difficult to deal with the insect pest problem, despite the efforts of many entomologists studying the biology of the pests. In cotton production, therefore, the purposeful adoption of strategies that help to minimize pest control costs has become one of the major cornerstones for profitability and sustainable cotton production.

The red bollworm, *D. castanea* is one of the major insect pests of cotton in all countries neighbouring Tanzania that lie to the south and south-western part of Africa. To date the red bollworm, which is one of the most dreaded pests of cotton in Africa, has not yet become a pest of commercially grown cotton in either the WCGA or the ECGA. The entry and subsequent establishment of the red bollworm on cotton in Tanzania has so far not happened mainly because all areas in the south and south western parts of Tanzania, comprising of the regions of Lindi, Mtwara, Ruvuma and parts of Mbeya and Rukwa, have since 1946 been banned from growing cotton in an attempt to prevent the possible entry of red bollworm into both the ECGA and WCGA. The absence of cotton which, apart from *Cienfugosia* and wild cotton is the only known host plant of the red bollworm, has been instrumental in preventing the possible spread of the red bollworm into Tanzania from the south.

Experimental cotton growing in the districts of Nachingwea and Masasi had shown increasing infestation by the red bollworm as one moved southwards towards Mozambique but not in the opposite direction. Unfortunately, the quarantine order that was also imposed over parts of Mbeya and Rukwa regions was in 1965 amended in order to allow for cotton growing only in one part of the Chunya district called Mwambani. As a consequence of the amendment cotton growing in part of Chunya district had spread out all over the district by 1999 and into some parts of Mbozi and Mbeya districts deep into the existing quarantine area. Such encroachment into the quarantine resulted in the red bollworm being first observed on commercial cotton in Chunya district during the 1999/00 cropping season. This stirred up a debate on the merits of continuing the ban, but the government immediately imposed the ban on cotton growing all over Mbeya region.

Unfortunately, by 2000 when the cotton ban was being imposed, Mbeya region had become the leading producer of cotton producing in the ECGA. During the 1992/93 marketing season Mbeya region alone had produced 7,497 tons of seed cotton. Consequently, as a result of the ban most of the activities involving the ginning, oil milling, textiles and apparel industries had to be either closed or scaled down considerably thus drastically affecting the livelihoods of many people in the region.

In the wake of such developments, most of the affected people and their leaders have been asking whether or not the decision to impose the ban was justified on economic and scientific grounds. Moreover, because most of the urban beneficiaries of the industry have been unaware of the dangers of the red bollworm, they have perhaps justifiably been asking just why the red bollworm seems to be more feared than the other common pests of cotton. In view of all this it can be discerned that the escalating demand to have the ban rescinded may have been fuelled by the decision by government to declare the entire Mbeya region part of the existing quarantine zone in the wake of red bollworm incursion into commercially grown during the 1999/00 cropping season.

Nevertheless, in spite of the wealth of existing scientific and economic reasoning behind the ban, some stakeholders and most notably the law makers have increasingly been questioning the continued validity of the ban as it has been in force for perhaps much longer than most other quarantines which have quite often been of a temporary nature. Thus in the past few years, there has been a lot of pressure being exerted on the government through lobbying and other subtle tactics to have the ban removed, thus allowing for the re-introduction of cotton cultivation in the affected areas. In this chapter I examine the existing debate.

5.2 The Debate: Why the Quarantine Zone?

The basis for the debate on the red bollworm is simple; if all countries to the south and south west of Tanzania have continued to grow cotton and to achieve relatively higher average yields than in Tanzania in spite of the red bollworm, why can't Tanzania do the same without resorting to the quarantine? This question was once put before Ali Hassan Mwinyi, Tanzania's second phase president when he paid a visit to Mbeya region. The question was passed onto TDT institutions for an answer. The scientific basis for the ban on cotton growing in certain designated areas of Tanzania is quite simply because we have a pest situation that lends itself to quarantine measures, plain and simple.

To date the red bollworm has not yet become a pest of commercially grown cotton in Tanzania and the rest of the Great Lakes Region. However, because the red bollworm is a pest of cotton of major economic importance in all the countries to the south of Tanzania, it lends itself amenable to control by merely legal measures for example by declaring all southern and southern highlands regions of Tanzania to be under quarantine. For over thirty years the Technology Development and Transfer institutions have stuck to the same answer, namely, maintain the quarantine zone regardless of whether politicians and others like it or not because the quarantine strategy makes more economic and entomological sense than any other pest management options.

On the basis of the above reasoning, Tanzania imposed a ban on cotton growing in all areas lying within a distance of up to 200 km from its borders with Mozambique, Malawi and Zambia. Such a decision was based on earlier observations by the colonial government which in its bid to introduce cotton growing to the then southern province in the early 1940s, decided to abandon the initiative after realizing that infestation of experimental cotton by red bollworms increased drastically as one moved southwards but not northwards from such fields. Through the imposition of the quarantine zone, Tanzania's decision went on to keep the country and the whole east African region free of this notorious pest until 1999.

As stated earlier, in 1965 the northward boundary of the quarantine zone within Mbeya region was amended in order to allow for "limited" cotton production in one part of Chunya district called Mwambani. Unfortunately, such an amendment which came as a result of sheer political pressure lead to the expansion of cotton cultivation within the whole district of Chunya as well as the rest of Mbeya region as a whole. The inadvertent expansion of cotton growing within the quarantine zone was further exacerbated by the entry into Mbeya region and Chunya district in particular of large numbers of pastoralists cum farmers fleeing from famine and drought in the WCGA in the late 1970s. As a result of all this the integrity of the quarantine zone in Mbeya region became compromised irretrievably.

Expanded cultivation of cotton within the quarantine area inevitably went on to re-establish the contact between the red bollworm and cultivated cotton. By breaching the mandatory 200 km distance separating cotton areas from the international borders had gone on to facilitate the insect to repeat its previous feat of spreading from near Zimbabwe to all over Zambia by using a few scattered perennial cotton plants here and there as 'bridges'.

It was not surprising therefore when by 1999 the red bollworm was found on commercial cotton in Chunya district just ten years after we had warned against the expansion of cotton into the quarantine zone. And so what was previously regarded as "lack of opportunity" for the red bollworm not to spread into commercial cotton during earlier years became a reality in 1999. Consequently, cotton growing in Mbeya region had to stop and the entire region brought back under quarantine. The brief encounter with the red bollworm in 1999 and the subsequent imposition of a quarantine zone over the entire Mbeya region has by and large been the main reason behind the recent upsurge in interest in the red bollworm and the need to understand it more.

5.3 Reasons on why the red bollworm is feared

The red bollworm, *D. castanea*, as stated previously is one of the several species of bollworms whose larval forms feed on the fruiting points of cotton plants thus affecting the final yield directly. However, unlike most other bollworms, the red bollworm has quite often been found to be rather difficult to control as a pest because of some rather unique attributes relating to its general biology, behaviour and ecology. Thus, unlike other bollworms, such as *H. armigera*, whose larvae are active and feed on a succession of buds, flowers and bolls and are relatively easy to kill by insecticides because of their mobility and exposure, larvae of the red bollworm are quite difficult to kill either chemically or biologically.

The difficulty to kill this pest derives primarily from the fact that upon hatching from eggs its larvae tend to burrow immediately into well grown up bolls and to remain there until the bolls have been completely eaten out prior to moving onto other mature bolls. It follows, therefore, that in order to kill such larvae chemically; sprays have to be carefully timed to coincide with either eclosion from eggs or their entry into the bolls. In practice, this is only achievable with scouted but not calendar based spray applications. In Tanzania's neighbouring countries where scouting is routinely practiced, a reasonable level of control of the red bollworm is quite often achieved after spraying more than eight times in one season. Such spraying frequency is not achievable in Tanzania where most farmers can often afford two to three sprays only.

Apart from the difficulties associated with trying to kill the larvae on the plant surface, *D. castanea* is perhaps the only bollworm pest of cotton known to undergo diapause in the tropics. Upon pupation, larvae of *D. castanea* may either emerge as adults within the same season or enter into a period of suspended growth commonly known as diapause during which it may remain underground for many months. By opting for the latter strategy *D. castanea* may in essence circumvent the long and hot dry spells typical of tropical weather or even the lack of suitable host plants. And where it emerges as an adult, it may either restart the breeding cycle or undertake long-range migration. These attributes tend to confer the red bollworm with a suite of adaptations that make it quite difficult to manage on cotton.

Finally, the red bollworm has a rather unusual distribution within Africa. Thus whereas *D. castanea* occurs in all countries to the south of the equator with the exception of Uganda, Kenya, Tanzania, Burundi, Rwanda and Democratic Republic of Congo (DRC), *D. watersi* only occurs on cotton in countries to the north of the equator in the so called CFA countries and in the Sudan where it is referred to as the Sudan bollworm. The other bollworm, *D. tephragrammais* restricted to Angola where it is referred to as the Angola red bollworm.

The absence of all red bollworms on commercially grown cotton in the East African countries as well as DRC up until 1958 was being attributed to mere "lack of opportunity". [It is possible that day length affects its ability to diapause in the equatorial regions of Africa.] In apparent recognition of the two unique aspects of the red bollworm ecology and biology, namely, its limited distribution as well as the difficulties being faced to control it relative to other pests, the colonial government in a desperate attempt to keep the feared pest away from the WCGA, ECGA and other cotton areas of the East African region, it imposed a ban on all forms of cotton growing in the southern and southern highland regions of Tanganyika in 1946. The area in effect became a quarantine zone.

6

COTTON PRODUCTION IN TANZANIA

6.1 A century of cotton farming in Tanzania

Cotton farming in Tanzania has been going on for just over a century ever since it was introduced by the Germans in 1906. Since then it has become a major economic undertaking in a number regions of mainland Tanzania, namely, Shinyanga (which has recently been split into Shinyanga and Simiyu regions), Mwanza (also similarly subdivided into Mwanza and Geita regions), Mara, Tabora, Kagera, Singida, Manyara, Morogoro, Coast, Tanga, Kilimanjaro, Iringa (recently subdivided into Iringa and Njombe regions) and Kigoma regions.

Cotton farming has had the potential to spread to virtually all parts of the country including the islands of Zanzibar and Pemba. On the two islands, efforts to have cotton farming introduced there proved unsuccessful as the islanders became more inclined to concentrate on spices. In spite of growing conditions being quite favourable there is no cotton at all being grown in Arusha and Dodoma regions. Similarly, in Manyara region some cotton is only grown in Babati and Hanang districts. Cotton farming seems to be less preferred in the said regions for what would seem to be purely socio-economic reasons such as the prevalence of a far bigger variety of other probably more lucrative enterprises such as livestock keeping and a multitude of food and cash crops.

In the southern and southern highland regions of Mbeya, Ruvuma and Rukwa and some parts of Iringa regions cotton farming has since the early 1940s been banned by law. These regions have since the late 1940s been collectively designated as a red bollworm quarantine area in a bid to prevent the entry into the ECGA, WCGA and the eastern African region as a whole a notorious pest of cotton called the red bollworm which is endemic in Mozambique, Malawi, Zambia, Swaziland, Angola and South Africa. Except for the 1999 incident when the red bollworm made an incursion onto commercially grown cotton in the Chunya district of Mbeya region, the imposition of such quarantine zone has so far helped keep both the ECGA and WCGA free of the red bollworm.

Wherever it is grown farmers preference for cotton would seem to derive from considerations such as its ability to perform well in the relatively semi-arid areas with an annual precipitation of less than 1000 mm per annum and for which reason it tends to be looked upon as some kind of an insurance crop. Similarly, on account of its better and more reliable marketing arrangements cotton tends to offer farmers far brighter prospects of being paid for their crop after harvest relative to other cash crops that also tend to be produced in the semi-arid areas. An even more important reason for farmer's liking for cotton in such areas would seem to derive from the fact that cotton tends to be much more suited for cultivation under either a low input/low output strategy or a high input/high output strategy both of which are good for the majority of the resource-poor farmers as well as the bigger commercial farmers respectively.

To date after just over a century of cotton farming how does the scenario for cotton production in the country look like? In this section an overview is given of the present status, challenges as well as prospects for increased cotton production in the country.

6.2 Cotton production is characterized by low average yields

Between 1960 and 2009 the area sown to cotton in Tanzania rose nearly threefold from 182,000 to 510,000 ha. During that period annual cotton output rose nearly fourfold from a low of 30,264 during the 1960/61 season to a high of 126,229 tons of lint obtained from a peak area of 510,000 ha during the 2005/06 marketing season. Thus, annual cotton output rose with increases in the area under cultivation rather than by increases in average yields per ha over time as has been the case in other countries outside Africa.

The average yield trend for Tanzania for the period between 1990 and 2008 when compared to that of other countries and the general global trend is shown in table 5. During that period Tanzanian average lint yields were only in the order of 19 to 53% of the global average. When compared to Mali and Burkina Faso where cotton is similarly grown under rain-fed conditions, Tanzanian average cotton yields were less by 55 and 56% respectively. When compared to Egypt where cotton farming is completely irrigated, Tanzanian average yields were only 21% in magnitude or less than 79%. When compared to average cotton yields obtained under partly irrigated conditions in Australia and Greece, Tanzanian average yields were lower by up to 81%.

Table No. 5: Trends in average cotton yields per ha in Tanzania versus the world for the period between 1990 and 2011

Year	Area harvested	Lint yield (kg/ha)	Total production (tons)	Global average lint yield (kg/ha)	Tanzania's average lint yield as % of global average
1990	320,000	150	47,900	572	26.2
1991	450,000	189	84,913	596	31.7
1992	430,000	223	96,017	549	40.6
1993	344,000	131	45,069	550	23.8
1994	172,000	233	40,062	582	40.0
1995	344,000	239	82,083	569	42.0
1996	283,000	308	87,091	581	53.0
1997	350,000	177	62,052	594	29.8
1998	180,000	200	35,925	570	35.1
1999	250,000	140	35,514	592	23.6
2000	182,000	225	40,933	606	37.1
2001	420,000	119	50,077	632	18.8
2002	387,000	158	60,963	644	24.5
2003	387,000	132	51,166	652	20.2
2004	500,000	229	114,306	740	30.9
2005	510,000	245	125,193	731	33.5
2006	300,000	145	43,545	765	19.0
2007	450,000	150	67,495	790	19.0
2008	510,000	245	125,193	785	31.2
2009	365,000	230	84,000	727	31.6
2010	480,000	196	90,000	738	26.6
2011	500,000	240	120,000	754	31.8

Source: ICAC.

Table No. 6: Average lint yields of cotton grown under different growing conditions

Country	Area.	Yield	100% irrigated	Supplemental irrigation	Rain-fed	Tanzanian yield as % of other countries
B. Faso	449,000	445	No	No	Yes	43.6
Mali	479,000	435	No	No	Yes	44.6
Tanzania	450,000	194	No	No	Yes	-
Zimbabwe	342,000	310	No	Yes	Yes	62.6
Greece	381,000	1043	No	Yes	Yes	18.6
Australia	357,000	1802	No	Yes	Yes	10.8
Egypt	300,000	928	Yes	No	No	20.9
Sudan	168,000	450	Partly	Yes	Partly	43.1

Source: ICAC.

Evidently the productivity gap between cotton farming in Tanzania and other cotton growing countries in Africa, let alone cotton growing in the AE, is quite enormous. In Egypt, the use of ELS cotton and irrigation is obviously one of the reasons for the higher yields there. In Greece and Australia yields are even higher in spite of irrigation being partial ostensibly due to cotton farmers' higher compliance with best farming practices including the use of GMO cotton. In these and other countries such as the USA, cotton farming has become extremely sophisticated involving the use of computer and satellite-controlled equipment during planting, spraying and harvesting.

In Tanzania as in Burkina Faso and Mali cotton farming is the undertaking of smallholders who are entirely dependent on seasonal rains. Nevertheless, average cotton yields per ha in Tanzania are much lower than those of their counterparts in the Francophone countries. The major explanation for this lies with the fact that in both Mali and B. Faso, cotton farmers tend to more closely abide with the recommended best practices for cotton farming including the routine use of pesticides and yield enhancing inputs such as inorganic fertilizers. In Shinyanga and Mwanza regions; two of Tanzania's leading cotton producing regions, the majority of cotton farmers there hardly ever use inorganic fertilizers on their cotton and are yet to comply with the basic best farming practices for the crop. In the said regions the practices of broadcasting cotton seed during planting as well as the haphazard intercropping of cotton with other crops and especially maize continue to be the norm rather than an exception.

Table No. 7: **Cost analysis of the productivity gap between Tanzania, Burkina Faso, India and Brazil**

	Unit	Tanzania	Burkina Faso	India	Brazil
Yield	Kg/ha	245	414	579	1,444
Acreage	Ha	510,000	510,000	510,000	510,000
Price	Dollars	0.50	0.50	0.50	0.50
Revenue	Dollars	137,732,385	232,739,622	325,498,167	811,777,812
Difference	Dollars	-	95,007,237	187,765,782	674,045,427

Source: **Tanzania Cotton Board**

Farmers' preference for a low-input–low-output approach to cotton farming in Tanzania does seem to have arisen in response to the need to deal with cotton farming in the absence of a viable and functional system for the provision of seasonal inputs and other services considered critical for the development of the cotton industry like the "filiere system" which proved to be extremely successful in the Francophone countries. The "filiere system" was developed by the French government to ensure that developmental, commercial, research and extension operations relating to cotton were fully integrated. Such system was retained after independence albeit with a different form of ownership under new state owned companies and remains quite attractive because apart from retaining a fully integrated supply chain for provision of seed to market services such as inputs, credit, transport, ginning and marketing; it also facilitates the provision of support services relating to research, extension and infrastructure. As a result, farmers in most Francophone countries tend to attain considerably higher average seed cotton yields when compared to their counterparts in Tanzania who for a long time have tended to lack both an integrated input supply and a producer-price support system.

6.3 Annual output fluctuates markedly between seasons

Apart from low average yields, cotton production in Tanzania is also characterized by marked fluctuations in annual output between seasons. Throughout the twentieth century, annual cotton output in the country has been fluctuating well below 100,000 tons of lint per annum. During the first decade of the twenty first century, annual cotton output rose and exceeded 100,000 tons of lint per annum on three occasions, namely, during the 2004/05; 2005/06 and 2008/09 marketing seasons. Nevertheless, just between 2001 and 2009 annual cotton output fluctuated dramatically between 43,525 and 126,229 tons of lint per annum in spite of the area under cultivation during that period remaining relatively stable between 300,000 and 510,000 ha annual.

Apart from cotton, tobacco is perhaps the only other major cash crop whose annual output similarly fluctuates quite substantially between seasons. For example between 1997/98 and 2007/08, its annual output swung quite widely between 19,400 and 58,000 tons of tobacco. Such drastic fluctuations in annual output are relatively uncommon in the case of other crops such as coffee, tea, cashew and sisal which are somewhat perennial in nature.

Table No. 8: Annual production trends of six of the major cash crops in Tanzania for the period 1997/98 to 2007/08 (in thousands of tons per year)

Crop	Marketing season										
	97/98	98/99	99/00	00/01	01/02	02/03	03/04	04/05	05/06	06/07	07/08
Coffee	37.0	41.9	48.0	58.0	37.0	52.4	37.5	56.7	34.3	51.1	
Cashew	95.9	106.2	116.1	122.5	67.3	89.7	78.9	71.9	90.4	92.3	
Tea	26.2	22.0	24.8	24.8	24.7	30.0	30.2	31.8	30.0	34.1	
Sisal	22.2	23.2	41.1	23.5	23.6	23.3	23.9	26.7	27.8	30.0	
Tobacco	51.0	38.0	24.4	19.4	27.7	25.1	33.6	47.5	56.5	58.0	
	86.9	62.3	35.5	41.4	50.9	62.9	46.9	114.6	126.2	44.5	
	229.7	232.5	210.1	316.6	289.8	200.3	295.2	204.2	212.3	217.7	125.2

Source: **Ministry of Agriculture, Food Security and Cooperatives**

Cotton and tobacco are two crops that tend to exhibit considerably wider swings in their annual output than the likes of say coffee and tea in part because as annual crops they tend to easily succumb to seasonal variations in the timing, distribution and amount of rainfall. For example, due to severe drought during the 2006/07 cropping season, annual cotton output was merely 44,000 tons of lint as opposed to 126,229 tons of lint obtained in the preceding season of 2005/06. Similarly, due to devastating effects of El Nino and La Nina annual cotton output during the 1996/97 and 1997/98 seasons declined significantly from 87,091 to 62,052 and 62,052 to 35,925 tons of lint due to flooding and drought in those seasons respectively. Such periodic and dramatic fluctuations in annual cotton output tend to be relatively unknown in countries such as Egypt where cotton production is entirely irrigated.

Apart from their direct effects on crop production vagaries of weather and especially the amount and distribution of rainfall during the cropping calendar has quite often tended to influence the decision by farmers on whether or not to grow cotton in a given season. Cotton as an annual crop tends to confer farmers with the flexibility to shift quite easily to other crops especially the food crops such as maize, paddy and upland rice, chickpeas and tomatoes with which it often competes for labour, land and price depending on season. In the WCGA for example, Kahama district which was until recently a major rice growing part of Shinyanga region has now turned into being one of the leading cotton growing districts in the region following increased incidences of drought. The increase in cotton output has in turn brought about increased crop competition and thus making the issue of relative prices between crops becoming quite critical in influencing farmers' cropping decisions.

Finally, although many factors have the potential to affect the level of cotton produced in any one season, the price paid to the farmer for each kg of seed cotton sold during the marketing season would so far seem to be the most crucial in influencing the magnitude of cotton produced in Tanzania. Cotton farmers in DE tend to make their planting decisions largely in relation to the price in shillings paid per kg of their seed cotton in the preceding season rather than on the basis of some projected future price as is the case in the more advanced economies. This might well be the reason for the present trend whereby any fall or rise in cotton output tends to come in tandem with price trends on the global cotton market as exemplified by the events during the Asian Financial Crisis in the late 1990s and the economic slowdown and financial meltdown during the 2008/9 marketing season.

During both crises, world prices for cotton declined significantly in part due to less demand for raw cotton by the textile and apparel manufacturers in China and the Far East in the wake of declining demand by retailers in the USA and Europe. Such scenarios went on to discourage cotton output in the subsequent season. During the 2009/10 marketing season the producer price for cotton soared to 1,200 shillings per kg of seed cotton for the first time in production history. Although such price was reached late in the season after most farmers had already sold their seed cotton at a suggested price of 600 shillings per kg, it was widely being anticipated that the area under cotton during the 2010/11 cropping season would increase quite significantly in the wake of such favourable producer prices.

6.4 In the ECGA production has stagnated

Cotton farming in Tanzania first began in the ECGA before spreading out to the rest of the country. With its head start in cotton production and being in possession of some key requisites for a successful cotton industry the ECGA was, at least in theory, anticipated to become a booming cotton belt for Tanzania. The ECGA is endowed with ample arable land with relatively more fertile soils than in WCGA; possession of large and relatively permanent rivers of the likes of the Rufiji, Ruaha, Wami, Pangani and Ruvu among others which tend to offer unlimited possibilities for producing both a rain-grown crop as well as an irrigated one in one season. The Germans, it would appear, opted to introduce cotton production in the Rufiji basin of the ECGA rather than anywhere else in the country possibly for these and other reasons. Moreover, it is one of the few areas in the country where up until the early 1970s two cotton crops could be grown in one calendar year; during the so called long rains between March and May as well as after the floods on the silt laden flood basin of the mighty Rufiji river.

Over the years the closer proximity of the ECGA to the major ports of Tanga, Dar es Salaam and Bagamoyo as well as the major textile mills located near these cities proved to be an added advantage for an industry based here. Finally, cotton varieties bred and grown in the ECGA have consistently been producing lint that is of far superior quality and hence in greater demand from overseas buyers than lint produced from the WCGA. For these and perhaps other reasons and initiatives during the pre-independence period cotton output in the ECGA increased culminating in this part of the country accounting for up to 71% of the total annual cotton output by 1938. Nevertheless, its contribution to annual national output has since then been on the decline reaching a magnitude of less than 10% and 2% by 1994 and 2009 respectively. To date the WCGA has become virtually the country's only cotton growing area.

Table No. 9: Cotton production trends for the WCGA and ECGA for the period between 1922 and 2010

Year	WCGA (Bales)	ECGA (bales)	TOTAL	% ECGA
1922	3,250	4,000	7,250	55
1923	4,250	7,750	12,000	65
1924	6,000	13,000	19,000	68
1925	10,000	11,500	21,500	53
1926	9,000	15,250	24,250	63
1927	7,000	9,000	16,000	56
1928	12,000	21,000	33,000	64
1929	8,000	19,500	27,500	71
1930	7,000	14,000	21,000	67
1931	7,500	3,000	10,500	30
1932	7,500	10,500	18,000	58
1933	15,000	26,000	41,000	63
1934	32,000	18,000	50,000	36
1935	41,000	18,000	59,000	31
1936	43,000	25,000	68,000	37
1937	31,000	31,000	62,000	50
1938	22,000	22,500	44,500	51
1939	40,000	16,500	56,500	29
1940	41.000	19,000	60,000	32
1941	50.500	22,500	73,000	31
1942	34,000	17,000	51,000	33
1943	23,500	13,500	37,000	36
1944	18,000	7,000	25,000	28
1945	36,000	6,000	42,000	14
1946	34,000	5,000	39,000	13
1947	32,500	7,500	40,000	19
1948	45,000	9,000	54.000	17
1949	38,000	14,000	52,000	27
1950	39,000	11,000	50,000	22
1951	42,500	5,000	47,500	11
1951/52	71,000	7,500	78,000	10
1952/53	44,500	10,500	55,000	19
1953/54	90,000	12,000	102,000	12
1954/55	109,709	12,291	122,000	11
1955/56	116,924	14,076	131,000	9
1956/57	119,000	14,127	133,127	11
1957/58	132,000	18,682	150,682	12
1958/59	155,000	18,786	168,786	11
1959/60	184,000	19.663	203,663	10
1960/61	162,000	24,817	186,817	13

1961/62	161,000	5,985	166,985	4
1962/63	198,000	17,843	215,843	8
1963/64	237,000	24,101	261,101	9
1964/65	272,000	23,639	295.639	8
1965/66	342,000	30,914	372,914	8
1966/67	408,500	30,023	438,523	7
1967/68	378,500	20,518	399,018	5
1968/69	275,000	9,929	284,929	3
1969/70	384,000	9,420	393,420	2
1970/71	405,378	16,835	422,213	4
1971/72	349,575	12,588	362,163	3
1972/73	411,221	10,020	421,241	2
1973/74	347,399	11,547	358,946	3
1974/75	371,208	21,841	393,049	6
1975/76	220,000	12,981	232,981	6
1976/77	348,429	18,881	367,310	5
1977/78	271,968	16,035	288,003	6
1978/79	282,701	25,335	308,036	8
1979/80	310,270	16,361	326,631	5
1980/81	280,699	14,059	294,758	5
1981/82	220,911	17,141	238,758	7
1982/83	212,213	12,864	225,077	6
1983/84	229,858	16,884	246,742	7
1984/85	256,656	12,761	269,417	5
1985/86	154,160	17,283	171,443	10
1986/87	352,238	20,985	373,223	6
1987/88	420,989	18,847	439,836	4
1988/89	279,712	19,610	299,322	7
1989/90	178,761	17,394	196,155	9
1990/91	255,883	13,113	268,996	5
1991/92	452,614	19,764	472,378	4
1992/93	497,314	35,126	532,440	7
1993/94	242,132	10,168	252,300	4
1994/95	212,177	11,199	223,376	5
1995/96	439,361	17,855	457,216	4
1996/97	460,635	19,648	480,283	4
1997/98	336,341	7,865	344,206	2
1998/99	190,032	11,368	201,400	6
1999/00	185,113	11,096	196,209	6
2000/01	228,317	317	228,634	0.1
2001/02	273,287	105	273, 392	0.4
2002/03	346,569	1,363	347,932	0.4
2003/04	257,230	1,720	258,593	0.7
2004/05	626,670	3,727	630,397	0.6
2005/06	690,528	3,281	693,809	0.5
2006/07	239,380	2,454	241,834	1
2007/08	370,285	1,315	371,600	0.04
2008/09	679,439	3,137	682,576	0.5
2009/10	493,100	437	493,537	0.1

Source: **Tanzania Cotton Board**

Notes: The standard net weight of a bale of lint is 181 kg and the seasons indicated refer to marketing seasons that normally start in July of the prevailing year and end in March of the next year.

In the ECGA, cotton farming has now become limited to just a few areas notably in Manyara, Morogoro and Coast regions. In these regions cotton farmers just like their counterparts in the WCGA have been growing cotton out of habit rather than coercion as was the case in the past. However, their attachment to cotton is now fast fading away for the main reason that in recent years cotton farming in the ECGA has become far less competitive relative to most other crops particularly the many food crops with which it often competes for labour, land and returns per unit cost of production. Similarly, due declining volumes of cotton in the ECGA ginners have tended to be reluctant to invest in cotton in the area and thence the immense marketing problems which the crop faces on an annual basis. Apart from the paucity of markets, other major factors constraining increased cotton output in the ECGA include its proneness to frequent and more damaging pest attack and weed competition than cotton in the WCGA.

In contemplating for a major and significant recovery of cotton production in the ECGA deliberate policy and institutional interventions are required. One seemingly very pragmatic strategy would be to heed the advice that was previously given to BCGA but which apparently could not make much sense at that point in time. BCGA had categorically been advised against pushing for cotton growing on soils and in locations where other crops proved to be more profitable to the grower than cotton. The challenge to date is whether cotton can be made more competitive than food crops through new incentives, policies or even new technologies that would improve its profitability and hence competitiveness relative to the numerous food crops grown in the ECGA. To this end, the introduction of contract farming (CF), warehouse, receipt system (WRS) and biotech varieties combining bollworm resistance and herbicide tolerance, may well be some of the options to think about now rather than later.

6.5 Policy changes tend to have a bearing on production
Cotton and six other so-called cash crops, have until recently been the only regulated crops in the country. As such their production, processing and marketing arrangements have quite often been liable to sudden policy and institutional changes initiated by government. Within the agricultural sector in general and commodity subsectors in particular, such policy and institutional changes have on more than one occasion culminated in drastic and quite often dramatic variations in the annual output of regulated crops in general and cotton output in particular. During the 1966/67 marketing season for example, the record cotton output of 75,373 tons of lint obtained that season declined to 42,179 tons by 1975/76 partly as a result of the effects of a combination of policy and institutional changes in the aftermath of the launching of the Arusha Declaration in 1967; the compulsory villagization of all rural people in mid 1970s and the dissolution of cooperatives as independent member organizations in 1976.

Similarly, the steady decline in cotton production from 96,372 tons of lint during the 1992/93 marketing season to 35,476 tons during the 1999/00 season was a consequence of several factors including a radical and wholesale liberalization of a key subsector; an unplanned restructuring of the marketing board and the simultaneous abolition of subsidies and devaluation of the shilling. The latter factor proved to be very critical because following the withdrawal of subsidies and a devaluation of the shilling, the cost of the much needed cotton insecticides increased significantly and in spite of increases in producer prices after the devaluation of the shilling, the margin of difference was inadequate to compensate for the high costs of farming inputs. Consequently,

94

annual pesticide use on cotton slumped from an average of one million litres by the 1992/93 season to just one tenth of it by 1999/00. Inevitably, cotton output dropped precipitously between 1994 and 2000.

A similar scenario emerged during the 2008/09 and 2009/10 seasons when cotton production dropped from 123,080 tons of lint to 88,837 tons respectively due to an abrupt termination of the "pass book system". Its withdrawal resulted in the majority of cotton farmers failing to buy the pesticides on a cash basis in spite of their prices being subsidized by government. As a result part of the crop was lost to insect pests. The subject of input credit and the "pass book" system will be discussed shortly.

Cotton unlike most of the perennial crops has tended to succumb more easily to the impacts of sudden and often frequent changes in policies and institutions that are associated with it. This, as explained in the case of prices, is partly due to its annual growth cycle and the farmers who grow it having the ability to switch relatively easily between cotton and other annual crops. During the 1994 reform of cotton subsectors in Africa several aspects of the cotton market were negatively affected and no doubt Anglophone countries that had adopted a fire brigade type of approach to the reforms have not fared quite well in their road to recovery. In the remainder of this chapter a discussion is made regarding some of the steps that were taken by the cotton industry in Tanzania to stop the decline in output and thence return the industry to the growth path.

6.6 How the jinx was broken

Cotton farming in Tanzania is characterized by conspicuously low average yields, dramatic fluctuations in annual output, vastly contrasting performance between the ECGA and WCGA and frequent policy and institutional changes. Such scenario is symptomatic of a subsector lacking a development strategy. Thus to get output up again in the aftermath of an unplanned, radical and wholesale liberalization of the cotton industry, the need for a development strategy could not be over-emphasized.

6.7 CSDS-1

Throughout the 20th century Tanzania remained unable to raise annual cotton output beyond 96,372 tons of lint obtained during the 1992/93 season in spite of its vast comparative advantages in cotton. Since then cotton output dropped to just 35,476 tons of lint by 1999/00 due to effects of liberalization. Such slump in cotton output had resulted in cotton's contribution to total export earnings declining from 24.6% by 1992/93 to 6% by 1999/00.

The idea of a development strategy was premised on the need for old and new market participants to have a shared goal on cotton development because after liberalization they had all resorted to pursuing their private agenda. Such attitude was quite clearly opposed to cotton development especially in the aftermath of the process of reduction and/or withdrawal of direct government involvement in the major processes of agricultural production, processing and marketing.

Prior to the reforms, the Dutch government had undertaken a series of tasks such as rehabilitating some of the old ginneries; constructing a couple of new ginneries; strengthening transport services for cotton and advising on how new investments in ginning should be optimized in the wake of crop marketing liberalization. In spite of such investments, the industry could not take off after the reforms. Thus, it became obvious that while further interventions were necessary in order to get the sub-sector moving again, such interventions had to be mainstreamed in an overall development strategy for the sub-sector. The formulation of CSDS-1 began in 1998 with the support of the Dutch Government, the European Union (EU) and the Government of Tanzania (GOT) and was finalized after extensive stakeholder consultations.

In summary, CSDS-1 sought to increase smallholders' income by raising the overall quantity of marketed cotton to 750,000 bales of lint or 135,000 tons of lint by the season 2006/07 and by establishing an institutional structure and capacity that allows for this growth. It was anticipated that CSDS-1 would achieve such results by creating a more secure inputs procurement and distribution scheme through CDTF; unifying the stakeholders by establishing a forum for consultation and coordination within the sub sector and putting in place an incentive scheme for rewarding best performers in the sub-sector, among other things.

6. 8 CSDS - 2

On 12th May 2010 cotton stakeholders conducted a post mortem of CSDS-1 and went on to adopt CSDS-2. The latter seeks to further revamp the industry by further raising annual cotton output to 270,000 tons of lint by 2015 as well as boosting domestic consumption of to 50%.

Box No. 1. Goals of CSDS-1

1. increasing smallholders' income by raising the overall quantity of marketed cotton to 750,000 bales of lint by the season 2006/07 by raising output in ECGA from 700 - 1000 kg/ha to 1000 - 2000 kg/ha and in the WCGA from 400 -700 kg/ha to 700 -1200 kg per ha;
2. increasing farmers income from between shillings 50,000 - 120,000 up to between shillings 120,000-250,000 per ha;
3. increasing ginning capacity to 400,000 tons of seed cotton within 6 months;
4. improving lint quality up to a level where up to 60% of lint samples are classed as Gany or Gany plus; and
5. Establishing an adequate institutional structure for the sub sector that would allow for attainment of the said goals.

Box No. 2. Objectives of CSDS-1

1. Appropriate and effective cotton production techniques;
2. Effective and efficient cotton extension services;
3. Timely availability of certified cotton seeds at village level;
4. Timely availability of good quality agrochemicals and farm implements at village level;
5. Effective and efficient marketing of seed cotton;
6. Effective and efficient marketing of lint;
7. A fair and transparent tax, levy and licensing system;
8. Increased cotton output through expansion of medium and large scale farming; and
9. Establishment of a forum for fostering common interest and understanding between stakeholders of the industry.

6.9 Setting up the CDF

One of the pressing issues after crop marketing liberalization was the need for a mechanism under which smallholders would get their seasonal inputs under a competitive market regime. During the single channel marketing system the procurement and distribution of seeds for planting, insecticides, sprayers and their spare parts involved only two institutions, namely, TCMB which facilitated their procurement and availability and RCU which then distributed them to farmers through a network of primary societies under a system widely known as interlocking contracts. The latter has been defined as the provision of seasonal inputs on credit using the borrower's expected harvest of the crop in question as a collateral substitute to guarantee loan repayment. Such input credit arrangements helped the single channel marketing system to circumvent the seemingly chronic problem whereby smallholders find themselves unable to purchase their seasonal inputs on a cash basis.

Nevertheless, the use of interlocked contract arrangements for provision of seasonal inputs proved quite difficult under a competitive market. As anticipated, most new cotton buyers cum ginners became reluctant to engage in such contract arrangements for fear of the so called "strategic default" whereby farmers deliberately avoid the repayment of the loans even though they know that they are under the obligation to pay up. Such fear was apparently based on experiences from Zimbabwe and Zambia where provision of seasonal inputs to farmers through contract farming arrangements had become plagued by a phenomenon commonly referred to as "side selling " whereby some of their farmers deliberately defaulted on paying back their input credit loans by selling their seed cotton to competing companies.

Of course there was also the issue of "side-buying" whereby cotton companies bought seed cotton from farmers who had not registered with them in the first place. Furthermore, with the collapse of most cooperative unions after crop marketing liberalization, agrochemical companies became increasingly reluctant to deal with smallholders on an individual basis given their large number and wide dispersion in space. For these reasons input use on cotton declined significantly between 1994 and 1999 resulting in annual cotton output declining significantly during that period.

Apart from seasonal inputs, the industry was also called upon to ponder on how it would finance cotton R & D as well. The latter was until 1993 being financed by the industry through TCMB by way of a statutory levy charged on lint exports. However, when TCLSB replaced TCMB there were no clear provisions on whether or not the cotton industry would continue to finance cotton research through TCMB's successor. An ensuing air of uncertainty over this issue went on to greatly disrupt cotton R & D programs at Ukiriguru and Ilonga between 1992 and 1995.

In 1995 a series of consultations between the government, TCLSB and cotton buyers cum ginners resulted in the formation of a Cotton Trust Fund as an interim facility for channeling funding to cotton R & D from the industry. However, for lack of a legal mandate its collection of cash became quite constrained as mere goodwill failed to compel some errant cotton buyers to pay up their dues. Similarly, by 1999 it had become obvious that apart from cotton R & D the industry also needed to address the financing of other public goods and services.

Thus, at a meeting held in Mwanza in 1999, CTF was replaced by a Cotton Development Fund (CDF). The latter became charged with the task of providing a centralized mechanism for the financing not only of cotton R & D but also the procurement and distribution of seasonal inputs; the provision of market information as well as the promotional aspects of the cotton industry. CDF was managed by a Steering Committee comprising of members from TCA and the Ministry of Agriculture, Food Security and Cooperatives (MAFC) with TCLSB as the Secretariat until 2001 when it became formally incorporated into the Cotton Industry Act No. 2 of 2001.

To raise the cash needed to run CDF a statutory levy was imposed on all seed cotton sales. Ginners collected the levy on behalf of CDF at the ginnery gate on the basis of seed cotton deliveries there. TCLSB monitored all levy collections by stationing collateral firms at all ginnery gates. The amount of levy to be collected varied annually in relation to expenses projected to finance the procurement of seed for planting; seed dressing chemicals; packaging and its transportation from ginneries up to the village level; insecticides and sprayers; provision of extension leaflets and brochures; financing of cotton R & D; promotion and general administration of the fund. Between 2000 and 2008, CDF and later CDTF undertook several major activities that helped the industry to attain the three bumper crops cited earlier. Some of the CDF's major milestones are discussed below.

6.10 Launching of the "pass book" system
One aspect of CDF that attracted a lot of interest as well as controversy was in relation to how smallholders' cash

contributions were used to finance their seasonal input needs. It may be recalled that in the wake of crop marketing liberalization, annual pesticide consumption by the cotton industry had declined from one million litres during the 1992/93 season to just 100,000 litres by 1999/00 not due to some rapid adoption of GMO technology or even IPM for that matter but due to the collapse of former input credit arrangements.

As a result smallholders became compelled to buy their seasonal inputs on a cash basis. However, for the vast majority of them, the buying of seasonal inputs on a cash basis was something that they were not used to. Furthermore, buying inputs on a cash basis became limited by increased prices of pesticides following the removal of subsidies and the devaluation of the Tanzanian shilling after SAP. Consequently, pesticide use on cotton dropped precipitously between 1992/93 and 1999/00. So, with the collapse of the "interlocked contracts" as described earlier, the industry became hard pressed to come up with an alternative financing arrangement for seasonal input supply.

To deal with the input credit crunch, CDF in 2000/01 imposed a levy on all seed cotton sales and used the cash thus collected to procure the requisite inputs as well as pay for the costs of their distribution up to village level. However, due to a small crop size only 100,000 litres of insecticides could be ordered on the basis of the levy collected. As a result only a few farmers could spray their cotton at least once. Other farmers ended up not spraying their cotton entirely. Such an approach to dealing with the input crisis also proved a non-starter because it entailed farmers being charged twice for the insecticide; by way of the levy charged earlier and for buying such insecticide on a cash basis during its delivery.

It is a truism that most smallholders hardly ever make any significant savings from revenues accrued after the sale of most of their agricultural products. It follows, therefore, that although they are likely to keep some seed or even pesticides for use in a subsequent season, they often find it difficult to keep their cash for long periods of time after the sale of their cash crops because their cash flow is often premised on uncertain harvests and an endless series of other expenses.

To enable such farmers to buy insecticides on a cash basis, CDF introduced the "pass book" system under which each farmer was urged to accept a deduction of 15 shillings per kg of seed cotton sold which was then entered into a pocket sized 10 to 15 page booklet dubbed the "pass book" provided to each farmer free of charge. Data that was also entered into the pass book included the weight of seed cotton sold on each occasion; the amount of cash received by the farmer; the amount of cash deducted per farmer for the weight of seed cotton sold; the date when the transaction was made; the signature of receiving clerk and the stamp of the buying company. Farmers were obliged to keep the cash receipts in respect of seed cotton sold on each occasion by affixing them to the "pass book" as proof of the transactions made.

The amount of money deducted per kg of cotton sold by each farmer was worked out to be 15 shillings. The computation was based on the assumption that at a prevailing average seed cotton yield of 750 kg per ha, a farmer would on average be able to save a minimum of 4,500 shillings per acre which, for the period between 2003 and 2008 was envisaged as sufficient to buy one sachet of pesticide worth 3000 shillings. In the WCGA farmers do on average spray their cotton at least 2 to 3 times and so one spray per acre per season was considered the barest minimum spray frequency given the prevailing economic realities. Farmers with savings greater than 4,500 per acre would be in a better position to afford more than a couple of sachets as well as other necessities such as sprayers.

The "pass book" system was piloted in the districts of Bukombe and Geita in Shinyanga and Mwanza regions respectively during the 2002/03 growing season in order to assess whether farmers would be readily persuaded to get started on the "new" culture of saving part of their earnings from cotton using the pass book for later procurement of their seasonal inputs. Findings of the study relating to farmers' opinions on the "pass book" as well as its utility were presented and discussed at a cotton stakeholder's meeting held in 2003 in Mwanza. Results from the pilot study confirmed that the "pass book" system was indeed quite capable of resolving the problem relating to farmers' inability to buy seeds and pesticides on a cash basis subject to implementation and supervision of the system being done properly. On the basis of the strength of the field results, use of the "pass book" system was endorsed and its subsequent rollout throughout the WCGA and the country as whole given a go ahead. One of the major assumptions underlying the use of the "pass book" system was that, at the start of each farming season, most smallholders do not have the cash needed to buy their inputs. Such an assumption proved to be reasonably correct as reflected by data gathered during the 2001/02, 2002/03 and 2008/09 seasons which showed that only 43%, 53% and 49% of all the pesticides bought by CDF/CDTF and distributed to the various outlets were actually sold on a cash basis thus leaving behind substantial quantities to be carried over to the next season.

Table No. 10: Patterns of pesticide use on cotton for the period between 1999/00 and 2009/10 with and without the "pass book"

Cropping season	Acre packs ordered	Acre packs used	Acre packs unused	% unused
1999/00	100,000	100,000	0	0
2000/01	397,381	350,000	47,381	12
2001/02	1,124,584	483,584	641,000	57
2002/03	1,118,000	600,000	518,000	47
2003/04	923,000	900,000	23,000	4 X
2004/05	1,223,000	1,100,000	100,000	10
2005/06	1,515,451	1,200,000	215,451	21XX
2006/07	1,415,416	849,416	566,000	40XXX
2007/08	1,837,655	1,564,238	273,417	14.9
2008/09	2,032,993	550,000	1,482,993	.9
2009/10	1,200,000	1,200,000	0	0

Source: **Tanzania Cotton Board**

KEY:
(i)   X - Season of commencement of the "pass book" system
(ii) XX – Severe drought affected crop growth.
(iii) XXX – "Pass books" were not used in that and subsequent seasons.
(iv) Units refer to "acre packs" or the quantity of pesticide in designated sachets required to spray an acre at a time.

The utility of the "pass book" system was demonstrated rather emphatically during the 2008/09 marketing season. In that season less 30% of the pesticides available on offer on a cash basis were purchased by farmers in spite of a 30% price subsidization by government per sachet due to a discontinuation of the " pass book" system. The repercussions of farmers' inability to buy insecticides on cash basis are threefold: cotton yields becoming depressed due to sub-optimal control of pests; increased likelihood of pesticides carried over between seasons expiring while in custody and hence depriving CDTF the revenue necessary to serve the industry and finally for lack of a predictable input credit arrangement for cotton, planning for the overall development of the industry becomes quite difficult if not impossible.

Some of the simplifying assumptions made about the "pass book system" turned out to be incorrect. For example it had been assumed that simply because the "pass book" system had readily been accepted in Bukombe and Geita districts, it would similarly be equally acceptable in other areas of the country. During initial tests in the two districts, it was learnt that some ginners were deliberately trying to sabotage the system for fear that if adopted it would render their practice of under-declaring purchase figures no longer tenable.

Similarly, after just a year or two after its adoption country-wide, some IFIs started to discredit the "pass book" system as some kind of a "forced saving scheme" implying that farmers were being coerced into saving their money. However, for lack of a suitable alternative to the "pass book" for dealing with the issue of seasonal inputs, stakeholders rejected the move to have it discontinued. Farmers were quick to appreciate the benefits of the "pass book" as it had helped improve the availability of seasonal inputs up to the village level and at considerably reasonable prices.

Another assumption underlying the introduction of the pass book system was that only *bona fide* cotton farmers would have access to pass books, that the books would be filled correctly using actual data generated at each buying post and that task forces at village, ward and district level would monitor the delivery and allocation of the inputs to farmers in accordance with "pass book" both effectively and efficiently. Unfortunately, this assumption went on to prove to be the pass book's Achilles heel because incidents of forgery and outright fraud quickly emerged as a result of the task forces never implementing their agreed upon roles. As a result, TCB with its meager staff was left to handle the monitoring of over 300,000 "pass books".

Admittedly, adoption of the use of the "pass book" was Tanzania's fire brigade type of approach to dealing with the "seasonal input crisis" facing the cotton industry in 1999 when national annual output had plummeted from a pre-liberalization record of 96, 372 tons of lint to merely 35, 476 tons by the end of the 20th century. Inevitably many challenges emerged in the course of the implementation of the "pass book" system largely due to a series of previously unforeseen events:

First, because average seed cotton yields of the majority of farmers tend to be quite low indeed, such farmers are obviously unable to raise the substantial amounts of cash needed to pay for all their input requirements. Thus, what they badly need is input credit if they are to raise their yields substantially. Unfortunately, the "pass book" system did not in any way provide a way of achieving that objective. Similarly, the "pass book" system was criticized for compelling farmers to use only certain kinds of insecticides cum formulations ordered by CDF. Such criticism came up following the introduction of water based formulations in the WCGA an area which was previously using oil based insecticide formulations only. Thus, although there were more than forty recommended pesticide formulations for use on cotton in Tanzania, more than 95% of those ordered by CDF via the pass book between 2002 and 2008 were water based ones. This was apparently necessitated by cost considerations because up until 2006 a sachet of a water-based insecticide was being sold to farmers at a price of 3,000 shillings as opposed to 5,500 shillings per sachet in the case of oil-based formulations. Thus, with inadequate savings in "pass books", farmers' continued use of oil based insecticides had become an awfully unrealistic proposition.

A CDF engineered paradigm shift from oil to water based spraying was also made on the basis of good science. Pesticides recommended for use on cotton come as either water or oil based formulations and hence can be applied on cotton using the ULVA+. The latter had been tested and recommended by both Ilonga and Ukiriguru as early as the mid-1980s but had not yet become widely adopted in the country. Thus in a choice situation, a switch from ULV to VLV spraying was not to be contemplated in the WCGA where ULV spraying had been going on since the early 1970s. Opposition to the adoption of VLV spraying was also partly due to the switch from ULV to VLV spraying being made too quickly for the comfort of some farmers and perhaps more importantly because the number of new sprayers distributed after the switch did not match up with that of farmers thus necessitating the sharing of such sprayers between them.

Such anomalies coupled with the limited capacity of some farmers to buy adequate quantities of insecticides in line with their needs as well as the lack of skills to dilute the insecticides correctly resulted in the emergence of sporadic complaints against the efficacy of the water based sprays of some insecticides. Occasionally complaints resulted in some pesticides being branded "fake". To emphasize the point, in the Sengerema district of Mwanza region it was alleged during the 2007/08 cropping season that samples of bollworm larvae that had been deliberately submerged in the stock solution of one of the so called "fake" insecticides had continued to live normally after such an exercise.

Such claim came up in an apparent attempt to further discredit the use of water based insecticides. Rather ironically those purporting to have emulated the biblical act of "baptism by immersion in water" neither specified just for how long the larvae remained immersed in the insecticide nor the stage of growth of the larvae. Because insects breathe through their skin, such larvae would have died anyway through suffocation or by intoxication. Nonetheless, reports on laboratory and field tests conducted independently by the Tropical Pesticides Research Institute (TPRI) and the Sokoine University of Agriculture (SUA) on samples of all insecticides distributed in Sengerema and other districts of the WCGA did not corroborate with the allegations from Sengerema.

Until 2007, water based VLV spraying had been going on in the whole country for over five years without any major hiccup until when the case in Sengerema came up. What happened in Sengerema helped to bring to light a few key lessons for the cotton industry. In that district, a farmer called Marco Nyala has for many years been designated the best cotton farmer in the district. By correctly complying with best farming practices including the appropriate use of water based insecticides he has been obtaining yields of up to 2,500 kg of seed cotton per ha. As a relatively well to do farmer, he often buys adequate quantities of insecticides and has become knowledgeable on how to use the VLV sprayers as well as how to correctly mix his insecticides with water. Unfortunately, most other farmers cannot afford to buy adequate quantities of insecticides to meet their spraying needs due to cash constraints. As a result such the little that is bought tends to be used for a much larger area by over-diluting it and no doubt farmers end not getting the desired results.

When oil-based insecticides were offered in place of water-based ones in the subsequent season, only 30% of them were bought by farmers. Such outcome confirmed once again that what was at stake in Sengerema during the 2007/08 cropping season was not the use of water based insecticides *per se* but rather farmers' inability to buy on a cash basis as well as their lack of training on how to use them appropriately.

As argued earlier, a switch from ULV to VLV spraying had to be made because there just was no other way by which the industry could hope to correct for the paucity of pesticides more economically then converting to water based spraying. In Francophone Africa such switch to VLV spraying was done much earlier and has resulted in significant gains in environmental safety as well by phasing out the use of insecticides such as endosulfan that have a high mammalian toxicity.

Thus, a major lesson learnt during the switch from ULV to water based spraying was that change is difficult under any circumstances, and when it involves a break with tradition, that difficulty is magnified further. The industry and indeed the government must now work out modalities which will help sustain the change by more training on how to use the new formulations as well as the need to institutionalize input credit so that most farmers can afford to gain access to the full package of recommended input use on cotton. The introduction of contract farming will, hopefully alleviate this and other needs.

The "pass book" system also came up for criticism on grounds that it lacked a strong institutional support and hence was considered unsustainable. By 2008 a perfunctory participation in the implementation and monitoring of the entire "pass book" system at district, ward and village levels had resulted in the bulk of the work being done by an overstretched TCB staff. Consequently, many "pass books" found their way onto wrong hands as "open cheques" and became willfully manipulated by both the rightful owners as well as clerks at buying posts for personal gain. To counter such malpractices, TCB undertook the task of verifying the correctness and authenticity of all entries in "pass books" numbering between 300,000 and 350,000 prior to their use by farmers. Inevitably delays in accomplishing this task became rife due to the sheer number of farmers involved as well as the scale of forgeries being done.

There was also a growing concern on the fate of farmer's balances in "pass books" after planting and spraying operations were over. Because pass books had to be issued on annual basis in line with the annual nature of crop operations as a whole and as a deliberate attempt to curb malpractices, farmers started demanding to know whether or not any remaining balances could be carried forward and if not how they would be compensated. Some politicians had earlier alleged that the cash balances were being pocketed by either CDF or TCB. To resolve the issue, farmers were either paid in kind in order to square off the balance in the book or where the balance in the book was say 2000 shillings, a farmer would be required to pay 1000 shillings in cash in order to offset the charge for a sachet of pesticide sold at 3000 shillings. Dealing with this and other related issues became an additional administrative burden to CDF and TCB.

Surprisingly many of the challenges facing the "pass book" system were not at all insurmountable. For example, CDF had earlier proposed for a series of amendments to the "pass book" system; for example on the need for "pass books" with transferability across seasons and on the need for the pass book to be mainstreamed into the savings and credit cooperative societies (SACCOS) in order to allow farmers to borrow money for cotton farming as well as to help them weed out all fake pass book holders and non cotton growers who until then had been accessing CDF money illegally. By linking smallholders to the SACCOS, the intention was to use the latter as an instrument for accessing agricultural credit from investment banks.

Unfortunately because the "pass book" had become extremely politicized, the idea of linking it to the SACCOS became a non-starter and so such line of thinking was abandoned in preference for the "voucher scheme" which came into effect during the 2009/10 cropping season. The voucher scheme which has for quite some time been used to facilitate farmers in the southern and southern highland regions to access government subsidized fertilizers for the maize crop, was recently expanded to include selected inputs for cash crops for example; planting seed and insecticides in the case of cotton; insecticides for cashew; and seedlings for coffee and tea. Interventions of such nature have been quite helpful in temporarily circumventing some input crunches facing the said crops. Nevertheless, the main snag with input subsidy programmes does seem to be the fact that they tend to be inefficiently administered and are unsustainable in the long run.

6.11 Jump-starting cotton production

One of the reasons for the steep decline in cotton annual output after crop marketing liberalization in Tanzania was that rather than investing directly in cotton production, incoming members of the private sector opted to engage in the relatively easier tasks of cotton buying, ginning and marketing of lint cotton. As a result most parts of the ECGA and a few parts of the WCGA where volumes of cotton harvest were relatively small stopped growing cotton completely altogether as no buyers ever went to them. Similarly, in most areas where cooperatives had until 1994 not yet paid farmers for cotton bought on credit in previous years, production ceased altogether. This was particularly true of the ECGA where liberalization had resulted in its contribution to total national output to decline from 10% prior to reforms to less than 5% by the year 2000.

CDF intervened to revive cotton production in the ECGA and parts of the WCGA by doing two things: in the first place, CDF facilitated the purchasing and ultimate disposal of all seed cotton in designated parts of the ECGA where it had remained unsold up until 2002. Secondly, CDF sought to revive cotton growing in the same areas by providing cotton farmers with the much needed seasonal inputs and engaging a buyer cum ginner to buy all the seed cotton produced by such farmers at the end of the season. Through such an approach CDF was able to facilitate the revival of cotton in the ECGA a task that went hand in hand with the rehabilitation of a few designated ginneries in strategic places in order to allow for the cotton thus produced to be ginned.

As a result of such interventions, cotton output in the ECGA picked up substantially from just 171 tons during the 2000/01 marketing season to 3,187 tons of seed cotton during the 2004/5 season mainly due to increases in output from Morogoro and Manyara regions. In the Urambo district of the WCGA, cotton output rose from 340 tons during the 2003/04 marketing season to 2,400 tons by 2008/09. Such increase in production has in part been due to some tobacco farmers switching to cotton. In the Kibondo district of Kigoma region output rose from less than 100 tons during the 2003/04 season to 600 tons in 2005/06 and production seems to have stabilized there.

In striving for the revival of cotton farming in the ECGA and parts of the WCGA, CDF and TCB learned a couple of important lessons. First, while both areas possess the potential for increased cotton output, the extent to which revival of cotton farming takes place largely depends on the level of support coming from the Local Government Authorities (LGA). Quite often the LGAs in the ECGA and WCGA were reluctant to take up agreed tasks especially those relating to the collection of payments in respect of seasonal inputs that had been loaned to farmers.

Similarly with regard to the task of monitoring crop performance there was a tendency for the LGAs to leave it all to TCB with its meager staff to do it but they were quite keen in demanding for their district crop levies to be paid in full. The lack of cooperation from LGA quite often resulted in CDF losing substantial amounts of cash by way of unaccounted for input loans. Until recently there has existed a tendency by some LGAs to still think that TCB can on its own manage to oversee production, processing and marketing of cotton in the country as was the case with the Tanzania Cotton Authority (TCA).

6.12 Promoting compliance to best farming practices
Tanzanian farmers do on average produce seed cotton yields

112

that are in the order of 750 and 1000 kg/ha in the case of the WCGA and ECGA respectively. Such yields fall well below the potential yields of varieties currently in use and are even lower when compared to the global average for the period between 1990 and 2008. Perhaps for lack of appreciation of this fact farmers have quite often been blaming the government and cotton buyers for the low producer prices on offer each year. As a result some farmers have been engaging in all kinds of adulteration in their attempts to increase the weight of their seed cotton prior to its sale to the ginners.

To encourage farmers to achieve higher average seed cotton yields per ha TCB with financing from CDF introduced, between 2004 and 2009, a series of nationwide competitions on cotton farming. The major objective of the such competitions has been to demonstrate to farmers how the yield gap between on farm and on station cotton yields can be bridged by promoting the adoption of best farming practices as recommended by TDT institutions. Preliminary surveys had shown that some cotton farmers were already realizing cotton yields in excess of 2,500 in both the ECGA and WCGA. Thus, apart from showing that higher average yields are indeed achievable on farm, the competitions have continued to be looked at as vehicles for the nation-wide campaign to boost annual cotton output to levels beyond 1.5 million bales of lint or 271,000 tons of lint by 2015.

Participation in the annual competition entails farmers fulfilling two simple conditions; that each farmer must have a minimum acreage of at least 0.4 ha under cotton; and that the farmer would strictly comply with the best farming practices prescribed for cotton growing in either the ECGA or the WCGA respectively. To qualify for any of the awards tenable at district, regional and zonal levels, participating farmers are annually being assessed for their level of compliance with the said recommendations the leaflets of which are provided to all participating farmers.

In addition, farmers are also assessed on the basis of the average seed cotton yields that they harvest at the end of the season. Nevertheless, to qualify as an overall winner at the zonal level, a farmer must have obtained a minimum weight of 2,500 kg of seed cotton per ha and having won at the district and regional levels as well. The 10th of October each year has been designated the National Cotton Day and all awards in respect of winners at the regional and zonal levels are presented to the winners on this date. Thus, cotton competitions have the added advantage of evoking some sense of belonging to cotton amongst farmers engaged in cotton farming.

In competitions carried out so far the average yields per ha for some of the best performing farmers rose from just below 2500 kg/ha in 2004 to 3875kg/ha in 2008. Such increases in average yields could not have happened without increased adoption of best farming practices as well as the utilization of farmyard manure. Increased compliance with best farming practices has also been due to farmers increasingly seeking to participate in the National Cotton Day festivities being held annually.

On such occasions farmers who have won at regional and zonal levels have the opportunity to rub shoulders with up to 1000 other stakeholders present at the event. The National Cotton Day has also become an occasion during which other similarly best performing actors in the cotton value chain are also being recognized for their contributions to `development of the industry. During the 2008/09 and 2009/10 marketing seasons for example, some ginners were rewarded for their outstanding work in relation to efficient provision of seasonal inputs to farmers, compliance with trading rules as well as observance of ethical trading practices.

6.13 Institutionalization of a one variety-one zone system
In the aftermath of crop marketing liberalization, the cotton seed industry suffered two setbacks, namely, the

demise of its system for multiplication of certified seed for planting and the subsequent mix up of existing cotton varieties. Up until 1994, the cotton industry had in place a functional system for multiplying seed for planting each year as well as maintaining the purity of varieties still in circulation (the wave system).

Thus, in the WCGA where varieties were being grown and ginned in conformity with the two existing ginnery zones, namely, northern and southern zones, (comprising of Mwanza, Mara and Kagera regions in case of the northern zone and the regions of Shinyanga, Tabora, Singida and Kigoma in case of the southern zone) any potential mix up of varieties as well as the spread of diseases such as *Fusarium* wilt and bacterial blight which occur in the northern and southern zones respectively was carefully monitored. Through such an accepted demarcation of the WCGA, it followed that cotton varieties bred to be grown in the southern zone could only be grown and ginned at any of the ginneries located within that zone and nowhere else. The same applied to cotton varieties bred for the northern zone.

Furthermore, avoidance of the mix up of varieties as well as the spread of the seed borne diseases across the seed zones was also helped by regulations governing ginnery construction. Before 1994, ginnery construction at any place within either the ECGA or WCGA was governed by two main requirements. First it had to be located at a site which is 45 km or more from the nearest ginnery in order to minimize undue competition for seed cotton from the same catchment area; and secondly, seed cotton from varieties grown in a designated ginnery zone had to be ginned within the same ginnery zone and not elsewhere in order to maintain the purity of cotton varieties then being grown in the two designated ginnery cum variety zones. The goal was quite simple namely; to link ginneries to rural areas where they would utilize available labour and thereby minimize the migration of the rural population into towns. The occurrence of small townships or so called "centres" near most major ginneries in the rural areas of the WCGA is perhaps a living testimony to the effectiveness of that policy.

However, conditions governing ginnery construction changed rapidly after 1994 resulting in the concept underlying the ginnery cum variety zones being changed completely. Prior to 1994, the Dutch Government had advised on how new ginneries could be accommodated without compromising the integrity of the existing ginnery zones. However, such advice was largely ignored and prospective ginners managed to erect more and more ginneries at any location of their liking particularly in towns rather than in the rural areas close to where cotton is grown and quite often such ginneries were built adjacent to each other as is currently the case for ginneries at the Ibadakuli area within Shinyanga municipality; in Kahama; in Igunga town of Tabora region; in the Nyakato area of Mwanza city and within the Bunda and Musoma townships of Mara region.

In the aftermath of crop marketing liberalization it became virtually impossible for the regulatory institution to prevent such outright infringements of the previous and present cotton statutes as well as regulations relating to the ginnery zone concept for reasons attributed to political capture. This happened at a time when cotton output was on the decline. Consequently, there occurred a burgeoning mismatch between the supply and demand for seed cotton and ginners became compelled to search far and wide for it and to compete by hooks and crooks to get it. Inevitably cotton varieties from the southern and northern zones became mixed as seed cotton started to move across the previous ginnery cum variety zones and the disease Fusarium wilt which was previously absent in parts of the southern zone started being spotted here and there in over time.

In the ECGA, the ginnery zone concept was largely nonexistent as a result of only one variety being grown all over the area. Nonetheless, some mix up of ECGA varieties with those from

116

the WCGA is presumed to have occurred in this area much earlier than in WCGA for the main reason that during the famines of 1974 and 1984 there was a mass exodus of people from the WCGA into the ECGA particularly Mbeya region. Most of the pastoralists cum farmers who moved into Mbeya region at that time came along with both their cattle and seed of cotton varieties from the WCGA into the Rukwa valley. The dramatic increase in cotton output from the Chunya district of Mbeya region up until 1999 was in part due to the arrival of cotton farmers from the WCGA.

To circumvent the seed mess as well as prevent any further mixing of newly released varieties without reverting to the former ginnery-cum variety zone system the industry opted to transform the WCGA and ECGA into one variety zones as was previously the case in the ECGA. To this end CDF, TCB and the two cotton R & D stations at Ilonga and Ukiriguru embarked on the multiplication of the varieties UK 91 and ALAI 90 for their eventual use in the entire WCGA and ECGA respectively. Such task was completed in 2005/06 and since then UK 91 and ALAI 90 have been in use these areas respectively. Nevertheless, in view of the diverseness of the agro-ecological conditions in both the ECGA and WCGA, the one variety-one zone strategy should best be regarded as a transitional arrangement pending further refinements in line with releases of varieties as well as the establishment of a more elaborate system for the production of certified seed.

6.14 Institutionalization of CDTF

In 2006, six years after it was formed, CDF and other commodity related funds came up for a major review. This was necessitated by two factors: first, the commodity funds in general were being faulted particularly by the IFIs for being government rather than private sector managed. Such criticism would seem to have stemmed from the fact that many of the commodity funds were formed under the same statutes that empower commodity boards to undertake regulatory and promotional functions. Thus, there was a perceived fear that such commodity funds would become government rather then stakeholder controlled.

Second, because the operations of CDF were based on levies being paid by farmers during the sale of their cotton crop sold each year, some people and indeed IMI reasoned out that CDF and other commodity related funds were in fact an unnecessary burden on such farmers in view of the administrative costs of the fund and by continued taxation of the resource poor farmers who they were purported to be serving. On the basis of such considerations and presumably others as well the stakeholders in the respective commodity subsectors were called upon to deliberate on whether or not commodity funds were serving a useful purpose and to suggest on how they should be managed without direct government involvement.

During a stakeholders' meeting held on 22nd April 2006, rather than opting to disband CDF, stakeholders unanimously resolved to retain the fund by converting it into a Trust Fund instead with a view to giving it the mandate to operate independently of any institution including the government. The operation of the Cotton Development Trust Fund took effect on January 2009 under a competitively appointed management team that reports to the Board of Trustees comprising of TCA, TACOGA and TCB (on behalf of the Government) and to the biennial meetings of cotton stakeholders on a regular basis. The initiative to transform CDF into CDTF in order to enable the latter to operate independently of direct government control was ostensibly made in good faith. However, if CDTF is to operate effectively and efficiently as CDF tried to do over the years, the pitfalls that led to the demise of CDF in the cashew industry have to be avoided at all costs. The cashew CDF ran into some administrative problems mainly due infighting between its major stakeholders on issues relating not only to the ownership of the funds but also on how such funds should be utilized.

Chapter 7

COTTON MARKETING IN TANZANIA

7.1 The cotton market prior to liberalization

Prior to crop marketing liberalization in 1994 cotton farmers in Tanzania were linked to the global market through the single channel marketing system. The latter was largely dominated by two institutions, namely, the cooperatives which supervised production, the purchase of seed cotton from farmers and its ginning into lint and the parastatal marketing boards which as state-owned and state funded institutions had the sole legal right to export cotton lint and to engage in any other related activity as deemed fit by the state.

Under the single channel marketing system an official producer price for seed cotton was fixed by government and then publicly announced on the 1st of May each year before the start of the marketing season in early July. Once set, the producer price became pan-territorial and pan-seasonal i.e. applicable all over the country and unchanged throughout the marketing season. Moreover, the government also provided a guaranteed market for the farmers' crop through the cooperative based marketing arrangement and their extensive network of crop buying and storage facilities all over the ECGA and WCGA. Marketing boards, by virtue of their statutory monopoly in the export of cotton, often tended to be used to generate revenues for the government by deliberately setting local producer prices for cotton below the international free on board (FOB) prices.

By the late 1970s and early 1980s the government became hard pressed by bilateral donors and IFIs to break up, restructure, sell off or at the very least commercialize the state–controlled marketing boards. The latter had become inefficient, wasteful and fiscally unsustainable by drawing enormous resources that might have been better utilized elsewhere. Such push was also in line with contemporary wisdom that visualizes governments as not directly managing or seeking to manage the process by which goods are produced and brought to the market. Such process, it is argued, would best be left to commercial, market-driven forces that will result, over time, in the most efficient allocation of resources.

The government acquiesced to crop marketing liberalization and to date up to 40 private companies including the RCUs tend to be involved in cotton buying and ginning on an annual basis. In this chapter, some of the challenges faced by the cotton industry during the transition from a state-controlled system of cotton marketing to one based on free market principles are discussed.

7.2 The "cotton season" controversy

As a matter of tradition the start of the "cotton season" that is the period during which buying, selling, ginning and export of cotton is allowed has had to be announced officially each year and the cotton board often does that on behalf of the government. Prior to 1994 such an announcement to that effect would be made concurrently with the producer price for the different grades of seed cotton as fixed by government. To date, TCB announces the date for the start of the cotton season but not the producer prices.

The need to announce the date for the start of the cotton season was found necessary for several reasons. First to ensure that the crop in both the ECGA and WCGA has matured well enough before it is harvested and sold as it is often sown over a range of sowing dates. Secondly, an announcement of such date confers the farmers enough time to grade their cotton prior to its sale. After crop marketing liberalization, the continuation of such practice often serves as some kind of a polite reminder to prospective buyers to finalize the necessary pre-season formalities relating to buying, licensing and financing requirements all of which take quite a lot of time to accomplish due to the red tape involved.

Fourthly and perhaps most importantly, prior to liberalization the need to announce the official date for the start of the cotton season stemmed from the need to safeguard the purity of cotton varieties then being grown in two so-called variety zones as discussed earlier. Up until 1994, cotton R & D institutions, TCMB/TCLSB and the RCUs had been cooperating closely to make sure that the buying and ultimate ginning of seed cotton originating from the regions in the two designated variety zones was carried out separately to avoid any mixing as well as the spread of diseases and by announcing a starting date for the cotton season early this helped to enhance monitoring.

Over the years the cotton season has tended to start between early June and late July and between early August and early September in the case of the WCGA and ECGA respectively. To date nearly twenty years after market liberalization, the justification for setting dates for the start of the cotton season has become questioned in light of recent developments within the industry. For example, following the designation of WCGA and ECGA as single variety zones where UK91 and ALAI 90 are now respectively the only varieties to be grown there, the fears regarding any potential mix up of varieties in these areas are no longer justified any more. Thus buyers-cum ginners feel that they should be able to buy seed cotton from any part of the two designated cotton growing areas. Nevertheless, fears regarding the increased spread of *Fusarium* wilt remain quite real following the demise of previous ginnery-cum variety zones.

Similarly, because cotton in the WCGA is sown over a range of dates between early November and late January; the crop tends to mature and become ready for sale at different dates of the calendar. Thus, a discontinuation of the norm of fixing a date for commencement of the season implies that farmers would be in a more flexible position to sell their crop. Conferring farmers the flexibility to sell their cotton whenever it is ready would also have the added advantage of circumventing two of their major problems; inadequate space for prolonged storage of their cotton as well as incidences of recurrent food shortages by disposing off their cotton early in the season and using the cash thus obtained to buy the much needed food. To date, delays in the commencement of the cotton season until late June and early July may have inadvertently promoted the pre-season buying of cotton by unlicensed buyers a practice commonly referred to as *"kuhelemba."*

Nevertheless, while evidence in favour of the discontinuation of the norm to announce an official date for the start of the cotton season seems to be quite compelling indeed, two factors may need to be considered very carefully before a decision is made to discontinue the practice. First, given the level of competitiveness of the cotton market and the paucity of viable systems for the collection, collation and dissemination of market information, there is a need for cotton stakeholders to ponder on how a level playing field will be provided in both the short and long term. TCB has to date found it very difficult to effectively and efficiently regulate the industry on its own for lack of adequate cooperation and collaboration with the LGAs. Without a *modus operandi* in place, issues relating to licensing, compliance with quality standards and payment of statutory taxes as well as the collation marketing may prove difficult to monitor and to enforce under such a liberal system.

Secondly, because the ECGA and WCGA are both so vast that none of them can be considered as being homogenous in terms of either soil or climatic conditions, the concept of a one variety one zone requires further refinement. Such

122

concept helped, at least on the interim, the need to circumvent the mixing of UK 91 and ALAI 90 with older varieties in both the WCGA and ECGA respectively in the immediate post-reform era by restricting ginners and farmers to dealing with just a single variety in each of the zones. In both the ECGA and WCGA, there are complaints already about the unsatisfactory performance of both ALAI 90 and UK 91.

In a nutshell, the present one-variety-one-zone concept does not allow for the exploitation of benefits arising from what breeders tend to refer to as "genotype by-environment interaction" a concept which was the basis of the former variety cum ginnery zones that were established over fifty years ago but which passed away unceremoniously after crop marketing liberalization. Cotton R & D institutions and TCB must therefore take leadership in guiding the industry on whether or not time has come for the reinstatement of the older system. Zimbabwe may well be the place to look for inspiration and guidance on this issue given the fact that in spite of the high level of competition there, the industry has continued to deploy a minimum of three varieties on an annual basis without the woes of mix-up as has been the case in Tanzania.

7.3 Producer prices during a free market era

The practice of fixing and announcing producer prices that became applied pan-territorially and pan-seasonally worked quite well during the era of the single channel marketing system. Such practice gave the government the flexibility to raise such prices in a stepwise manner from one season to the next simply because the prices it fixed were considerably lower than the prevailing FOB prices. However, such practice hit a snag during the 1990/91 marketing season when the price of 90 shillings per kg of seed cotton announced by government was found to be considerably higher than the prevailing price at that point in time. Inevitably, the government was compelled to reduce the producer price to 70 shillings per kg and since 1994 the tradition of price fixing came to an end.

News of the abandonment of both price fixing and announcements regarding official producer prices prior to the cotton season was not well received by farmers all of whom had become used to government involvement in the fixing of producer prices. With the advent of free market economics, farmers feared that they had been left out in the cold to fall prey to the profiteers.

To allay such fears and indeed reduce the possibilities of farmers in some remote areas from selling their cotton at prices below the cost of production, the use of the so-called "indicative or suggested price" became adopted. Such prices were determined by a panel of representatives of a select group of stakeholders namely; TCA, TACOGA, TCB and the ministries responsible for agriculture and industries after having taken into consideration the prevailing world market price as reflected by the Cotlook A Index, exchange rate, GOT, cost of cotton seed, taxes/levies, operational costs and a margin for the cotton buyer. The estimated producer/ indicative price was then communicated to the rest of cotton stakeholders a week or so prior to the start of the cotton season.

The use of indicative producer prices began during the 1999/00 cotton marketing season and worked quite well until the 2002/03 marketing season resulting in farmers being paid reasonable prices that tended to increase over time during each of the seasons. That this happened at all was due to the fact that the numbers of cotton buyers cum ginners were relatively low and crop size was also not big and so they could afford to offer higher prices over time. Unfortunately, with such an increasing price trend some farmers went on to believe that cotton prices would always behave that way every season and so they resorted to withholding the sale of their cotton until very late in the season in anticipation of higher prices.

Table No. 11: Producer price trends for the period between 1989/90 and 2010/11

Season	Producer price	World market price.	Producer price as % of world market price
1989/90	28	96	29
1990/91	41	114	35
1991/92	70	121	57
1992/93	60	142	42
1993/94	80	190	41
1994/95	120	308	39
1995/96	207	350	59
1996/97	170	329	51
1997/98	180	373	48
1998/99	185	301	61
1999/00	123	264	46
2000/01	180	323	55
2001/02	175	271	63
2002/03	180	296	61
2003/04	280	440	64
2004/05	250	363	69
2005/06	220	337	65
2006/07	360	442	81
2007/08	450	584	77
2008/09	480	650	62
2009/10	440	623	71
2010/11	650	845	77

Source: **Tanzania Cotton Board**

Such beliefs apparently misfired on more than one occasion when some farmers who had held back the selling of their cotton found themselves unable to sell it at all because cotton buyers had already closed shop. Since then the saying that "it is the early bird that gets the worm" started to make sense to them. In the final analysis, the entire system became questioned because farmers who had sold their seed cotton very early say during the first week of the season also complained for having been given a raw deal by selling their cotton when prices were at the lowest threshold.

The worst risk in connection with the use of indicative prices surfaced during the 2005/06 season when, rather than going up, producer prices fell from 300 to 250 shillings per kg of seed cotton and considerably less by the end of the season. During that season, global cotton prices tumbled as a result of some unforeseen market developments in China mainland. As expected, farmers reacted quite angrily to the turn of events because they had become accustomed to seeing cotton prices going up but not down.

The unexpected fall in both global and local prices occurred, rather unfortunately, at a time when Tanzania was bracing for a general election. Such coincidence came in quite handy for politicians from opposition parties who quickly cashed on farmers' discontent to make outright political gain. One prominent politician from Bariadi took issue with the ruling party by alleging that its government had deliberately lowered the producer prices in order to generate the revenues needed for the financing of its election expenses. Such allegations prompted the government to explain both in parliament and in public on what had actually occurred on the cotton global market. To appease the farmers, the government through a statement given in parliament by Frederick Sumaye, who was the former Prime Minister at that point in time, scrapped off once and for all the education levy and scaled down quite substantially the levels of other statutory levies on cotton in a bid to stabilize producer prices. In the wake of such interventions the producer price bounced back from 250 to 275 shillings per kg of seed cotton.

The saga on indicative price had two significant implications to the cotton industry. In the aftermath of the 2005/06 "crisis", the "double-edged" nature of the so-called indicative price became revealed over and over again starting from 2008/09 onwards. While the likelihood of smallholders' lack of market information tends to predispose them to exploitation by the better informed and more organized buyers, it is the high level of illiteracy amongst cotton growers and their continued perception of cotton as a "government crop" which tends to somewhat complicate the utility of indicative prices. During the era of the single channel marketing system farmers had become used to administered prices which once fixed never went down apparently because they were always set below world market prices. Thus, in a post-reform era farmers went on to believe that indicative prices would similarly continuously go up but not down.

Rather paradoxically, while most cotton farmers are well aware that prices for most other merchandise tend to go up and down in accordance with the law of supply and demand, they apparently feel and quite strongly for that matter that such law should not be applicable to cotton which in their opinion is a *de facto* government crop. Farmers have grown to feel that way simply because politicians and the government in general tend to show more sensitivity and sheer attachment to cotton than probably any other so-called cash crop. This assertion is amply corroborated by the fact that the cotton market has over the past half century been the target of by far more frequent policy and institutional changes than any other commodity market. Thus, in farmers' opinion, the government should not at any one time abscond from the noble task of fixing prices for cotton.

In order to allow stakeholders to ponder and reflect on the events of the 2005/06 season the use of indicative prices was suspended during the 2006/07 marketing season. Nevertheless, indicative prices were again put into use during the 2007/08 marketing season in spite of the advice given by Premier Sumaye against their use. Indicative prices were re-introduced following the establishment of the Tanzania Cotton Growers Association (TACOGA). It was thought that by mainstreaming TACOGA in the process of setting the

127

indicative prices as well as educating farmers on their limitations, the utility of indicative prices would become appreciated. Stakeholders sought to continue using indicative prices within the cotton industry for one major reason, namely, as tools to help them and especially the farmers to keep track of market price movements from some set point either upwards or downwards. Unfortunately, rampant farmers' ignorance and lack of mechanisms to disseminate market information resulted in the issue of indicative prices becoming manipulated for political ends. This fact was vividly confirmed by events that started to unfold starting from the 2008/09 seasons onwards.

During the 2010/11 marketing season for example, the cotton market became an exciting circus like scene when some prominent legislators cum politicians sought to gain political capital from the indicative price crisis by publicly inciting farmers not to sell their seed cotton on the basis of an indicative price of 800 shillings per kg of seed cotton. They instead insisted that farmers should only sell their seed cotton on the basis of an earlier indicative price of 1,100 shillings. The latter had apparently been proposed at the start of the buying season in early June, but it soon became untenable after cotton prices on the global market had tumbled yet again.

Nevertheless, as time went by most farmers began selling their cotton at the prevailing market price after realizing that neither the government nor the legislators could guarantee them against any further decline in the global market price. On the other hand they had become aware, on the basis of previous experiences with cotton prices that they only stood to lose if they did not sell their cotton at the revised price as cotton prices in general tend to be quite volatile. Perhaps more importantly, farmers had become fully aware that even if it wished to intervene by way of subsidizing cotton prices, the government lacked the financial clout to do so as is the case in the USA and EU.

In the aftermath of commodity marketing liberalization, the switch to competitive markets has apparently not been similarly followed up by a change in the mindset of both farmers and some armchair politicians regarding the law of supply and demand versus the traditional approach of setting and fixing prices under the single marketing channel system. A question to be asked is why has this been more difficult for cotton than other cash crops and food crops?

7.4 New marketing challenges after liberalization

The premise for liberalization was that the introduction of competition all along the production, processing and marketing chain would improve efficiency, reduce marketing costs and hence raise farmer's share of the FOB price. The latter was in turn expected to motivate farmers to boost production and productivity. However, rather than rising as was initially anticipated, cotton output kept on falling rapidly during the period between the 1994/95 and 1999/00 marketing seasons. At the same time the industry witnessed a rapid and unregulated entry into the market of new participants reaching 40 within a period of five years largely due to the inability of TCLSB to stamp its authority at that time. Because the number of buyers cum ginners increased quite quickly at a time when annual cotton output was declining, they began competing quite vigorously among themselves and against the RCUs for a reasonable market share of seed cotton stocks.

As a result of increasing competition most ginners resorted to adopting a series of strategies such as locating their ginneries close to a major cotton growing area; putting up numerous buying posts in key strategic areas and engaging the services of the so-called "Marching Guys" or simply cotton agents in a bid to maximize volumes at reasonable cost. Nevertheless, given the high level of competition that exists from time to time some of the ginners have tended to resort to rather unfair trading practices in order to meet their objectives. Some of such malpractices are discussed here.

7.5 Institutionalization of the practice called "Pamba hewa"
One of the hallmarks of the single channel marketing system was the apparent institutionalization of the phenomenon commonly referred to as *pamba hewa;* two words often used as a euphemism for theft or pilferage. The terms *pamba hewa* were coined prior to liberalization to denote the frequent but unexplained weight differences between seed cotton delivered at ginneries with the expected actual weights of seed cotton on the basis of cash handed to primary societies at the start of the season.

In their attempts to quickly optimize seed cotton volumes, most ginners increasingly found themselves loosing the cash destined for purchasing seed cotton through either outright thefts or sheer misappropriation by their field staff via a phenomenon popularly known as *pamba hewa* as described above. In the past, cooperatives covered up for such losses by either deliberately delaying the ginning operations until the next season on anticipation that the malpractice would not be detected or by deliberately setting the seed cotton under storage on fire in order to destroy any incriminating evidence.

How to deal with *pamba hewa* has now become a major institutional problem because after having started during the era of the cooperatives it has kept growing and has now become quite widespread. Thus if the *pamba hewa* malaise is to be solved further reforms to the present marketing arrangements would be necessary. Some ideas to this end are discussed in the penultimate chapter. To deal with other forms of operational cash losses, the onus remains with the cotton buyers cum ginners who must decide carefully on whether or not they will continue buying cotton all over the place or in few designated areas; whether they intend to use their own working staff and warehouses or hired facilities belonging to either PS or private individuals; and finally whether or not to buy cotton either through commissioned agents or the "Marching Guys".

Table No. 12: Trends in the number of cotton buyers and buying posts between 1994/95 and 2008/09

Season	No. of buyers	No. of buying posts
1997/98	37	2912?
1998/99	21	2398?
1999/00	15	1110
2000/01	5	192
2001/02	19	2504
2002/03	11	1271
2003/04	29	2822
2004/05	35	5552
2005/06	29	5225
2006/07	30	4761
2007/08	42	8362
2008/09	40	8284

Source: **Tanzania Cotton Board**

7.6 Increased contamination and adulteration of cotton

In their attempt to maximize seed cotton volume quickly in order to comply with contractual obligations for shipment of bales within specified periods, ginners resorted to buying seed cotton hurriedly from farmers and became more than willing to offer good prices regardless of the quality status of the seed cotton bought. Farmers responded by selling their cotton prior to its harvest in an unpicked form as is often the case for paddy rice and by increasingly leaving their seed cotton on farm for extended periods of time and then taking it directly to a buying post without any prior sorting at home. However, as a result of increased tendencies by ginner's agents to steal from farmers' sweat by way of cheating through the use of tempered weighing scales, cotton farmers retaliated by adulterating their seed cotton prior to its sale in a bid to compensate for the weight losses incurred.

131

During the single channel marketing system the cooperatives were renown for the rigorous enforcement of grading of seed cotton prior to selling as well as adhering to strict best ginning practices. At each selling point seed cotton was routinely inspected to ascertain whether or not each farmer had sufficiently separated cotton which is white, unstained and without any extraneous matter from that which is stained by either insects or rainfall splash. After grading, seed cotton was categorized in two grades, namely, Grade A and Grade B on the basis of whiteness and staining respectively.

To encourage grading, the producer price on offer for Grade A cotton was more than double that of Grade B cotton and farmers who sold their Grade A cotton during the first few weeks of the buying season were often given a bonus. To keep out contaminants such as PP and what have you, seed cotton had to be brought to the buying post either in an ox-driven cart where this was possible or just carried in a large piece of cotton cloth or in jute canvas bags. As a result of doing all these things on a countrywide basis Tanzanian cotton earned two things: a good reputation as reflected by its being called "white gold" and premiums of up to six, four and two cents per pound for type 1, 2 and 3 roller ginned cotton respectively. A further premium of 7 cents per kg was also offered due to cleanliness of hand picked cotton.

Nevertheless, as a result of most cotton buyers failing to pay prices in accordance with the two grades during the scramble for seed cotton; this went on to discourage farmers from grading their cotton before its sale and increasingly less and less Grade B seed cotton was bought. Similarly, at the ginnery, the old age of most of the roller gins as well as the inadequate servicing and maintenance of the saw gins occasioned by lack of spares for some of the older models led to further contamination of lint from extraneous matters such as whole and broken seeds; oils and grease; plastic, jute, hessian and PP and most importantly sand and dust.

Table No. 13: Trends in seed cotton grading between 1997/98 and 2007/08

Marketing season	Tons of Grade A cotton	Tons of Grade B cotton
1997/98	197,706	140.9
1998/99	93,961	472.7
1999/00	97,042	125.8
2000/01	123,418	11.6
2001/02	147,575	858.2
2002/03	187,314	124.0
2003/04	188,916	575.0
2004/05	338,322	152.6
2005/06	374,815	520.9
2006/07	129,197	19.0
2007/08	200,000	450.9

Source: **Tanzania Cotton Board**

The issue of contamination became further worsened by the emergence of an even more destructive form of contamination of cotton involving the deliberate adulteration of seed cotton by farmers prior to its sale and by company clerks prior to its delivery at the ginneries. The most common forms of adulteration in the WCGA have invariably involved the addition of water, fine sand and lately some hygroscopic chemicals to seed cotton ostensibly to increase overall weight just prior to either its sale at a buying post or delivery to the ginnery.

Interestingly, the adulteration of seed cotton was unknown prior to liberalization and so its emergence after market reforms must have been motivated by some new market developments. The general slackening in the enforcement of grading at buying posts as well as increased indiscipline in the market place in the aftermath of crop marketing liberalization would seem to have greatly contributed to the emergence of these malpractices. For example, due to a return, by some company clerks to the old practice of cheating on weights and measures that flourished in the late 1940s, farmers have this time opted for a more direct approach to countering it by adulterating their cotton both physically and chemically. During the two seasons of bumper crops, namely, the 2005/06 and 2008/09 marketing seasons, deliberate use of limestone or calcium carbonate by some farmers and agents of private buyers resulted in significant amounts of lint becoming spoiled through rotting and/or discoloration of lint.

Table No. 14: Weights of fine sand recovered from seed cotton delivered at some ginneries during the 2005/06 marketing season

Ginnery	Seed cotton Bought (kg).	Weight of sand (kg)	% of sand
Afrisian	15,155,527	120,168	0.80
Alliance	31,842,766	618,237	1.94
Al-Adawi	1, 254,029	6,091	0.49
Mwanhuzi	8,663,443	357,535	4.13
Cargill 39sand	21,557,298	649,215	3.00
Fresho	15,503,724	402,180	2.80
Gaki	23,498,043	464,270	1.98
Jambo	26,283,010	160,060	3.80
Luguru	2,707,221	61,408	2.30
Malampaka	5,503,724	55,037	0.99
Mhunze B	2,560,290	64,007	2.50

Source: **Tanzania Cotton Board**

Table No. 15: Tons of seed cotton damaged through chemical adulteration during the 2005/06 and 2008/09 marketing seasons

| Company | Marketing season | |
	2005/06 season	2008/09 season
S & C Ginning	2,000	300
Virian	800	-
NCU	120	-
Nsagali	26	115
Mwatex	-	238.7
Alliance	1,700	24
Birchand	3,000	-
Dynamic	600	-
Hassanali Walji	65.2	-
Olam	-	980
Badugu	-	1,500
ICK	-	375
KBL	-	500
Chesano	-	30
New Sam	-	182.1
Grand total	8,311.2	4,244.8

Source: **Tanzania Cotton Board**

In a nutshell, the compulsion by ginners to buy seed cotton regardless of its grading status in order to maximize volume in the shortest period of time inadvertently led to the creation of a new culture of deliberate adulteration of seed cotton as well as the emergence of a new breed of unlicensed cotton buyers commonly known as "marching guys" who often buy seed cotton under the cover of darkness with lorry trucks as their mobile buying posts and tend to be very active both prior to and during the official cotton season.

In the end, the industry became confronted by problems relating to increased contamination and adulteration. These problems went on to tarnish the otherwise good name of Tanzanian cotton resulting in the cessation of it being called white gold as well as the loss of premiums and started being sold at discounted prices on end markets.

7.7 Emergence of the "Marching Guys"

In the quest to maximize volume while minimizing operational costs, most efficient cotton buyers opted to locate their buying posts in a few strategic places capable of being easily reached by own or hired transport. Nevertheless, others preferred to engage the services of a new breed of "middle men" commonly referred to as "marching guys". The latter are *de facto* unregistered cotton buyers who specialize in buying cotton illegally long before the official season starts and during the main cotton season. They quite often use open lorry trucks as mobile buying posts; a phenomenon commonly referred to as "mobile buying". They have become so versatile over time that they are capable of meeting the seed cotton requirements of any prospective ginner upon demand.

To date, such a new breed of cotton buyers has become both an asset and a threat. Thus by buying seed cotton from farmers prior to the official cotton season they may be helping the them get the cash needed to buy food at a time when some farmers are in dire need of food prior to the harvest of food crops - a phenomenon commonly referred to as *"kuhelemba"* in Sukumaland. It is probably for this reason that information regarding the identity of the "marching guys" who are apparently very well known at local level, is never ever divulged to regulatory authorities. However, because of the tendency by the "marching guys" to operate at rather awkward hours for fear of being apprehended by the regulatory authorities, they quite often do not attach any seriousness to the quality of seed cotton which they buy during such hours. Such unmonitored trade has no doubt contributed quite substantially to the deterioration of the quality of Tanzanian cotton in recent years. During the two seasons when chemical adulteration of seed cotton occurred, the bulk of that cotton is said to have originated from the "marching guys".

Interestingly, the so called "marching guys" never existed

during the single channel marketing system under the cooperatives and parastatal marketing boards and so they are largely a creation of crop marketing liberalization which does seem to have created the necessary incentives and motivations for such niche marketing arrangements as argued before. Unfortunately, the rise of "marching guys" as a vehicle for procuring seed cotton from farmers parallel to a system involving genuinely registered cotton buyers with certified buying posts has brought about substantial regulatory challenges.

Due to their mobility and elusiveness the monitoring of seed cotton quality has become almost impossible. Because the buying of seed cotton is often transacted at night or other times when official recording of sales cannot be made, it is obvious that estimates on average yield, total production as well as the accuracy of projected revenues from applicable taxes and levies will be liable to significant underestimation. Perhaps more importantly, the ginners who engage the services of the "marching guys" tend to gain an unfair trading and hence competitive advantage over their competitors by not paying some of the statutory taxes and levies. As a result, serious ginners may not be expected to make substantial investments in new ware houses cum buying posts and the personnel needed to manage them if the "marching guys" can offer similar services at less cost. Dealing with the issue of the "marching guys" has therefore become a major institutional problem and the cotton industry is unlikely to win its war against contamination and adulteration of cotton so long as this form of cotton marketing continues to flourish unabated.

7.8 Paucity of warehouses
One critical non-marketing function which marketing parastatals performed prior to crop marketing liberalization was with regard to the establishment of a network of buying cum storage ware houses throughout the ECGA and WCGA.

Such storage facilities were quite often strategically located within the production areas and at railway stations in order to speed up transportation of such cotton to either the ginneries in the case of seed cotton or to the port in case of bales.

Up until 1994, there were up to 1000 buying posts with own warehouses in both the ECGA and WCGA where seed cotton was bought and stored. The warehouses were constructed using high quality aluminum sheets and were collectively capable of storing up to 300,000 tons of seed cotton per annum. Such storage capacity did suffice up until the 1992/93 marketing season when crop harvest just barely exceeded the 300,000 tons threshold. At the port of Dar es Salaam, TLSMB had put up an elaborate warehouse system capable of receiving, storing and facilitating the shipment of up to 600,000 bales annually. By linking such system to both the rail and shipyard, TLSMB ensured that the export of cotton was relatively fast and efficient especially during the critical third quarter of the cotton calendar.

After liberalization, most private buyers sought to lease the existing warehouses the majority of which are under the custody of either the PS or RCUs rather than putting up new warehouses of their own. To date most of the warehouses belonging to PS and RCUs are in a terribly pathetic state given the lack of repair and maintenance for many years and as a result they could hardly cope with the modest increases in crop output between 2000 and 2009.

Thus, with cotton output anticipated to rise to 271,000 tons by 2015, the need to quickly revamp the warehousing situation cannot be over-emphasized. At the port, the infrastructure that handled cotton storage as well as facilitating its shipment quite efficiently in the past also requires a major overhaul and modernization given the fact that up to 80% of the lint produced in Tanzania will continue to be exported for yet some time to come. In the WCGA a few new ginners notably Virian constructed their own warehouses to ease the competition for PS owned warehouses and some privately owned houses that became turned into temporary cotton stores.

In the Igunga district of Tabora region, the lack of suitable privately owned storage structures became quite a big problem and with the collapse of the Igembensabo cooperative union in the late 1990s this further meant that PS in this district could not, on their own, participate in cotton trade. As a result, the LGA for Igunga intervened by directing all prospective private cotton buyers within the district to procure their seed cotton only through the existing PS. However, due to the paucity of PS owned warehouses within the district, the buyers became further compelled to share the existing warehouses, a practice which has now become the norm rather than an exception in this part of the WCGA.

Partly as a result of buyers having to share the warehouses, the district has somewhat managed to avert some of the malpractices that are commonly associated with buying at non-PS sites, namely, tax evasion and the under-reporting of purchase figures among other unethical practices. The practice of two or more cotton buyers having to share a warehouse owned by a PS in the purchase of their cotton has increasingly spread to the neighbouring districts of Meatu, Kishapu and Maswa all of Shinyanga region. It is arguable whether the situation in those districts lends itself to true and fair competition between buyers where one cooperative society acts as an agent for two or more competitors because quite often price competition between them stops to cxist.

In Igunga district, farm gate prices have, as rule, tended to be much lower than elsewhere in the WCGA and at buying posts a single buying price is quite often displayed thus confirming that buyers had agreed to buy cotton at the same price. The dissatisfaction by farmers with such practice is corroborated by seed cotton from peripheral parts of Igunga district finding its way to buying posts in neighbouring districts where prices are higher due to competitive procurement. In other places, where warehouses owned by PS are in short supply or just do not exist buyers have tended to rent residential houses which are then turned into buying cum storage places. Unfortunately, most such houses have tended to be too small for the intended purpose.

The proliferation of many buying posts cum storage sheds of varying design, size and location even within the same district or region has tended to complicate the enforcement of rules governing licensing, data collection and quality control in general. Given the vastness of the WCGA, TCB has quite often found itself too thinly spread over the area to be able to efficiently and effectively monitor the buying process and hence the quality of seed cotton being bought given its limited staff, finance and institutional support. In view of these realities, agents of most cotton buyers tend to find it relatively easy to flout the Cotton Industry Act of 2001 with impunity.

7.9 The cotton market is without a level playing field
One of the key outcomes of crop marketing liberalization was that it eventually brought private sector participation back into commodity marketing. However, unlike in the past where the major actors were just the Indians, to date there are a series of other ethnic groups comprising of the Africans, Arabs and Europeans although the Indians continue to feature more prominently. These together with other players, namely; the cooperative unions, TCB and the LGAs tend to constitute a far more heterogeneous team of players some of whose major interests lie outside cotton business per se.

The increase in the number of participants in cotton business undoubtedly resulted in some positive benefits such as farmers being paid promptly for their cotton as well as getting up to 70% of the FOB price apart from increased new investments in ginning and oil milling. However, increased competition has also resulted in increased factionalism as revealed by rampant market manipulation, price fixing, infighting as well as incidents of one company buying seed cotton belonging to another company. In short there has emerged some kind of distrust among and between the ethnic groups.

The level of participation in cotton business by most cooperative unions has left a lot to be desired. Their significant loss of market share between 1994 and 2008 has become an issue of great concern given their prominent legacy in the history of cotton. In spite of their enormous infrastructure, massive subsidization from government as well as other forms of support which they have tended to enjoy from time to time, none of cooperatives that are operational today have been able to face up to the competition from private companies. Regrettably, their failures have quite often tended to be blamed on private buyers in general and TCB in particular.

Ironically, in recognition of their financial and operational predicaments, TCA frequently tried to be accommodative or soft to many issues affecting them for example by agreeing to defer the payment of their statutory levies relating to CDTF. Nevertheless, the RCUs often sought for total exemption from such payments and therefore went on to blame TCB for not agreeing to their wishes. As a regulator, TCB insisted on the payment of such levies by all cotton buyers cum ginners because without such revenue CDF would not have been able to service the industry. TCB's insistence on the payment of statutory fees and levies by both RCUs and private ginners resulted in the RCUs accusing TCB for being "anti-cooperatives" and for siding with private interests under TCA.

7.10 The business environment has worsened

Prior to 2006 prospective cotton buyers, ginners and exporters were required under the law to pay up a series of levies such as the TCB levy, CDF levy, district crop cess or levy, education levy and licensing fees in relation to cotton buying, ginning and export of cotton before they could engage in any of the cotton related businesses. Most such payments have since July 2006 been abolished by government except for the district council crop levy and CDF levy that still remain in force.

However, in what now appears to be an obvious attempt to make up for the revenue losses resulting from such action by central government, some LGAs using the legal powers vested in them have lately been coming up with new demands from cotton buyers. Thus, the education levy has become reinstated in Meatu district in spite of its earlier abolishment by central government. Similarly, cotton buyers are now being subjected to an even longer licensing procedure whereby their applications for cotton buying licenses have to be approved at the district, regional and TCA levels prior to TCB finally giving the relevant buying licenses. Although buying permits are now being offered by TCB free of charge, ginners must however pay up the so called "optional contributions" such as sitting allowances for LGA officials and for the "Uhuru torch" before their applications are passed on from one to the next stage of the approval process.

Such an arduous licensing protocol coupled with the compulsion to pay up non-statutory payments has been to the dislike of most cotton business people. Some of the manifestations of buyers' dissatisfaction with a non-conducive business environment include rampant under-declaration of the true volumes of seed cotton purchased; tempering with weighing scales and using one buying permit to procure cotton at more than one place or to use a photocopy instead of an original one.

In what is perhaps a more extreme case, some buyers have often resorted to buying without a license at all even though licenses are now being issued free of charge. At the ginneries other malpractices such as the deliberate duplication of lot numbers; the non-labeling of bales produced at any one time; manipulations involving the ginning out-turn (GOT) values and of course the outright smuggling of bales across territorial borders or their diversion to local textile mills without being accounted for in terms of applicable taxes etc tend to take place in an obvious bid to compensate for operational costs involved with licensing.

Partly as a result of such malpractices in general and the falsification of production, purchases, ginning and exports data in particular, TCB and the government as a whole have become completely ill placed to fully track the actual trends in crop production. As a result the feeling amongst most cotton stakeholders is that in the aftermath of crop marketing liberalization data on actual cotton output in Tanzania is only being partly reflected by official figures released by government.

So while most buyers agree to paying the CDTF levy in view of its critical role in financing seasonal inputs; cotton R & D and market information, they find paying the district crop levy unjustified because the monies thus collected are hardly ever utilized for the intended purposes let alone servicing the cotton crop. thus ginners tend to evade its payment or to pay just a smaller portion of it by under-declaring their actual seed cotton purchases for the season.

Chapter 8

THE GINNING INDUSTRY IN TANZANIA

8.1 The need for a paradigm change in ginning

All over the world, cotton is grown primarily for its fibre to be used in the manufacture of textiles and garments. However, as it comes from the field after harvest as seed cotton, it is by weight, approximately two-thirds seed and one-third lint. Thus the first major processing operation needed to convert it into cloth is its separation from the seed by a process called ginning.

One of Tanzania's major competitive advantages with regard to cotton trade prior to crop marketing liberalization was its ability to deliver its lint to the world market during the 3rd quarter of the year in time before cotton from the northern hemisphere hit the global market. This was of great strategic significance for Tanzania and all cotton producing and exporting countries of the southern hemisphere which collectively account for only 10% of total global cotton output. Furthermore, by delivering cotton to the global market during that critical trading window, Tanzanian lint became amenable for a premium of up to 2 USA cents per kg of lint sold. Thus, by virtue of its geographical location on the eastern coast of Africa Tanzania has tended to command a major strategic and hence a comparative advantage in cotton trade.

However, due to stagnation of cotton production coupled with severe operational and financial challenges which the cooperatives faced in mid-1980s, Tanzania, which had become the third largest producer of roller ginned cotton in the world after India and Turkey, began to lose its competitive edge in cotton trade largely for failing to deliver reasonable quantities of its cotton to the market during the requisite period as a result of the difficulties which faced both production and ginning. Thus, one of the overarching objectives for crop marketing liberalization was to revamp production as well as promote competition, efficiency and most importantly to encourage private sector investments in new ginning technology.

There are currently four main ginning technologies available world-wide, namely; *saw ginning,* used mainly in the USA, China, Australia, Greece, Pakistan, Uzbekistan, Brazil, West Africa and other countries accounting for 55% of all cotton ginned globally; *double roller ginning* used mainly in India, Tanzania, Myanmar, USA-California/Arizona, Zimbabwe, Uganda, Zambia, Kenya and Sudan accounting for 35% of all cotton ginned world-wide; *ginning by rotobar* or *rotary knife roller gin* mainly in the USA and Turkey accounting for 5% of total cotton and *single roller ginning,* accounting for the remaining 5%.

The choice on which technology to use is increasingly being influenced by factors such as the type of cotton being grown-whether short or long staple, the volumes of seed cotton produced at any one time and the history of ginning in the respective country among other factors. In recent years, the concept of ginning has been broadened to include the drying and cleaning of the seed cotton prior to ginning as well as undertaking further cleaning of the lint fibres after the ginning process.

Thus, apart from just separating the fibre from seed during the ginning process in the conventional sense, the modern ginnery also plays an increasingly significant role of enhancing the value of cotton lint by removing objectionable foreign matter while preserving as nearly as possible the inherent qualities of the fibre. It is worth pointing out that by virtue of being entirely handpicked, hand graded and almost entirely roller ginned, Tanzanian cotton fetched premiums of up to 7 and 6 cents per pound respectively prior to 1994 merely for its cleanliness and for being roller ginned.

8.2 Present status of the Tanzanian ginning industry

By independence in 1961 there were already 27 ginneries in place in the country with Kilimanjaro Native Cooperative Union (KNCU) ginnery built in 1917 being the oldest followed by the Nyanza Cooperative Union (NCU) ginnery at Ukerewe built in 1923. By 1993 just prior to liberalization the number of ginneries in the country had reached 37 a number which rose to 79 by 2009.

Prior to 1993, the only saw ginneries in operation were those located at Nyambiti and Luguru under NCU and the Shinyanga Regional Cooperative Union (SHIRECU) respectively. In spite of many of the ginneries owned by the cooperatives having been considerably rehabilitated between 1980 and 1992, only up to 40 out of the 79 ginneries tend to be operational annually.

Table No. 16: The status of ginneries, ginning and storage capacity in Tanzania

Region	Roller gin stands	Saw gins stands	Bales produced per day	Bales produced per month	Actual bales per month	Storage capacity in tons
Shinyanga	432	60	7,794	187,376	146,922	59,100
Mwanza	481	19	4,944	121,668	82,565	36,000
Mara	192	8	2,288	54,912	41,400	22,000
Kagera	40	-	240	5,760	4,320	2,000
Tabora	74	-	444	18,456	8,856	4,000
Singida	24	-	144	3,456	2,592	1,000
Mbeya	34	-	204	4,896	3,672	1,300
Morogoro	87	-	422	12,516	9,396	4,900
Tanga	5	-	30	720	540	700
Kilimanjaro	4	-	24	576	432	1000
Coast	24	-	144	3,448	2,592	1,400
Grand total	1435	89	16,778	413,796	303,287	145,400

Source: **Tanzania Cotton Board**

147

Table No. 17. The present status of ginnery ownership in Tanzania

Region	Total Number of gins	Saw gins	Double roller gins	Cooperative union	Private company
Mwanza	24	6	18	12	12
Shinyanga	29	18	11	7	22
Mara	8	2	6	3	5
Tabora	1		1	-	1
Kagera	1		1	1	-
Singida	1		1	-	1
Morogoro	7		7	6	1
Mbeya	1		1	-	1
Tanga	1		1	-	1
Kilimanjaro	2		2	2	-
Coast	2		2	2	-
Kigoma	1		2	1	-
Total	79	26	53	32	47

Source: **Tanzania Cotton Board**

148

The rapid increase both in ginning capacity and in private sector participation within the cotton market between 1994 and 2009 was motivated by brighter prospects for increased cotton output in the country and by the decision by government to bring an end to the cooperatives' monopoly in crop procurement, ginning and marketing after the reforms. Over the years, the cooperatives had become increasingly unable to process the entire crop in one season thus resulting in the ginning of one season's crop overlapping with that of the next season's crop. It was for this reason that the Netherlands government had tried during the late 1980s to help ease the situation via a bilateral aid programme with the government. The new market entrants circumvented the capacity constraint that had long plagued the cooperative unions by installing their own ginning equipment.

Private companies felt compelled to put up their own ginneries after their attempts to lease the idle ones from the cooperatives were turned down. This as can be imagined was an obvious strategy on the part of the cooperatives to stifle an emerging competition. However, this only worked to their disadvantage because when they later agreed to leasing some of their ginneries to the competition, the latter had already invested in the construction of their own ginneries and often times on locations quite close to ginneries belonging to the cooperatives.

Initially, most private companies sought to introduce saw rather than roller gins. This would seem to have been largely motivated by the major advantages associated with the use of the saw gin technology namely; faster operation resulting in more lint being produced per gin stand per unit time; lower labour and energy costs as well as the ability to clean up trashy seed cotton. However, after working with saw gins for almost two decades ginners are increasingly returning to the roller gins again. Ginners have apparently realized that apart from the higher price offered for roller ginned cotton, the roller ginning technology offers significantly higher ginning out-turn values, better retention of fibre length, less neps in the yarn, fewer short fibres with lengths less than 12 mm being left un-ginned and it is by far cheaper to operate. Thus, in spite of roller ginning having higher maintenance, labour and energy costs, such factors are by and large offset by the savings on seed cotton due to higher GOT and the saw gins higher total variable costs.

Table No. 18: **A comparison of variable costs for different ginning technologies**

Ginning variable costs at average value of factors (US cents/kg lint)	Double Roller Gin		Rotobar		Saw Gin	
	Standard	Jumbo	Standard	High speed	116 saws	170 saws
Seasonal labour	0.67	0.27	0.08	0.07	0.05	0.04
Energy	3.14	3.14	2.25	2.05	1.63	1.46
Maintenance	0.67	0.67	0.67	0.67	0.44	0.44
Seed cotton	83.33	83.33	83.33	84.34	87.50	87.50
Total variable costs	87.81	87.41	87.33	87.12	89.63	89.44

Source: **Gerald Estur**

8.3 The status of lint production, export and consumption in Tanzania

One immediate outcome of the rapid increase in the number of ginneries in general and the increased adoption of the saw ginning technology, in particular, was an increased timeliness in ginning operations within the industry. As a result, the previous capacity related constraints that had necessitated the ginning of one season's crop to overlap with that of the next or subsequent crop came to an inevitable

150

end. Such outcomes may have further been helped by inadequate quantities of seed cotton available at the time due to the continued decline in production of cotton between the 1992/93 and 1999/00 marketing seasons.

To date less than 40 ginneries are operational between July when the cotton season starts and March the following year when it comes to a close. If, for argument's sake, the 40 ginneries were to run for a period of 3.5 months at 75% of their installed capacity they would need 405,000 tons of seed cotton. Because such level of output has not yet been reached most ginneries are currently operating well below their installed capacity. The scenario would be even worse if all the 79 registered ginneries were to be operational each year. In the context of Tanzania's projected cotton output of 810,000 tons of seed cotton projected to be produced by 2015, it follows that ginning capacity would have to increase quite substantially as well. That would enable the industry to comply with the need to have lint shipped between September and December. However, not all of the lint would need to be exported as the country also seeks to boost the processing of lint into textiles and apparel domestically.

To date, the bulk of the cotton lint produced in Tanzania is exported leaving just a little to be used by the domestic textile and garment industries. Between 1990/91 and 2005/06 between 60 and 98% of the lint was exported as compared to between 2 and 40% that was used locally.

Table No. 19. **Lint production, consumption and export trends for the period 1990/91 and 2009/10**

Marketing season	Total production (tons)	Lint exported (tons)	% exported	% used locally
1990/91	48,688	39,265	81	19
1991/92	85,500	62,724	73	27
1992/93	96,372	58,177	60	40
1993/94	45,666	43,893	96	4
1994/95	40,431	35,379	88	12
1995/96	89,157	60,645	68	32
1996/97	93,551	73,169	78	22
1997/98	67,120	65,654	98	2
1998/99	39,273	29,490	75	25
1999/00	38,220	33,825	89	11
2000/01	44,499	34,178	77	23
2001/02	54,821	40,085	73	27
2002/03	67,702	52,475	72	28
2003/04	50,467	37,182	63	37
2004/05	123,337	90,519	73	27
2005/06	135,991	106,124	78	22
2006/07	47,157	20,935	44	56
2007/08	67,259	31,514	47	53
2008/09	122,719	49,498	40	60
2009/10	89,495	50,213	56	44

Source: **Tanzania Cotton Board**

Some of the major destinations of Tanzanian lint are countries in the Far East, namely; Indonesia, India, China, Thailand, Vietnam and Malaysia in that order. Some cotton is also exported to Kenya in Africa and to Switzerland and Portugal in Europe. As can be seen, this is in line with the global geographical shift in the consumption of lint away from Europe and the USA to the Far East. Consequently, Tanzanian lint competes with lint from the rest of the world for a market share in the Far East global textile engine. Due to the large quantities of cotton traded in the region, the market for lint has become quite competitive. Thus, for Tanzania to be able to continue selling its lint to such markets it must quickly resolve some of the problems relating to the quantity as well quality of lint which it exports there.

Table No. 20: **Trends of exports of cotton versus other cash crops for the period between 2001 and 2007 (Tons in thousands) Crop Years**

Crop	Years													
	2001	%	2002	%	2003	%	2004	%	2005	%	2006	%	2007	%
Coffee	57.1	6.7	35.2	3.6	50	4.1	49.8	3.8	74.3	4.4	61.4	3.6	98.1	4.9
Cotton	33.7	3.9	28.6	2.9	46.5	3.8	74.6	5	111.5	6.7	55.8	3.2	66.4	3.3
Sisal	6.7	0.8	6.6	0.7	7.3	0.6	7.2	0.5	7.3	0.4	6.1	0.4	6.8	0.3
Tea	29	3.4	29.6	3.0	24.8	2.0	30.1	2.0	25.6	1.5	31	1.8	28.7	1.4
Tobacco	35.7	4.7	55.5	5.7	39.9	3.3	57.6	3.9	80.8	4.8	65.2	3.8	72.9	3.6
Cashew	56.6	6.6	46.6	4.7	41.8	3.4	68.1	4.6	46.6	2.8	39.4	2.3	13.2	0.7
Cloves	12.3	1.4	4	0.4	10.3	0.8	10.3	0.7	8.5	0.5	8.2	0.5	4.2	0.2
Minerals	302.2	35.4	383.8	39.2	552.2	45.4	680.2	46.2	711.3	42.4	823.9	47.8	886.8	44.2
Industrial product	131.1	15.3	142.9	14.6	170.7	14	247.1	16.8	283.2	16.9	324.1	18.8	309.2	15.4
Other product	189.9	22.2	246.9	25.2	272.8	22.4	248.1	16.8	327.3	19.5	308.2	17.9	520.4	25.9
Total exports	854.4		979.7		1216.3		1473.1		1676.4		1723.3		2006.7	

Source: **Ministry of Industries, Trade and Marketing**

153

Table No. 21: **Lint exports by destination between 1999/00 and 2008/09 (tons in thousands)**

Marketing seasons

	1999/00	2000/01	2001/02	2002/03	2003/04	2004/05	2005/06	2006/07	2007/08	2008/09
1	India 6.33	India 7.3	India 10.64	Indonesia 10.20	Indonesia 10.25	India 24.2	China 35.2	Indonesia 5.24	Pakistan 9.10	India 28.80
2	Indonesia 5.22	Indonesia 5.9	Indonesia 7.54	India 8.14	India 6.52	China 7.29	Thailand 7.61	Pakistan 4.18	Indonesia 8.17	Vietnam 6.75
3	Malaysia 3.41	Bangladesh 5.3	Thailand 4.50	China 4.52	China 4.10	Indonesia 5.57	Indonesia 5.99	Thailand 3.11	Thailand 5.40	Indonesia 6.74
4	Taiwan 3.31	Thailand 3.99	Portugal 1.95	Pakistan 2.74	Pakistan 2.55	Thailand 5.36	Vietnam 4.64	Vietnam 2.90	China 3.17	Thailand 4.16
5	Bangladesh 3.03	Malaysia 3.2	Malaysia 1.81	Thailand 1.73	Switzerland 2.24	Kenya 1.99	Bangladesh 2.67	Portugal 1.71	Vietnam 2.93	Pakistan 2.06
6	Thailand 2.26	Portugal 1.69	China 1.72	Taiwan 1.21	Thailand 1.24	Switzerland 1.78	Pakistan 2.25	India 1.07	Bangladesh 1.36	Taiwan 1.73
7	Portugal 2.02	China 1.25	Kenya 0.97	UAE 1.17	UAE 0.98	Malaysia 1.46	Turkey 2.19	Kenya 0.56	Mauritius 0.92	Kenya 1.41
8	Kenya 1.82	Taiwan 0.91	Bangladesh 0.81	Kenya 1.09	Vietnam 0.91	Taiwan 1.40	India 2.12	Belgium 0.31	Kenya 0.59	China 1.11
9	UK 1.33	Zambia 0.39	Taiwan 0.60	Madagascar 0.95	Kenya 0.90	UAE 1.27	Taiwan 1.76	Bangladesh 0.26	Malaysia 0.52	Malaysia 0.79
10	Turkey 1.03	Italy 0.27	S. Africa 0.49	Vietnam 0.91	Portugal 0.77	Pakistan 1.21	Portugal 1.20	Mauritius 0.23	Belgium 0.33	Switzerland 0.63

Source: **Tanzania Cotton board**

8.4 Challenges facing ginning and lint trade

After a seemingly long period of domination by marketing parastatals and cooperative unions, the cotton market responded in several different ways to the initiatives that were brought about by liberalization. On one hand, the chronic capacity constraint facing the ginning operations at most of the ginneries under the cooperatives subsided quite quickly as a result of increased ginning capacity after the entry of private buyers cum ginners. However, due to an unregulated entry of market participants, there soon emerged a burgeoning mismatch between ginning capacity and the volumes of seed cotton to be ginned. Due to declining annual cotton output between 1994 and 2000, buyers cum ginners increasingly engaged in the scramble for the declining seed cotton stocks. Such competition went on to precipitate a number of challenges some of which are discussed below.

8.5 Supply-side challenges

As a result of most cotton buyers cum ginners failing to procure adequate volumes of high quality seed cotton needed for profitable ginning, they resorted to buying cotton rather indiscriminately in an attempt to maximize such volumes. Unfortunately, the competition that quickly ensued went on to trigger a range of buying and selling malpractices by ginners and farmers respectively. Some of the negative outcomes of such competition included the increased delivery at buying posts and at the ginneries of ungraded seed cotton and of seed cotton that had been adulterated by water, sand and some hygroscopic chemicals. In addition, the purity of varieties designated for planting in the southern and northern zones of the WCGA became in the wake of buyers moving seed cotton across the former ginnery-cum variety zones.

Due to ungraded and badly contaminated seed cotton increasingly finding its way to most ginneries, the quality of lint coming out of the ginneries deteriorated quite rapidly and this tended to be exacerbated by the age and technology of equipment then in place. It may be recalled that most of the cooperative owned ginneries were built at a time when handpicked cotton was quite clean and thus did not require any physical cleaning prior to the ginning process. For this reason none of the ginneries was built with auxiliary equipment for cleaning the seed cotton before ginning as well as the lint after ginning as is the case in most countries today. The same has apparently been true of all private ginneries constructed after market liberalization.

Due to the lack of such auxiliary equipment for cleaning badly contaminated seed cotton prior to ginning, all kinds of contaminants, the major ones of which are PP, broken and/intact seed have quite often become associated with Tanzanian lint sold overseas. In surveys conducted by the International Textile Manufacturers Federation (ITMF) between 1999 and 2007, Tanzania was ranked 26th amongst 29 participating countries having the most contaminated cotton with India, Pakistan, Turkey and Turkmenistan in that order being the leading countries in the world. Similarly, in surveys conducted by ITMF in 2001 cotton from the WCGA and ECGA ranked 12th and 23rd respectively amongst the most 30 contaminated descriptions. Thus, there was a case of clear increase in the level of contamination of Tanzanian lint up until 2001.

Apart from the challenges relating to inadequate volumes of seed cotton available for purchase, contamination, adulteration and within bale variability, cotton buyers cum ginners found themselves unable, at that point in time, to fully capitalize on the benefits of lint exports from Tanzania as a result of their continued use of varieties with very low average ginning out-turn (GOT) values. With all Tanzanian varieties having GOT values around 34%, ginners had to forego the benefits of recent increases in lint yield output had they used varieties with higher GOT say 40 to

42% as is currently the case in most other cotton growing countries. Recently, Ukiriguru released two varieties; UK-08 and UK-M08 with average GOTs in the order of 40 and 42 percent respectively. Such varieties could not be released earlier due to a discontinuity in funding for research brought about by SAP in the early 1990s coupled with a collapse of the systems for seed multiplication and distribution.

8.6 Demand-side challenges

To optimize ginning margins in the face of increased competition for seed cotton and high operational costs, all ginners sought to engage in one or more strategies. For the vast majority of ginners their strategy remained one of "wait and see" by continuing with their businesses as normal and adjusting to the rapidly evolving market situation as they saw fit. Such ginners invariably found themselves partly engaging in one or more aspects of outright infringement of one or more of the existing cotton regulations either during the procurement of seed cotton or processing into lint. The proliferation of buying, ginning and marketing malpractices, which were totally unheard of prior to liberalization, became quite common and no doubt the otherwise good image of Tanzanian cotton became tarnished.

Some ginners such as Lintex who found the competition not to their liking opted to exit from cotton business. Other companies such as Afrisian, Alliance, Birchand, SM Holdings, Olam and Cargill chose to open up new cotton businesses in one or more of the countries within the Southern African Development Convention (SADC) region where they have found the business environment to be more conducive. Amongst the remaining companies, some such as Jambo, Lintex, Afrisian, Dynamic, Olam, and S & C Ginning decided to diversify their business portfolio by increasingly engaging in multiple businesses such as oil milling, textile manufacturing, rice milling or even trading in other commodities such as cashew, coffee, chickpea and general merchandise in a bid to smoothen incomes and risks.

157

To help increase the profitability of cotton ginning, Tanzania has embarked on a program the goal of which is to raise annual cotton output to 810,000 tons of seed cotton or 271,000 tons of lint or 1.5 million bales each of 180 kg by 2015 by simply tripling the current average yields of about 750 kg of seed cotton per ha. As discussed earlier, the current ginning capacity involving only some 40 ginneries would need to double or even treble in order for such a crop to be ginned quickly enough if it is to be ready for shipment during the most opportune period between September and November.

To date, ginning remains just marginally profitable for the main reason that most of the machines that were imported into the country up until 1999 were second or even third hand acquisitions being up to ten years old or older when they were delivered in the country. Thus, there has been quite some increase in the cost of running and maintaining them due to frequent breakdowns exacerbated by lack of appropriate spare parts, inadequacies in trained mechanics and fitters. As a result, many ginneries are often unable to run at full capacity and thence failing to capitalize on the September to November export window.

Apart from the age and type of technology in use, the inadequacy of professionalism in running and managing most ginneries, in part due to the lack of properly trained fitters and mechanics, has quite often been one of the main reasons for the increased contamination of Tanzanian lint by whole or broken seeds, oils and grease. Perhaps more importantly, the current system of manually feeding seed cotton to most of the roller gins has tended to worsen the contamination problem. To date, there are just a handful of ginneries that have been respectively fitted with systems for automatically cleaning the seed cotton and lint prior to and after ginning. Thus, strategies that seek to revamp production must go hand in hand with those that aim to improve ginning capacity and contamination free cotton.

To further increase the profitability of ginning, the projected rise in cotton production has to go hand in hand with a push towards an accelerated increase in the utilization of the by-products of ginning. To date, only about half of the ginners also engage in oil milling. That the latter is still largely under-developed is reflected by the fact that with the exception of a few companies that produce double-refined oil, the rest produce low quantities of low quality, semi-refined cottonseed oil. Furthermore, there has been very little effort devoted to developing and promoting the use of other by-products of both the ginning and oil milling industries such as linters, cotton seed cake and husks. Hopefully, as other sectors of the economy, most notably livestock, tend to grow, the demand for them will grow as well.

8.7 Global trade issues

For over half a century, Tanzania has been exporting the bulk of its cotton as lint largely in the hope of generating the foreign currency needed for the importation of capital and other goods as well as debt servicing. After crop marketing liberalization, Tanzania's lint export price has increasingly tended to become affected by factors such as the untimely delivery of the crop in designated markets, lack of consistency in the quality of the lint being exported and difficulties faced at times in trying to meet the quantities of the crop required as per contractual obligations. These factors have collectively tended to affect Tanzania's position in the global cotton market. Other drivers of international trade, which ginners must face time and again, or risk losing their cotton business are highlighted below.

8.8 The need for increased classing of cotton

In cotton like any other commodity, quality in general and quality parameters in particular, tend to largely determine prices because they constitute the main source of differentiation between the cotton origins traded on the international market.

Tanzanian cotton is sold on the basis of Grade, together with the corresponding staple length known as Type. There are altogether seven (7) grades of cotton out of which five (5) are physical and two (2) are descriptive. The basic selling grade is Gany, as adopted by the International Cotton Association (ICA).

Table No. 22: **Tanzanian lint classification by grade**

Tanzanian Grade	Universal Grade	Remarks
Tang	Good middling	Physical
Gany	Strict middling	Physical
Gany	Middling	Physical
Gany	Strict low middling	Descriptive
Gany	Low middling	Physical
Gany	Strict good ordinary	Descriptive
Yika	Good ordinary	Physical
Under grade (UG)	Below grade	No grade

Source: **Tanzania Cotton Board**

Table No. 23: **Tanzanian lint classification by type**

Type	Millimetres	Code
Type 1 staple length	28.2 1	16
Type 2 staple length	27.4 2	15
Type 3 staple length	26.7 -27.2	14

Source: **Tanzania Cotton Board**

The Type is independent from Colour grade; for example Type 1 Tang, Type 1 Gany, Type 1 Gany minus a quarter and Type 3 Tang.

To date, the global emphasis has been for cotton to be sold on the basis of quality criteria determined by instrument based testing methods such as the high volume instrument (HVI)

160

or any other similar equipment rather than the traditional methods based on manual and visual classing of cotton. The latter methodology has for many years been used for the determination of grade, extraneous matter and preparation at TCB's Kurasini laboratory.

The need for cotton to be subjected to quality tests prior to its export has in part been necessitated by the advent of high speed spinning machines as well as increased automation in the textile and apparel industries. As a result of such developments, the two categories of industries have become increasingly demanding for lint which is completely free of extraneous matter contamination as well as stickiness in addition to conforming to the conventional quality attributes such as requisite staple length, strength and micronaire values. As a result, the majority of overseas spinners or international merchants (IM) and their intermediaries categorically demand for information on quality as evidenced by a classing certificate based testing done by high volume instrument (HVI).

Information derived from HVI testing is increasingly being used as a tool for price negotiation using the applicable price quotations based on the Cotlook A Index. The latter, also simply referred to as the A Index, is one of the pricing systems for world cottons being an index of the level of offering prices on the international market. The daily quotation is an average of the cheapest five quotations from a selection of sixteen upland cottons traded internationally. Prices for cotton tend to be expressed in USA dollars or cents per pound, CIF (cleared, insured and forwarded) for delivery to a northern Europe port.

Tanzanian lint has up till now continued to be classed both manually and by HVI. Nevertheless, due the growing trend towards cotton trade based on quality determined by instruments, Tanzania and other cotton exporting countries of SSA must seek to build their own capacities in order to be able to class all their cotton prior to export because as HVI classed lint becomes increasingly traded internationally, any failure by DE countries to join the instrument testing band wagon will result in their automatic exclusion from global cotton trade as there would be no objective basis for the comparison of the quality of their lint vis a vis that of competing countries.

8.9 The need for price risk management

Until recently a significant number of ginners in Tanzania preferred selling their lint ex-ginnery on free on truck (FOT) terms to engaging in forward sales. The major reason for this trend would seem to be the fact that selling their lint ex-ginnery confers them with the flexibility of putting their cash into circulation at a faster pace than if they had to export it. In so doing, one would assume that the ginners would be capable of running their ginneries more efficiently given the competitive nature of the industry. This would seem to be indeed the case for most of the "smaller fish" in the ginning industry. The more professionally run as well as well-seasoned ginning companies have, as a rule, been selling their lint worldwide on other terms.

Nonetheless, a closer examination of practice involving selling lint ex-ginnery would seem to suggest that most of the ginners who opt to sell their lint locally tend to do so for lack of an understanding of international cotton trade, its rules, price discovery as well as knowledge about the major spinners. So, rather than seeking to understand such trade, ginners have tended to opt selling to the local textile and apparel manufacturers where the need for classing data tends to be optional.

However, by circumventing the need for classing data and hence TCB's regulatory control mechanisms, such trading malpractices have tended to fuel practices such as sale of lint bales through unofficial channels or even smuggling them across borders in desperate attempts to evade payment

162

of statutory taxes and levies. On the other hand, overseas merchants as well as spinners are as a rule very discerning with regard to whom they trade with. For example, one merchant told me that and I quote; "we merchants often seek for reliability, flexibility and on the capacity of the ginner to observe and accept international trading rules as-*sine qui non*-conditions".

Thus, unless and until ginners change their way of doing cotton business, they may not be able to fully benefit fully from international trade in cotton. Most ginners who sell ex-ginnery or on the spot market, quite often tend to forego their margins more substantially than if they sold their lint through forward sales on a cost and freight (C & F), CIF and FOB basis. The reason is that by selling their lint on the spot market rather than on forward sales they are unable to achieve price protection in the event of price and trade shocks (respectively defined as declines in real prices of at least 10 percent from one year to another and a 10% year-on-year decline in terms of trade).

Forward sales, on the other hand, tend to protect ginners from the risk associated with price shocks happening between the time of buying cotton from farmers and that of selling their lint to mills or cotton merchants. Thus, buying on the spot market in an era of rapidly changing world prices, is quite often the reason why ginners who do so are unlikely to pass on to farmers the benefits that they would have gained had they sold their cotton ahead of time.

The need for more ginners to be introduced to the use of price risk instruments for protecting their profits was vividly illustrated during the 2008/09 marketing season. In that season, the commodity boom that had started in late 2007 led to cotton prices rising up to 72 cents ex-ginnery by July in 2008. A few enlightened ginners entered into forward contracts and sold their cotton at prices ranging between 60 and 69 cents with a closing on prices as high as 72 cents.

However, following the financial crisis that came to a head in September and October, prices declined to 47 cents per pound by the end of October. By 31st December 2008, an estimated 240,000 bales out of the projected 680,000 bales for the 2008/09 marketing season remained unsold as ginners were not in a position to sell them at a loss. Under such circumstances, ginners who often sell their cotton on the spot market are the ones who end up suffering most.

8.10 Trading via the International Merchants

One enduring norm of the global trade in cotton lint is the involvement of the so-called "international merchants" (IM). The latter, or more correctly "third parties" or "middle men" together with their agents distributed worldwide tend to play a crucial role in cotton trade linking the ginners and farmers in cotton producing countries with spinners in the importing countries.

Unlike most other trading relations where the "middle men" can quite easily be removed or "done with", by mutual agreement between the seller and the buyer, this has not been easy in the case of cotton trade. The IM as a "niche profession" has persisted over time apparently due to the dispersion of producers and consumers, the geographical fragmentation of global cotton production and the propensity by spinners to prefer certain blends from different national origins and qualities.

Under such circumstances any direct trade links between ginners and spinning companies would be too difficult to undertake without the involvement of the IMs. A prominent merchant had this to say, and I quote: - "cotton merchants are the necessary link between farmers and textile mills. The most important single function of a cotton merchant is that of a market maker. By buying cotton from farmers when they want to sell, and selling cotton to the mills when they want to buy, the merchant effectively creates a market where cotton can be bought and sold at all times" unquote.

Nevertheless, in the aftermath of market liberalization, some of the Tanzanian novices in international cotton trade found out that "all that glitters is not gold". They learnt and quite bitterly for that matter that just as there are good and bad agents in all kinds of trade, the case for cotton trade was not different. Between 2000 and 2006 high-level consultations made between cotton exporters from Tanzania and spinners from China, Viet Nam, Thailand and Indonesia revealed that some agents of IMs operating within these countries engaged in deliberate acts of disinformation and deception to steal from both the unsuspecting ginners as well as spinners.

One popular way of disinformation and manipulation was with regard to the confusion between staple length and whether or not cotton was roller or saw-ginned. Thus, whereas Tanzanian cotton can be sold as type 1, 2 or 3 on the basis of staple lengths regardless of whether it has been roller or saw-ginned, agents of certain IMs lied to the "uninformed spinners" by alleging that all roller and saw ginned cotton originating from Tanzania belonged to Types 1 and 2 categories respectively. Thus, an unsuspecting spinner would have to buy either Type 2 or Type 3 cotton at a price meant for Type 1 lint cotton (which is considerably higher) just because it was roller ginned. Similarly, a spinner would be compelled to buy his saw-ginned cotton at a price meant for Type 1 when in fact such cotton probably belonged to Type 2.

Consequently, spinners in importing countries ended up losing sizeable amounts of cash through such unethical tricks. On their part, ginners who had sold their cotton ex-ginnery and without classing certificates ended up losing cash through underpayment. To stop such malpractice, spinners only needed to insist for HVI classing data for all their imported cotton; information which is currently available free of charge from TCB for all cotton exported from Tanzania. In order to guard against any possibility of spinners ever finding out about such malpractices, IM sought to carefully sever all kinds of direct links between spinners and the ginners in the country where cotton came from. One preferred strategy for achieving such objective was to feed spinners with false and greatly distorted information about the lint exporting country in general and the ginners in particular.

In the case of Tanzania, it was being alleged that the country was at war and thence an unsafe destination to visit. For people who had never travelled to Africa where civil war and conflicts are commonplace, such news is indeed very bad news. In an even more extreme case it was being alleged that Tanzanian ginners are such big novices in international trade that they cannot even process a letter of credit (LC). Thus, it became apparent to both the spinners in the Far East and the ginners from Tanzania that trading through a third party is not entirely without cost or risk.

However, because trading through the third party was seemingly making the ginner and spinner worse off, getting rid of the middlemen became a viable proposition. In light of malpractices being perpetrated by such *de facto* "middlemen" ginners and spinners had started to increasingly look at them in the same light as excess baggage, which in an era of shrinking trading margins, should best be off-loaded and left behind rather than taken on board. Simple computations showed that by trading directly with a spinner based in Viet Nam, a Tanzanian ginner would gain up to 4 cents more per pound of lint sold in 2005 than if he were to sell his lint through a third party.

Over time, lint exporters from Tanzania and spinners from the Far East have grown to know each other quite well as well as each other's dislikes and preferences. Thus, opening up direct trade links between themselves would most probably help to cut down costs as well as circumvent some of the malpractices being perpetrated by some unscrupulous agents of IMs. To reinforce the notion of direct trade between ginners and spinners given the savings and revenues to be gained on both sides, one of the options proposed for circumventing the necessity of trading via the agency of IM, involves Tanzanian ginners opening up warehouses say in Djakarta, Shanghai or elsewhere in the Far East. Such warehouses would be used to stash lint bales for use by the spinners on a consignment basis. IMs, such as Olam, have been using such strategy because they tend to handle relatively large quantities of cotton in designated markets.

To remain viable economically, ginners face some quite formidable challenges. To date their biggest challenge would seem to be how to make ginning a profitable undertaking given the difficulties associated with the procurement of cotton in a rapidly changing cotton business environment. To survive, they will need to improve efficiency and reliability in their business deals if they are to forge viable direct dealings with the spinners. Selling lint these days is no longer just simply where to sell and how much to sell but rather to whom, how and why. With an unending mismatch between the demand and supply of seed cotton in the country, it has become necessary for all ginners to change their perception of farmers from being mere suppliers of seed cotton to being valuable partners in a cotton value chain. Similarly, as competition for the Far East Global Textile Market intensifies, the imperative to improve the quality of lint as well as the proportion that is HVI classed prior to sale will become crucial for Tanzania.

Chapter **9**

THE TEXTILE AND APPAREL INDUSTRIES
IN TANZANIA

9.1 Moving from production of lint for export to production of textiles and apparels for export

When cotton farming was introduced in SSA, the primary objective was to turn the area into an alternative source of cheaply produced raw cotton for use by the colonial textile and apparel industries based in their countries. This, it may be recalled, arose out of the need to diversify sources of raw cotton during the "cotton famine" when supplies from the USA became halted by war.

After independence, Tanzania like most other cotton producing and exporting countries in SSA sought to switch from the colonial legacy of "production of lint for export" to "production of textiles and apparel for export". The motivation was quite simple; to demonstrate to the public that the newly independent states were determined not only to create the jobs for the local population but also to show that they were determined to replace imported textiles by locally made ones. It had dawned on Tanzania and other cotton producing and exporting countries that investing in a locally based textile and apparel industry was also justified on socioeconomic grounds because all over the world, such industries tend to constitute a potential and significant first step for DE that are embarking on the path of industrial development.

Nonetheless, after more than fifty years of independence, most cotton producing and exporting countries of SSA have by and large failed to facilitate such paradigm change. In fact the legacy of "production for export" does seem to have become even further entrenched over the years. Thus, by the first centenary of cotton farming in Tanzania, the country was still exporting more than 70% of its cotton as lint on an annual basis. That the country only manages to convert up to 30% of its lint into textiles and apparel is quite clearly symptomatic of an industry facing immense challenges throughout the process of the conversion of fibre to fabric and fabric dyeing, printing and finishing.

It may be recalled that between 1960 and 1980 the late President Julius Nyerere sought to seriously reverse the trend of "production for export" by adoption of trade policies centred on the strategy of import-substitution industrialization in an apparent attempt to achieve structural economic development and hence lessen Tanzania's dependence on exports of primary products. As a result by 1968 several textile and apparel industries such as the Mwanza Textiles; Friendship textiles; Kilimanjaro Textile Corporation, Tanganyika Dyeing and Weaving Mills; Calico; Moshi Textiles and Tanganyika Textile Industries had been already been established.

In trying to promote domestic industrial production, the government among other things advocated for the protection of the domestic market from foreign competition through a series of non-tariff measures, preferential licensing for capital goods, provision of subsidized loans and raw material costs among other privileges and measures such as exchange rates manipulation; policies normally associated with import –substitution. Inevitably the government became extensively involved in the direct management of production and marketing via a series of parastatal bodies that were formed to spearhead some of these activities.

In its 2nd Five Year Plan for the period 1969 –1974 the government sought to further expand the local textile and garment industry with the objective of eventually processing up to 60% of Tanzania's annual lint production into textiles and garments. By the early 1980s the textile and garment industry had grown to become the second largest sector after agriculture with over 40,000 employees deployed at its 50 factories where it produced up to 85.2 million square metres of textiles per annum.

However, starting from the mid-1980s onwards, the performance of the textile and apparel industries declined considerably resulting in a severe shortage of fabrics and hence garments. Such decline came in the aftermath of the disengagement of government from involvement in the daily management of the industries as well as the removal of most of the government protection that the industries had enjoyed prior to the launching of the national economic recovery program at that point in time. By 1994 when market liberalization came to a head, 10 out of the existing 22 textile and garment mills had already closed down and manufacturing output had declined to just 33.4 million square meters per annum. By the year 2000; 8 of the 14 previously publicly owned mills had become privatized.

Table No. 24: **The status of textile and garment industries in Tanzania by 1994**

Privately owned before 1994	Now
A to Z Clothing	Private
Karibu Textiles Ltd	Private
Sunflag (T) Ltd	Private
Commercial and Industrial Combine (CIC)	Private – now called Afritex
Calico	Private – closed
Coast Textiles (COTEX)	Private – closed
J.V. Textiles and garments Ltd	Private – closed
Publicly owned before 1994	Privatized
Blanket Manufacturing	Privatized
Mbeya Textile Mill	Privatized
Morogoro textile Ltd (Polytex)	Privatized
Musoma Textiles Ltd (MUTEX)	Privatized
Tabora Spinning Mill (TABOTEX)	Privatized
Tanzania Package Manufacturers Ltd	Privatized
Ubungo Garments	Privatized
Ubungo spinning Mill Ltd	PPP
Friendship Textile Mill (Urafiki)	Closed down
Kilimanjaro Textile Corporation (KIL TEX)	Privatized
Mwanza Textiles Ltd	Privatized
Tanganyika dyeing and Weaving Mills Ltd (SUNGURATEX)	Closed down
Tanzania Bag Corporation	Privatized
Tanzania Sewing Thread Manufacturers (UZI BORA)	

Source: **Tanzania Cotton Board**

One of the immediate fallouts of the impending collapse of the textile and apparel industries was the inevitable loss of most of the trained and experienced staff. Their loss went on to impact quite adversely on the ability of the industries to manage the various manufacturing processes as well as the maintenance of the machinery then in place. To redress the situation, most mills resorted to utilizing expatriate for the bulk of their technical, skilled and management jobs.

9.2 Massive entry in the county of "mitumba"

The near demise of the textile and apparel industry after liberalization was also partly facilitated by the rather massive entry into the country of imports of pre-owned or 2nd hand clothing popularly referred to as *"mitumba"*; new clothing and those under the donated category. Most of the new clothing enters into the country as either under-invoiced or just plainly dumped stuff. Consequently, locally made and legally imported clothing started to face increasing competition from them, the outcome of which was reflected by the closure of some well known local textile and apparel industries such as Calico etc.

Recent studies have shown that many Tanzanians tend to prefer second hand garments to new locally made or imported garments on considerations largely relating to price and fashion trends. Other factors that are increasingly influencing most peoples' preferences for the type of clothing to buy include rising living standards, changing life styles and an increasing trend towards more informal approaches in the organization of work. Such considerations tend to reinforce an increased demand for variety.

Trade in second hand or used clothing has thus become a multi-million dollar business providing "employment" as well as low-cost clothing to the disadvantaged segments of the population. Nevertheless, its longer term implications on the budding garment industries remains worrisome and this does not seem to be helped by dumping which has also become increasingly a major threat to the blanket, *kanga* and *kitenge* industries all of which currently constitute the cornerstone of the Tanzanian textile manufacturing industry.

Table 25: **Imports of clothing into Tanzania for the period from 2003 to 2009 (Millions of Tanzanian shillings)**

	2003	2004	2005	2006	2007	2008	2009
New clothing	286	133	176	334	384	747	710
Pre-owned	31,036	34,094	29,327	34,364	41,102	43,223	50,065

Source: **Foreign Trade Statistics 2009-National Bureau of Statistics**

By the close of the 20th century, liberalization related and other developments within the textile and apparel industry had virtually rendered the Tanzanian industry completely uncompetitive by any standard. Most of the existing mills as well as those that had been brought into the country by the private sector either as 2nd or 3rd hand acquisitions were in fact too old to operate efficiently and their technology quite outdated as well. To date, for example, only 20% of the machines deployed in spinning are under 10 years of age. So, while modern equipment is faster, less dependent upon manual inputs and geared at producing high quality yarn, Tanzanian old equipment is unable to produce standard yarns for the global market at an acceptable price and quality. Thus the bulk of the spun yarn is in the 1/24 Ne, which is used mainly for the production of the base fabric for printed *kanga, kitenge* and sheeting.

The rather pathetic status of the textile and apparel industry both before and after liberalization, became one of the compelling reasons for Tanzania to seek to revamp it. Nevertheless, there were other considerations as well. First, it had become evident that cotton farmers were unlikely to reap the benefits of increased cotton output after liberalization if Tanzanian cotton continued to be exported in raw form as lint instead of textiles and apparels. Trading in lint no longer seemed to make economic sense because along the cotton value chain, the value of its products per kg during trade tend to increase as follows; 0.32; 0.76; 1.32; 3.80 and 25.00

dollars for seed cotton, lint fibre, yarn and finished product in terms of their selling prices respectively. Thus the selling of cotton in any of the other form of the finished products was to be preferred to selling it as either seed cotton or lint.

After market liberalization, most smallholder farmers have regularly been complaining about producer prices for cotton being too low to cover for their production costs. The truth of the matter though is that because of the tendency for commodities to exhibit a secular long-term decline in their prices over time, ginners cum lint exporters have similarly been finding it difficult to pass onto farmers the benefits of international trade due to their trading margins being on the declining trend as well. Thus, unless and until Tanzania processes increasingly more and more of its cotton into textiles and apparel, the urge to export more and more raw cotton to the global market will persist regardless of price as it strives to obtain the foreign earnings that are badly needed to pay for imports and debt servicing.

The implication of the scenario cited above to the overall economy of the country can best be illustrated by a more practical example. In 1988 the cost of buying a 75 horse power Massey Ferguson tractor with its full complement of a disc plough, a disc harrow and a trailer was 460,000 Tanzanian shillings. In 2008, twenty years later, the cost for the same package had risen to 35 million shillings. In other words, while 23 bales were required to finance the purchase of one tractor in 1988, 128 bales were needed in 2008 mainly due to factors such as declining export price and exchange rate fluctuations. The long-term decline in global prices for commodities has, as discussed earlier, been due to the global supply for commodities getting out of balance with demand.

Table No. 26: **Effect of changes on exchange rate and unit export price for lint on the capacity for Tanzania to import capital goods.**

Year	Exchange rate (Shillings/dollar)	Export price (dollars/kg)	Tractor Price (Shillings)	Tractor Price (dollars)	Price/181kg bale (dollars)	Number of bales needed per tractor
1988	83	1.34	460,000	5,542	243	23
2008	1,200	1.26	35,000,000	29,167	228	128

Source: **Tanzania Cotton Board**

Finally, Tanzania with an estimated population of 50 million in 2012 and an estimated per capita consumption of 10 square meters of textiles and apparel per annum needs some 500 million or more square meters to meet the growing demand. However, the country only produces an estimated 240 million square meters of textiles and apparel per annum part of which is being exported. Thus, there is a considerable gap that is currently being filled up by imports of second hand clothing rather than new garments. It has perhaps been for this and other considerations that the country now seeks to process up to 50% of the projected lint output of 270,000 tons by 2015 into yarn, fabric and apparel.

9.3 Improving the prospects for increased textile and apparel manufacturing in Tanzania

Unlike most other SSA countries Tanzania has an enormous potential for the development of a big and vibrant textile and apparel industry. Such an assessment is based on the fact that Tanzania has a significant comparative advantage in relation to cotton production as well as the processing of such cotton into textiles and apparel products.

By the end of the first decade of the 21st century Tanzania had become one of the ten leading producers and exporters of cotton in Africa. In spite of liberalization related challenges that threatened the future of the cotton industry as a whole, the country managed to raise its annual cotton output to levels of 114,573, 126,229 and 123,080 tons of lint during the 2004/05, 2005/06 and 2008/09 marketing seasons respectively. It may be recalled that throughout the twentieth century annual cotton output never went beyond 96,372 tons of lint that were obtained during the 1992/3 marketing season just prior to market liberalization. Under the recently announced Cotton and Textile Development Programme, annual cotton output in the country is projected to rise to 270,000 tons of lint per annum by 2015 mainly through the adoption of contract farming.

However, as discussed earlier, profitability along the cotton value chain is only likely to be improved if increased cotton output goes in tandem with an increased processing of Tanzanian cotton into textiles and garments. Tanzania already has some 21 textile and apparel mills but most of them are operating below 50% of their installed capacity due to operational and structural problems and for which reason they are only utilizing up to 35,000 of Tanzanian lint on annual basis.

In spite of existing setbacks, the prospects for increased production of textiles and apparel through further investments are quite bright for Tanzania. Apart from a plentiful supply of locally produced cotton, the country also has abundant and lowly priced labour with fair labour standards already in place. Perhaps more importantly, the country provides huge possibilities for potential investors to export their textile and apparel products to several overseas countries such as the USA and Canada; Turkey, Switzerland, and Norway; and Australia, New Zealand and Japan because of Tanzania's textiles and apparel products being eligible for entry into such countries on the basis of preferential Least Developed Country market access often under very relaxed trade rules of origin. Such considerations coupled with Tanzania's reputation as one of Africa's most politically stable democracy should at least in theory confer to the textile and apparel industries far more attractive conditions for investment and better comparative advantages than their counterparts in most other countries.

In spite of such endowments, the textile and apparel industry must urgently address some fairly serious issues before it can finally takeoff. To date, the biggest problem facing the Tanzanian cotton to garment value chain is the chronic shortage of high quality unprocessed fabric at the local level. Yarns that are currently being produced in Tanzania are generally neppy and irregular thus making it impossible to make high quality fabric out of them. Thus, most of the yarn goes into making woven fabric for production of *kanga* and *kitenge* (K & K) for sale to both the local and regional markets.

As a result of the prevailing shortage of high quality fabric, the production of knitted garments is virtually non-existent in Tanzania. Because the production of knitted goods constitutes over 50% of the global apparel market, the absence of a functional knitting industry in Tanzania which has been necessitated by the prevailing acute shortage of high quality fabric has in turn compelled the companies such as A to Z, Mazava, Ellen Knitwear and Kibo Trade (with the exception of Sunflag) to source for the polyester and cotton fabrics that are needed for the manufacture of knit garments destined for the retail markets in the US, EU and South Africa from outside Tanzania. Fortuitously, Sunflag is the only mill that produces its own cotton fabric for use in the production of knit garments for export to the same destinations.

Similarly, due to quality considerations cited earlier, the bulk of the yarn that is currently being produced by spinning mills such as Tabotex, Afritex, 21st Century, Urafiki (the Tanzania-China Friendship Textile Mill), Jambo, Mbeya Textiles and Musoma Textiles is mainly used to manufacture the fabric that is needed for the production of *kitenge, kanga* and bed linen. The fabric required to make such products is far less demanding in terms of quality requirements than for say knit garments. Thus, most spinners focus on the internal market for K & K and have a 25% duty protection against imported products although they are still vulnerable to imported fabrics.

To date the making of *kanga, kitenge* and bed linen has become the most remunerative undertaking for the majority of the existing industries simply because the combination of factors such as low operating hours due to power disruptions, age, speed and the condition of existing machinery, levels of productivity and cost of finance does not allow for the production of good quality yarn that would go into making high quality fabric for garment manufacturing. Instead, the mills tend to end up with a final product cost structure that does not allow for them to compete internationally.

To encourage garment production in the country, it is imperative that the production of high quality yarn and fabric at local level must be increased in the first place. To date, this is being approached as a three-pronged thrust involving the upgrading of some of the old mills; installing entirely new investments at some of the existing export processing zones (EPZ) and finally attracting new investments in the industry through either joint ventures or green field investments and the like. Such interventions are aimed at helping the textile and apparel industry to get operational to full capacity again. To complement these efforts, the industry must also address the issue of skills development that has so far necessitated the use of expensive expatriates mainly from India. Without such a programme the industry will not be able to improve the work performance at the mills where machines use new technology.

Tangible steps towards the realization of such goals were taken following the launching of the Cotton and Textile Development Program (CTDP) in 2007 with funding from the Gatsby Charitable Foundation (GCF). To date GCF through the Cotton Textile and Development Programme has been striving not only to boost cotton production and productivity but also to promote the increased sale of Tanzanian textiles and garments. Similarly, the CTDP has been facilitating new value chain investments as well as supporting both the University of Dar es Salaam and the Vocational Education Training Authority (VETA) to develop not only a Textile and Fashion Design Training Programme but also a new cadre of skilled small scale textile and apparel producers respectively.

So far Tanzania's garment industry is mainly focused on the export of sportswear with the USA and Europe as its principal markets. Exports of knitwear currently comprise of T-shirts as well as men's and boys' knitted shirts. Nevertheless, Tanzania has so far failed to sufficiently capitalize on both AGOA and EBA. Two of Tanzania's largest garment factories continue to exist because they do not make use of cotton but instead use synthetic knits as their raw materials because of the favourable trade preferences that Tanzania enjoys as a Least Developed Country under AGOA. The ability to use 3rd country fabric and still be eligible for duty free access into the USA is highly attractive to garment manufacturers whose products are made out of synthetic materials, as these attract a higher level of duty (about 30%) into USA compared with cotton garments (about 16%).

Apart from the shortage of quality fabric that would allow for the emergence of a garment industry, the textile and apparel manufacturers in Tanzania are similarly facing formidable supply and demand-side constraints and challenges. On the supply side manufacturers continue to face frequent and prolonged power cuts due to load shedding and voltage fluctuations; transport related problems due to the rail infrastructure being grossly under-invested. Thus, they have become heavily dependent on costly road transport. Other challenges relate to lengthy and often cumbersome customs clearing processes and difficulties being faced while obtaining permits.

As a result the Tanzanian textile and apparel industry has become largely uncompetitive by world standards. For example, factors for a successful short staple spinning operation include; an assured supply of quality cotton at or below world market prices; an assured and competitively priced electrical power supply; a well trained and competitively priced labour force; access to capital at competitive interest rates for fixed asset and working capital investments; the ability to work for the maximum possible number of hours annually and reliable infrastructure to deliver cotton and transport yarns.

Amongst the factors cited above, Tanzania does seem to score positively for at least two critical factors, namely, labour and power. In the case of labour, the average spinning operative cost for Tanzania is 0.40/hour, which is very low and compares very favourably with Bangladesh which has the world's lowest labour rates. However, such cost advantage tends to be lost by low productivity, high labour turn over and rampant absenteeism. With regard to power supply, the variable energy charge per kilowatt hour in

Tanzania in 2011was 5 US cents which is quite favourable indeed when compared to the global variable energy charge average of 3 to 20 USA cents per kilowatt hour. However, the major problem with Tanzania's power supply is with regard to the rather frequent and prolonged cuts due to load shedding and voltage fluctuations.

In view of the existing constraints and challenges it is not entirely surprising that most textile and apparel related industries have tended to be more heavily involved in the production of just a few printed fabrics, namely, *kanga*, *kitenge, kikoi* and bed linen. This is further reinforced by the high rate of duty protection which is currently being enjoyed by the textile industry makes the production of these products. Most of the existing mills seem to prefer to focus on increasing their market share in the existing product segments of finished and processed printed fabrics rather than to compete in the highly competitive international yarn and fabrics markets.

Furthermore, the rather cumbersome process of getting access to and clearing imported fabrics on international markets provides a huge disincentive for going into making other products. A deliberate reduction in the level of duty protection would perhaps help to allow the emergence of non-integrated printed fabrics processors. The latter would provide the incentive for additional investments in garment manufacturing which is currently the major undertaking of only Sunflag, A to Z, Ellen Knitwear, Mazava Fabrics and Production and Kibo Trade.

Table No. 27: **Present status of the textile and apparel industry in Tanzania**

	Spin	Weave	Knit	K_K_K	Bed linen	Blanket	Bed-net	Thread	Clothes	Made-up	Jobs
New Tabora Textiles	Yes	No	No	No	No	No	No	No	No	No	245
Jambo Spinning Mills	Yes	No	No	No	No	No	No	No	No	No	150
Namera/Nida	Yes	Yes	No	Yes	Yes	No	No	No	No	No	1,700
21st Century Textiles	Yes	Yes	No	Yes	Yes	No	No	No	No	No	1,300
Afritex	Yes	Yes	No	Yes	No	No	No	No	No	No	1000
Mbeya Textiles (2001)	Yes	Yes	No	Yes	Yes	No	No	No	No	No	775
New Mwanza Textile Mills	Yes	Yes	No	Yes	Yes	No	No	No	No	No	1,100
Urafiki (Tz-China Friendship)	Yes	Yes	No	Yes	Yes	No	No	No	No	No	1,200
Karibu Textile Mills	No	No	No	Yes	No	No	No	No	No	No	600
African Pride Textile Mills	No	No	No	Yes	No	No	No	No	No	No	150
Sunflag Tanzania	Yes	Yes	Yes	Yes	Yes	No	Yes	Yes	Yes	No	1,900
Morogoro Canvas Mills	Yes	Yes	No	No	No	No	No	No	No	Yes	1,300
21st Century Sisal	Yes	Yes	No	No	No	No	No	No	No	Yes	400
A to Z Textile Mills	No	No	Yes	No	No	No	Yes	No	Yes	No	7,500
Ellen Knitwear	No	No	Yes	No	No	No	No	No	Yes	No	100
Kilimanjaro Blanket Corporation	No	No	No	No	No	Yes	No	No	No	No	100
Blanket & Textile Manufacturing	No	No	No	No	No	Yes	No	No	No	No	100
Kibotrade	No	No	Yes	No	No	No	No	No	Yes	No	45
Mazava Fabrics & Production	No	No	Yes	No	No	No	No	No	Yes	No	600

Legend: K-K-K stands for *kanga, kitenge & kikoi* respectively

Table No. 28: **Comparative exports of textiles and apparel to the EU from selected East and Southern African states for the period between 2000 and 2008 (in million Euros)**

Country	Calendar year								
	2000	2001	2002	2003	2004	2005	2006	2007	2008
Tanzania	15.8	20.4	14.4	12.6	15.4	11.8	13.0	10.9	11.9
Kenya	9.3	7.0	7.4	8.4	11.0	9.8	9.8	8.2	7.1
Uganda	8.0	8.5	8.6	8.2	4.8	5.8	3.0	3.9	3.8
Ethiopia	5.2	3.0	5.4	5.8	7.0	8.1	8.0	9.1	8.1
Rwanda	0.0C1	0.003	0.34	0.27	0.008	0.009	0.024	0.027	0.0004
Burundi	0.049	0.124	0.001	0.7	0.29	0.092	0.18	0.021	0.25
Madagascar	277.3	281.8	153	137.6	170.6	191.4	240.1	257.3	229.2
Mauritius	690.6	682.5	629.7	561.8	524.3	450.9	498.3	491.6	436
Botswana	18.3	19.8	8.0	5.6	10.2	4.8	5.5	7.8	7.1
Lesotho	8	3.8	2.0	1.3	1.4	0.65	0.86	1.7	1.9
Namibia	0.32	0.53	0.9	0.6	0.9	0.7	0.6	0.7	0.8
Swaziland	10.2	9.4	7.6	7.6	4.7	1.9	2.5	2.5	1.4
S. Africa	283.1	280.1	292.1	307.5	295.7	248.1	227.5	212.9	170.1

Source: **European Union Eurostat**

183

Table No. 29: *Comparative exports of textiles and apparel to the US from selected Eastern and Southern African states for the period between 2000 and 2008 (in million dollars)*

Country	Calendar year								
	2000	2001	2002	2003	2004	2005	2006	2007	2008
Tanzania	0.24	0.43	0.33	1.9	3.4	4.1	3.7	3.3	1.9
Kenya	44.0	64.7	126.0	188.0	277.3	270.9	263.8	249.1	246.9
Uganda	0.004	0.001	0.0001	1.6	4.0	4.8	1.3	1.2	0.4
Ethiopia	0.028	0.7	1.3	1.8	3.4	3.6	6.0	4.9	9.6
Rwanda	0.022	0	0.002	0.003	0.001	0.001	0.001	0.005	0.02
Burundi	0.009	0.0004	0.008	0.001	0	0	0.0001	0	0
Madagascar	109.7	178.1	89.4	196.1	323.2	277.2	238.5	289.8	279.4
Mauritius	244.9	238.3	254.7	269.2	227.6	167	119	114.7	101.6
Botswana	8.4	2.5	6.3	7.2	20.2	30.1	28.7	31.7	16
Lesotho	140.2	214.8	320.7	392.7	455.8	390.8	387.2	383.6	339.7
Namibia	0.02	0.012	6.7	42	78.9	53.2	33.2	28.6	0.07
Swaziland	31.9	48	89.1	140.7	178.7	161	135.3	135.3	124.9
South Africa	175.6	209.8	212.8	268.1	180.1	102.2	87.1	58.2	46.7

Source: **US Government's Office of Textiles and Apparel (OTEXA) and the US International Trade Administration (USITC).**

In conclusion, it can be said that the textile and apparel industry has the potential to rise again and hence give a greater contribution to economic growth and poverty alleviation. However, for this to happen, new investments in infrastructure and training are necessary. Opportunities exist that will allow Tanzania to sell quota and duty-free to the US and EU; to recapture its traditional regional markets as well as to sell on the local market by replacing imports. Nevertheless, this will require a re-examination of the policy framework, regulations, tax regime and enhanced public –private- partnership (PPP). With regard to the latter aspect, the need to strengthen stakeholder associations cannot be over-emphasized. The textile and apparel industry quite rightly deserves to be designated a priority sector but this has so far not been stated out for the simple reason that its stakeholders have not yet seen the wisdom of the saying that "the future belongs to the organized".

10

THE COTTON STAKEHOLDERS IN TANZANIA

One of the anticipated outcomes of the liberalization of the cotton industry was that with the broadening of stakeholders participation along the cotton value chain efficiency in production, processing and marketing would be improved significantly due to the competition arising at each of such processes. It may be recalled that between the early 1950s when PS and VFCU took over the purchasing and domestic marketing of cotton from private ownership up until 1994, the number of key stakeholders operating within the cotton industry was merely limited to farmers, NARS, cooperatives, marketing boards, agrochemical companies and the government. To date, the stakeholder complex has broadened rather significantly to include private banks, non-government organizations (NGO), collateral firms, the LGA and perhaps most importantly private cotton buyers cum ginners of both local and international origin.

In the context of the present discussion, stakeholders are defined as individuals or organizations that are affected by the activities of a business who may have a direct or indirect interest in the business and who may be in contact with such business on a daily basis or just occasionally. The broadening of the stakeholder complex in general and the re-entry of private buyers- cum ginners in particular had quite far ranging implications on the functioning of the industry.

Thus, while competition during the processes of buying, processing and marketing of cotton became accompanied by improvements in the timeliness of such processes as well as farmers being paid on a cash basis and obtaining a higher portion of the FOB price, the rather unregulated entry of cotton buyers cum ginners precipitated some major challenges too. First the very survival of some stakeholders became extremely threatened due to their failure to adapt to the new market circumstances. Perhaps more importantly, the future destiny of the subsector became in doubt.

As a result of the rapid increase in the number of stakeholders with diverse and often conflicting interests, a series of coordination related problems started to emerge within the industry culminating in its failure to deliver some of the vital services such as seasonal input credit as well as assure the upkeep of lint quality and financing of cotton R & D and extension services. The extent to which the subsector suffered as a result of such unforeseen consequences of liberalization was discussed earlier. This chapter examines the status of each of the major stakeholder groups after liberalization and how they collectively sought to deal with the emerging challenges.

10.1 Farmers

Up until 2009, the extent of their involvement in the cotton to garment value chain can most objectively be visualized by the fact that they are collectively responsible for the cultivation of cotton in 13 regions as opposed to 7, 5, 4 and 3 regions in the case of coffee, cashew, tobacco, tea and sisal respectively. Based on records from "pass books" issued to individual farmers between 2002 and 2006 under the national input scheme (NIS), the number of farmers who actually registered and participated in the "pass book" system varied between 300,000 and 400,000 per year for the entire WCGA and less than 50,000 in case of the ECGA. The number of cotton farmers unlike those of other crops such as coffee, tea, cashew and sisal has tended to vary seasonally because of farmers' propensity to switch between cotton and other crops, particularly food crops, depending on location and season.

Thus, it has quite often proven a daunting task to accurately establish their actual numbers as well as the acreage under cotton. Farmers' decision to switch between crops has quite often tended to be influenced by the competitiveness of the price of cotton relative to that of competing crops as well as the extent to which prevailing weather conditions favour the production of cotton relative to competing crops. The relative ease with which farmers shift between cotton and other crops would seem to be one of the major reasons for the dramatic seasonal fluctuations in annual cotton output. Such situation is relatively uncommon for most other crops such as coffee, tea, sisal and cashew that last beyond one growing season.

Cotton farmers practice a mix of commercial and subsistence production where the family provides the bulk of the labour while the farm provides the principal source of income. Their farms are typically small of between 0.4 and 5 ha. They largely depend on family labour for all farm operations and their cotton is grown under totally rain-fed conditions. Cotton farming under smallholder conditions benefits from extremely limited use of insecticides. The use of farm inputs such as inorganic fertilizers and herbicides by smallholders is virtually unknown and rather not surprisingly, there is absolutely no price support from the government. Faced with such limitations, it is also not surprising that for many years Tanzanian cotton farmers have tended to adopt a low-input-low-output approach to farming; a strategy which has tended to keep their average seed cotton yields only in the order of 400 to 750 kg/ha and 750 to1000 kg/ha of seed cotton in case of the WCGA and ECGA respectively.

Prior to economic and market reforms, cotton farmers in Tanzania were quite often assured of the provision of some of the fairly basic support services such as input supply, input credit and marketing as well as stable prices set by the government via the marketing parastatals and the cooperative. However, following the advent of a competitive market, smallholders became increasingly disadvantaged under the new market place that could no longer provide the same services and no doubt annual cotton output declined precipitously after liberalization.

The situation in Tanzania was quite opposed to that in Francophone Africa in general and in Burkina Faso (Africa's leading cotton producing country) in particular where farmers have a countrywide representative body that speaks on their behalf. In Tanzania, cotton farmers have until recently not been as properly and cohesively organized as was the case in the past due challenges being posed by liberalization. Thus, they have proven to be too small individually, to make cotton price rise for example, by reducing the acreage under cotton.

In recognition of the difficulties involved in trying to revive the cooperatives of the kind and stature that existed prior to 1976 under the likes of the late Paul Bomani, as well as the need to establish a truly farmers' association with grass root support all over the country, an attempt was made in 2004 to form a farmers' association dubbed TACOGA. Its main task was to unite cotton farmers all over the country for the sole purpose of fending for their interests and rights and speaking with one voice when interacting with either the government or other lobby groups within the cotton industry.

To ensure its credibility as a genuinely farmers' organization TACOGA has been striving to mobilize only cotton farmers to join the association. As a start all farmers who had previously participated in the annual countrywide cotton farming were asked to form the nucleus members. Such process was implemented during a meeting called by TCB on 21st April 2006. The formation of TACOGA just like that of TCA in 1997 was facilitated by TCB which, under the mandate of the Cotton Industry Act No. 2 of 2001, is obliged to do so as part of its regulatory and promotional functions within the industry.

Unfortunately, due to inadequate grass root mobilization and uncertainties on modalities for its financing arrangements, TACOGA continues to face the challenge of establishing its credibility to a wider group of farmers all over the country. Although the general awareness about TACOGA's roles and functions would seem to have increasingly spread out to many farmers and especially those partaking in annual competitions relating to best farming practices, by far the vast majority of cotton farmers remain largely unaware of TACOGA. Its other major emerging challenge would seem to be the sheer reluctance by some government officials and politicians to recognize and promote the rise of TACOGA as some kind of alternative instrument for genuinely representing cotton farmers' interests in the country.

Such reluctance would seem to be based on some apparently misplaced fears or perhaps political reasoning that the recognition of TACOGA would somehow hasten the demise of the cooperatives which up until 1976 had served as the only genuine and legitimate representative of cotton farmers. Unfortunately, today's cooperative movement has so far failed to organize farmers and to cater for their interests in a manner reminiscent of the cotton cooperatives of the late1950s and early1960s. Farmers' lack of a viable instrument for uniting them and strongly fending for their rights as is the case say for most civil servant organizations or trade unions has quite certainly been a major set-back for them.

Given cotton's importance to the broader socioeconomic development of the WCGA it goes without saying that the subsector in general, and farmers in particular, who constitute the critical bulk of the electorate tend to wield considerable political clout as well. It follows, therefore, that whoever manages to fight for their cotton related interests and other welfare/economic needs as was the case under the VFCU will get their unwavering support in any arena. While time will soon or later tell whether it will be either TACOGA or the Cooperative Unions which best serve farmers' interests and needs, both these institutions should best be left alone to pursue their objectives because after-all they are legal institutions trying to act in cotton's best interest.

10.2 The cooperative unions

Cotton cooperatives arose as African's response to unfair trading practices as well as exploitative tendencies on the part of non-African traders in the early 1950s. Since then they became promoted by both the colonial and post-colonial governments as a potential source of decentralized grass root participation in agricultural credit, input, and commodity markets. Old cooperatives sold cotton on forward contracts and hence enabled smallholders to obtain a higher share of world prices cooperatives and they maintained widespread, multipurpose assets and facilities. Their activities tended to be concentrated in, or even limited to, those segments of the cotton value chain that were close to farmers such as farm supply and first stage commodity handling.

In the aftermath of institutional and policy reforms implemented between the early 1970s and early 1990s, it was widely expected that the AMCs would become more specialized and more interlinked up and down the value chain than in the past. On the contrary AMCs remained virtually stuck in their past in terms of outlook by failing to cope with modern economic realities. Thus, they have to date become virtually indistinguishable from the multinational corporations (MNCs) and/or private ginners with whom they are competing for the cotton market share. For example, rather than collecting the seed cotton from their constituent members through an extensive circuit of primary societies as was the case in the past, they now buy cotton from virtually any cotton grower just like the private buyers.

Similarly, while in the past the AMCs bought seed cotton on credit and determined producer price levels as a post-cost and post-margin residue, with the opening of the cotton market to private participation, they are now being obliged to buy seed cotton on a cash basis and to offer competitive prices for it something which they have so far miserably failed to accomplish due to chronic liquidity problems. Thus, between 1994 and 2008, their market share for seed cotton declined countrywide from 100% to well below 5%. Due to worsening marketing conditions the profitability of their operations has similarly deteriorated and as a result they been unable to pay competitive prices.

In the wake of their increasing failure to provide any useful service to their members, AMCs have witnessed a continued flight of their bona fide members. At the primary society level, their limited participation in cotton business under the RCUs has resulted in most of them becoming agents of private buyers and not RCUs any longer simply because with credit-based input supply no longer being undertaken, the smallholders' loyalty to them has lost all its rationale. So, although RCUs have continued to own and manage a numerically significant ginning capacity, their prevailing structural, financial and organizational challenges and hence limited participation in cotton business has, to say the least, more or less rendered them completely redundant.

Prior to the institutional reforms the AMCs rather than the RCUs were indeed the true cooperatives in the sense that they were businesses owned and controlled by the people who used their services and whose benefits were being shared by the users on the basis of use. On the other hand, the RCUs which came about in the aftermath of the reforms cannot be strictly labeled as cooperatives because as enterprises they did not conform to the spirit and intent of the definition of a cooperative enterprise as universally accepted and presented here. The widely held view of a cooperative movement as a model organization based on freedom of association, democratic equality with one member one vote, and independence from the state is totally inapplicable in case of the RCUs for the main reason that farmers were more or less obliged to join the PSs which, as alluded to earlier, functioned as extended arms of government by gaining exclusivity in agricultural marketing, fiscal exemptions, credits, donations and what have you.

Under such circumstances, the leadership that took over the RCUs and PSs never truly got to understanding the meaning of the cooperative organization, and as a result, could not defend it for the main reason that farmers joined the PSs on a compulsory membership basis and no doubt the image of AMCs turned into RCUs became tarnished due to mismanagement, poor business practice and perhaps most importantly, corruption. In the wake of these factors and uninhibited state intervention and micro-management, the "Regional Cooperative Unions" found it increasingly very difficult to live up to the earlier objectives of the AMCs in the face of market competition which they managed to tame quite well during the 1950s.

In view of the above challenges, as well as a myriad of constraints faced while engaging in cotton business, the number of cooperatives actually involved in cotton buying and ginning declined over time to just a handful of them such as ; SHIRECU, NCU, Biharamulo Cooperative Union (BCU), Kahama Cooperative Union (KACU), Oridoyi PS, Coast Region Cooperative Union (CORECU) and Kilimanjaro Native Cooperative Union (KNCU).

In spite of the numerous challenges and constraints that they have been facing over time, their critical role in uniting the numerous resource poor smallholders who individually cannot fend for their interests is indisputable. The challenge then is how farmers can regroup in a bid to become stronger and more efficient again and hence compete against the private companies. Because previous cotton cooperatives were borne out of a crisis situation, it should be possible to resuscitate that spirit for the main reason that the present market scenario in cotton is not so different from what existed at that point in time.

Nevertheless, for true and strong AMCs to re-emerge, some of the prerequisites or preconditions would be: the need for such AMCs to be strictly member-driven, member-controlled and member-responsive organizations. However, AMCs meeting such criteria would still be liable to fail unless and until they are managed efficiently by professionally qualified staff who in turn are under the supervision and control of democratically elected boards of directors. The intention here would be to ensure that the management of AMCs is subject to principles of accountability and answerability, ethical behavior and good governance and independent of government intervention.

The good name of past cooperatives during the era of the late Paul Bomani and his colleagues owed quite greatly to their efficient and effective management based on discipline and principles of good governance. The fact that they were managed in a business-like manner helped them to be non-political, self-reliant and hence neither charity organizations nor social clubs. Thus, with regard to the future of the cooperatives, the government has the formidable task of putting up sound policies that will foster such a rebirth of such spirit again. The promulgation in 2005 of the Cooperative Reform and Modernization Programme as well as the initiative in 2009 to decouple cooperative development from government ministries by creating a semi-autonomous Cooperative Development Commission are extremely welcome initiatives. Hopefully, that will promote the formation of truly member driven and professionally managed cooperatives.

10.3 Cotton R & D
Under the National Agricultural Research Service (NARS), research into aspects relating to the economic production of cotton in both the WCGA and ECGA has since the early 1930s been the mandate of two main research stations, namely; Ukiriguru and Ilonga respectively. The former, located just 30 km from Mwanza along the road to Shinyanga was established way back in 1932 and has been undertaking research that rather broadly addresses the needs of cotton

production in the WCGA where the major researchable constraints continue to be low and declining soil fertility as well as damage by insect pests and plant diseases.

Increased cotton production in the ECGA has for many years tended to be constrained by severe attacks from insect pests; intense weed competition, the tendency for cotton plants to grow very tall and thereby making spraying operations difficult and strong competition from food crops for land, labour and producer prices. Research into aspects of alleviating these and other related constraints is being undertaken at Ilonga. The latter which is located about 10 km north of the town of Kilosa along the road to Dumila was established in 1949 by the British colonial government to solve the cotton related production constraints in the ECGA.

Cotton R & D at both research stations has traditionally been undertaken using multidisciplinary and demand-led approaches. To date, the research work going on at both stations mainly relate to the development, testing and adaptation of new farm level production technologies as well as packaging the results obtained from such research into forms considered to be useable by extension staff and farmers. In chapter 4 some of the research agenda as well as the major challenges and constraints facing cotton R& D were discussed and so will not be repeated here.

10.4 Extension services

In Tanzania, as in other countries, the primary task of the extension service has been to package information on pro-poor production technologies for cotton and delivering it to farmers in an effective way. The other equally important task, at least in theory, has been to provide a feedback mechanism to cotton R & D personnel regarding problems that are being faced by the cotton farmers.

Up until 1973, the extension service in the country was under the Ministry of Agriculture where, together with research, they have continued to remain close to one another albeit as separate departments and thence retaining a history of functional specialization. Unfortunately, as a consequence of such administrative separation and hence specialization, the two departments have quite often not been collaborating as closely as they should be in part due to the rather regular changes in the structure and functions of the agricultural ministry itself.

Following the formation of the so-called crop authorities in 1976, a step was made towards the institutionalization of commodity specific extension services under the newly established crop authorities as a strategy to improve the effectiveness of extension services in the country. Under the new structure, the newly formed Tanzania Cotton Authority (TCA), for example, was mandated to engage agricultural extension service agents in each of the designated cotton growing districts who would engage with cotton farmers directly.

Unfortunately, such system of commodity based extension services only operated until 1984 after which the extension services were transferred from the agricultural ministry to the newly re-established Local Government Authorities (LGA). Such move came in the aftermath of new policy changes that also saw the so-called crop authorities being reconstituted into mere marketing boards. As a result of such changes, the nature of the delivery of extension services also changed from being commodity specific to being rather generalized in nature. Such a simplifying approach to extension services was probably in line with another policy change which, while allowing the department of extension service to be moved to the LGA, the fundamental task of agricultural policy formulation remained with the agricultural ministry.

The separation of the tasks of policy formulation and extension service delivery in relation to agriculture and their placement under two separate ministries, namely of agriculture and that of Regional Administration and Local Government respectively, was not generally well supported by agricultural stakeholders. The latter have been explicit in pointing out that the new arrangement requiring two separate line ministries to promote agriculture that way is neither feasible nor sustainable in the long run.

Apart from the effects of frequent policy and institutional changes, the provision and delivery of extension service in the country is widely being seen as outdated, paternalistic, top-down, subject to bureaucratic inefficiencies and thence unfit to cope with demands of an increasingly market oriented farming. Such an assessment may in part be due to the fact that agricultural extension services in Tanzania continue to be provided free of charge by the government through the LGAs.

That the extension service has so far not been able to deliver in Tanzania has in part been necessitated by the chronic and glaring mismatch between the numbers of staff that are actually required for the delivery of such service as compared with the number that is actually out there serving the farmers. By 2007, for example, there were only 3,379 agricultural extension officers in the country out of whom 2027 were village extension officers and 1,352 as ward extension officers. These figures do not augur well with the national requirement for extension officers estimated at 15,082 out of whom 12,227 and 2,855 are in respect of villages and wards respectively.

The other and even more critical factor behind the poor state of extension services in the country is with regard to the fact that they have tended to be deployed to undertake activities that do not at all relate to their training in agriculture. The LGAs by virtue of their being engaged in a multiplicity of non-agricultural activities, tend to deploy extension officers to collect levies, taxes and the like. Consequently, most of the extension staff have tended to be poorly motivated at their places of work.

There has been a lot of talk on the need to restructure and manage extension services in a bid to make them more effective and efficient in addressing the major problems facing farmers and several schools of thought have emerged on how that can be achieved. The well-known Training & Visit or simply T & V system under which extension service agents are simply seen to act as a bridge by facilitating a two way information flow between researchers and smallholder farmers is increasingly being adapted into a simple, demand driven, decentralized, pluralistic extension delivery system using the farmer field school (FFS) approach. The latter, by its nature, encourages group-based approaches to achieving increased diffusion of information between and amongst farmers.

There has also been some suggestion on the need to privatize and commercialize agricultural extension services, for example, by initiating private-public-partnerships involving the government and the private sector. Similarly, due to a declining trend in government funding for public services, including extension services after SAP there has emerged a need to privatize as well as commercialize such services. Nevertheless, the operationalization of such an idea has so far not happened as yet on account of the imperative to carefully balance the needs for subsistence and commercial farms as well as the modalities for pricing the services to be provided to them. In addition, the government will have to carefully consider both the short and long-term implications of a restructuring process that will have to take place prior to the privatization and thence commercialization of such services.

Fortunately, there has been some progress already made to that effect in relation to cotton. Within the cotton subsector, there has been some kind of a return to the system which existed during the era of crop authorities in the mid to late 1970s, whereby extension field staff under TCA provided cotton specific extension services. Under the contract farming arrangements for cotton, that are currently being promoted all over the country, ginners will be required to provide cotton related extension services by recruiting qualified and properly motivated extension staff who will be working in their designated areas of operation. It is hoped that through CF the speed of delivery and uptake of best farming practices from cotton R & D institutions will improve and thus lead to the rapid transformation of cotton production in the country.

10.5 Input providers

One of the major factors contributing to the rapid expansion of cotton growing in Tanzania after the 1950s, was the increased availability of some of the basic farming inputs, notably, seed for planting and pesticides. Throughout the 20th century annual input use for cotton peaked during the 1992/93 marketing season when 30,000 tons of seed, 150 tons of seed dressing chemicals and one million litres of insecticides were used. Coincidentally, the biggest crop output in Tanzania during the 20th century also occurred during the 1992/93 marketing season.

Up until 1992/93, inputs such as seed dressing chemicals, insecticides and sprayers were being supplied to the cotton industry by several local and international agro-chemical companies such as BASF, Bayer, Ciba Geigy, Hoechst, Nordox, ICI/Twiga Chemicals, Shell, Sumitomo and Tanzania Pesticides among others. The number of agro-chemical dealers increased quite rapidly during the early 1980s. Some of the factors behind such increases included the introduction of endosulfan as an alternative to DDT which along with dimethoate were the two main products being used on cotton up until 1975; the introduction of the use of ultra low volume spraying involving the application of insecticides formulated in oil and perhaps most importantly the arrival of a series of synthetic pyrethroids as alternatives to both DDT and endosulfan for the control of bollworms and sucking pests on cotton. The appearance of many new agrochemical companies was thus in response to the need to market the new pesticides in their different formulations and the sprayers needed to apply them.

By 1999/00 marketing season, the use of insecticides on cotton had dropped from 1 million litres in 1992/93 to just 100,000 litres. The drop in insecticide use on cotton after the 1992/93 marketing season was correlated with a rapid decline in the number of agrochemical companies operating in the country. The dramatic drop in input use was a direct outcome of the abolition of input subsidies and devaluation of the shilling after Tanzania's adoption and implementation of austerity measures under SAP. As a consequence of the reforms, farmers found themselves unable to afford to buy their pesticides whose retail prices had significantly gone up. Inevitably, the agrochemical companies found themselves compelled either to exit from business or to cut down on their pesticide imports into the country.

After liberalization, most of the new cotton buyers cum ginners were reluctant to maintain the input credit arrangements that had previously been handled by cooperatives for fear that price competition at the farm gate would encourage side selling by farmers and hence affect their profitability. Similarly, by 1994 most of the larger chemical companies were increasingly shifting to new investments in other areas of research on plant protection most notably in the biological sciences. To date, some of the former agrochemical companies have been replaced by smaller and perhaps less well-known companies the most active of which are Mukpar, Balton, Helm, Arista Life Science, Baytrade, SubaAgro among others. Present companies operate just a few retail outlets in strategic areas where they quite often maintain limited quantities of their products. They have quite often preferred to deal with the Cotton Development Fund (CDF). The latter, like the marketing parastatals, has been procuring agrochemicals and applicators in bulk on behalf of smallholders by way of a centralized tendering system.

The reluctance by most agrochemical companies to get fully involved in the retail distribution of cotton pesticides would seem to have arisen because of four major considerations. Firstly, because input use by farmers is usually tied to access to credit, the failure of rural credit markets to develop on a sustainable basis in sub-Saharan Africa has meant that seasonal input use has generally declined over the years. Secondly, agricultural input use has quite often been tightly linked with the research and extension services, both of which have been significantly cut down during the market reform period. Thirdly, because most inputs are imported, there is an inherent foreign exchange risk that a small trader may not be able to bear. Fourthly, because of the inherent variability in rainfall, there has also been the risk on the part of the agrochemical company of being stuck with a large carry-over stock in case the rains do not come.

To fill up the vacuum there has, unfortunately, been an explosion of unlicensed and uncontrolled dealers in the agrochemical industry as well as a proliferation of unregistered, unlabeled, expired and often repackaged products obtained through an emerging informal trade, smuggling and unauthorized cross border trade. This has occurred contrary to the original objective of liberalization of the agrochemical input market which sought to induce a more competitive market leading to lower prices, higher quality products, more timely procurement and delivery and encouragement of more rational use of inputs according to economic signals. Regulation and control of pesticide use has thus become more complex due to a bigger number of actors to deal with than in the past.

10.6 Tanzania Cotton Association
Increased private sector participation in the cotton industry after market reforms brought with it the need for the actors to have a forum for interacting amongst themselves and with policy-making organs of the state. Such forum was

created after the formation of the Tanzania Cotton Association in 1998 some four years after the liberalization of the cotton industry in 1994. With the tacit backing and support by the Cotton Board, TCA came into being as a legal and legitimate platform for articulating and defending mainly the interests of all private cotton buyers, ginners and exporters in a unified manner.

Regional Cooperative Unions and later TACOGA also joined TCA in spite of their perceived philosophical differences in the way they tend to approach or engage in cotton business. To date TCA has 43 members most of whom are ginners. Between 1994 and 2004 Paul Reinhart, Cargill and Olam were the only international companies operating in Tanzania. The rest of the ginners were local companies owned by individuals belonging to three major ethnic groups namely; African, Indian and Arabian Tanzanians. Conspicuously absent from the association though are the other members of the value chain including most notably the textile millers, shippers and input providers.

In other cotton producing and exporting countries, TCA would be the equivalent of an apex organization where all major stakeholders involved in cotton business such as cotton growers, buyers, ginners, oil millers exporters, textile and apparel manufacturers and others are all represented. This is not yet the case in Tanzania. Nevertheless, it is widely foreseen that by soon or later that will be the case. In the meantime TCB has been striving to facilitate the formation of individual associations along the value chain, which like TACOGA and the textile manufacturers of Tanzania (TEXMAT) in the case of growers and textile manufacturers respectively, will be represented in TCA.

Since its inception, TCA has quite often striven to provide representation for its members when speaking to government as well as striving very hard to influence government policy and action. Thus, it has often sought for government action to improve the quality of delivery of some public services most notably railway services and local road maintenance. TCA has also actively participated in discussions relating to specific cotton industry legislation and regulations. Over the past ten years, TCA has most importantly managed to put up before government three major policy proposals. The first proposal related to the need by the industry to be empowered to raise the bar and thereby limit market participation to credible companies and firms capable of investing in the sub sector. Unfortunately a fee of 500,000 dollars that was proposed to be mandatory before one engaged in any cotton business was rejected by government for being a potential barrier to market entry. And so an opportunity to keep out opportunistic firms was lost.

The second proposal required all ginners to participate in a mechanisation program by contributing to the purchase of tractors to be used on hire basis. Such proposal had sought to boost cotton output by assisting smallholders to get their fields ready for planting in time. A few ginners tried to object to an otherwise excellent initiative but due to support from government the initiative went on as planned. So although contract farming arrangements for cotton had not yet been instituted in Tanzania at the time, the initiative had been designed to boost cotton output.

Finally, in an attempt to make seed cotton buying more transparent and genuinely competitive, ginners advised the government to introduce the auctioning of cotton at a few designated posts. The latter were perceived to be a better option than the current system whereby each ginner maintains his own buying posts in several different places of cotton producing districts. Under the present arrangement TCB has often been unable to provide adequate monitoring due to an existing mismatch between its capacity to do so in terms of logistics, finances and personnel relative to the size of the operational area.

To further improve its status within the sub-sector, TCA must continue to seek to promote a positive public image of the institution itself as well as that of the cotton sub-sector as a whole through its products and services. To date TCA has an obvious image problem. Smallholder farmers tend to look at buyers in general as being dishonest due to price manipulation, tempering of weighing scales and price fixing through collusive behaviour by forming cartels. Unfortunately, most malpractices are largely being perpetrated by their agents and the so-called "Marching Guys". The latter have become quite a force to reckon with in the aftermath of market liberalization.

Some of the issues which have been of some concern to the government and the general public relate to the under-reporting of figures by most ginners in a bid to evade the payment of statutory levies and taxes as well as the deliberate exploitation of smallholders by way of low producer prices on offer. It has perhaps been for this reason that cotton buyers tend to be castigated as thieves or just outright daylight robbers. Thus TCA must improve the quality of membership as well as the representation within TCA.

TCA can achieve that in two ways; first by trying to ensure that all cotton related businesses are duly registered with TCA and secondly by urgently putting in place a code of conduct or service. The latter is a set of guidelines and regulations to be followed by members of the association although it does not normally have the force of law. TCA stands to gain substantially by introducing this facility as it will help to enhance self regulation within the industry, something which is currently conspicuously absent.

10.7 Tanzania Cotton Board

The Tanzania Cotton Board officially came into operation on 1st July 2004 after the passage by parliament of the Cotton Industry Act No. 2 in 2001. The major functions of TCB as set out under the new legislation relate to the regulation and promotion of the cotton industry as well as to help in all aspects that facilitate monitoring, coordination and development of the subsector in general.

As a quasi-government institution TCB plays key advisory and representation roles as well. TCB is by all intents and purposes a culmination of several policy and institutional reforms undertaken by government since 1952 when the Lint and Seed Marketing Board was first formed by the British colonial government. It was retained after independence as a vehicle for facilitating the provision of marketing services, input supplies, and seasonal credit disbursement in line with other considerations for strategically valued commodities in general.

Between 1984 and 1994 the functioning of the commodity market became questioned on several grounds. The marketing board and regional cooperative unions as state sponsored and state financed bodies did not quite operate with a profit motive in mind; they were inefficient; they were overly politicized; they were basically acting in ways that served to stifle rather than promote the growth of the sub sector; they were not serving their clients well in terms of the quality of delivery and the timeliness; they were taking the lion's share of the world market prices for cotton; they were quite often being used as vehicles to support vested interests and were often paying cotton farmers late if at all. Such a diverse array of basically anti-market sentiments went on to form the basis for the ultimate reform and restructuring of all commodity boards under the umbrella of the structural adjustment and liberalization programs.

After nearly two decades of continuous policy reforms and concerted restructuring of commodity boards in particular, their functions became redefined in ways that theoretically go on to strengthen public-private-partnership within respective industries. Thus, the roles and functions of all the commodity boards have become entirely regulatory in outlook and scope while those relating to production, buying, processing, marketing and exporting have been left to the private sector. Nevertheless, functions such as the financing of cotton R & D; extension service delivery; the provision of seasonal inputs; promotion and advisory services are now being jointly shared with the private sector. The financing of such functions also became redefined to reflect the split in responsibilities.

Box No. 3: Functions of the Tanzania Cotton Board

1. To license persons engaged in cotton buying, processing and marketing;
2. To collect, refine, maintain and disseminate information relating to cotton;
3. To advise the government on matters of strategy and policy relating to the development of the cotton industry;
4. To convene an annual general meeting of all cotton stakeholders;
5. To ensure quality standards and enforce the compliance to such standards by persons licensed by the Board to oversee the quality of cotton sold locally and overseas
6. To ensure fair trade and competition and monitor prices as determined by market forces;
7. To supervise the execution of contract farming in cotton;
8. To register cotton growers
9. To supervise the production of correct standard monthly reports showing monthly lint bales produced
10. To enter and inspect premises and collect information

In spite of the redefinition of the roles of all the key stakeholders, the mindsets of some stakeholders are still stuck in the past. For example, until recently some politicians still thought of the present TCB as some kind of a replica of the former Tanzania Cotton Authority (TCA) which during its hey days unilaterally carried out all the functions relating to seasonal input supply, quality control, extension service delivery and marketing among other services as was the case prior to 1984. Understandably, such thinking has tended to be a reflection of their disappointment with the failure of crop marketing liberalization to live up to their expectations. As a result sentiments have tended to emerge that call for TCB to re-engage the tasks and activities that were previously under TCA.

The failure by TCB to take up its rightful roles just as liberalization took effect in 1994 was probably one of the major reasons for the poor performance of the cotton industry in Tanzania in the aftermath of market reforms. Between 1994 and 2004, TCLSB i.e. TCB's predecessor was on a life support machine in view of the predicaments facing it. Because it had been formed after a mere amendment of the previous marketing law, it inherited many of the liabilities of TCMB the major one of which was the legal issue involving the unfulfilled contracts which arose as a result of its predecessor having defaulted on contracts which it had entered with overseas cotton buyers on behalf of the cooperative unions. TCLSB was being required to pay up on behalf of the defunct TCMB or risk sanctions as well as the seizure of its landed assets; an issue which could not be resolved until 2004.

Secondly, due to an ill-defined regulatory and promotional mandate TCB ended up spreading its meager human and financial resources rather thinly in an attempt to deal with the complex of problems from the field to the garment. TCB also became faced with a considerable miss-match between its responsibilities and the size of its human resources needed to accomplish its mission given the large size of the operational area. Thirdly, following the removal of its statutory levy on cotton in 2006, TCB found itself increasingly unable to oversee and regulate the cotton industry due to the inadequacy and erratic nature of the subventions coming from government coffers. This issue as will be discussed later has further been compounded by the erroneous belief that vide decentralization by devolution LGAs will compliment TCB's regulatory functions.

10. 8 Oil Millers

The extraction of edible oil from cotton was until 1994 the preoccupation of just a few private companies, namely, the Mwanza and Morogoro based VOIL and MOPROCO companies respectively. In addition, some fairly small scale crushing of cottonseed for semi-refined or crude oil was also being undertaken by all RCUs at some designated ginneries. However, after liberalization most of the new entrants into the ginning industry also became engaged in the crushing cotton seed for oil and the large scale of sale of the by products such as seed cake and cotton husks. By 2007 some thirty ginners had installed oil mills at their business premises, capable of processing 16,121 metric tons of cotton oil; representing only 14% of the installed capacity of 115,150 tons per annum. To date, these and other oil mills produce an estimated 52,000 tons of cotton seed cake annually.

The recent trend towards increased crushing of cottonseed for oil extraction on their sites has come in the wake of increased demand for edible oil for which Tanzania is currently facing a deficit. The latter was until recently being met through imports mainly from South East Asian countries. The demand for edible oil in the country is currently estimated at around 200,000 metric tons annually and if the Food and Agricultural Organization's (FAO) recommendation for a minimum per capita consumption of 5 kg per annum is taken into consideration, the demand for a population of around 50 million Tanzanians would amount to around 250,000 metric tons of edible oil. However, with an estimated 100,000 metric tons of edible oil being produced locally, it is obvious that a production gap of around 150,000 metric tons must be met through imported semi-refined and refined palm oil.

The recent tendency by almost all ginners to engage in both ginning and the crushing of their cottonseed for the production of oil and other by-products does seem to have been prompted by other economic considerations as well. Most ginners have now realized that at current retail selling prices for cottonseed, the oil industry more than compensates for the total operational costs involved in the ginning process. Thus, in the context of the relatively harsh business environment which makes ginning only marginally profitable, such windfall savings/revenues arising out of their involvement in oil extraction would tend to provide them with the much needed additional cushion necessary for business comfort. Furthermore, it would appear that increased interest in oil extraction business has also been fuelled by rising awareness within much of the WCGA that cotton husks can be an extremely valuable dry season feed for cattle prior to their shipment to Dar es Salaam. In recent years, the demand for cottonseed husks between July and November has been quite high, thus, necessitating payments being be made ahead of time just to guarantee delivery.

10.9 Textiles and Apparel Manufacturers
The textile sector is one of the key components of the cotton to garment value chain and so it provides a very important link between cotton and lint production on one hand and the garment and apparel production on the other. Prior to liberalization, the sector had a strong and functional association (TEXMAT) that comprised of members from the entire segment of the textile and apparel industry. Unfortunately TEXTMAT collapsed after market reforms. Its demise was very strongly linked to that of most textile mills. Until recently, the textile and apparel sector has tended to be represented

by a committee that operates under the broad auspices of the Confederation of Trade and Industries (CTI). The latter, also represents the interests of the other segments of the manufacturing sector and so lobbies for the textile sector as well as other industries by interacting with government.

Unfortunately, having to lobby through CTI rather than its own sector-wide association puts the textile sector in a disadvantaged position. Because of its rather unique constraints and challenges, it may not be able to lobby for its own interests as well as clearly define its priority goals within the sector. The danger which is likely to arise from a situation like this one is that individual textile companies may quite easily fall into the trap of pursuing their own agenda thus further thwarting the ability of the industry to come up with a unified approach to dealing with its welfare.

To avert such fears, TEXTMAT was recently resuscitated and will now constitute a new vehicle for lobbying and promotion of its interests. Such revival of TEXTMAT has come at a time when TCB is increasingly being called to oversee the promotion of the entire cotton to garment value chain. This is a significant milestone in the cotton industry because the previous compartmentalization of production and processing on one hand and that of value addition and export on the other between the two ministries of agriculture and industries tended to constrain rather than nurture the emergence of a viable global value chain strategy for the cotton industry.

10. 10 Local Government Authorities
In its attempt to quickly spearhead rural development, environmental sustainability and poverty reduction, the government has increasingly been pushing for a process designated as decentralization by devolution or just simply D by D. Under the new kind of decentralized administration, the government has sought to assign clear and legally recognized geographical boundaries to local government authorities (LGA) within which they assume the authority to

perform a series of public functions such as raising revenues, undertaking investment decisions, overseeing the delivery of public services and supervising some key economic activities such as agricultural production.

The goal of decentralization by devolution has thus been to confer high local autonomy as well as accountability in a bid to improve service delivery to the rural poor and thereby making them feel being party to their own development. Unfortunately, with regard to agricultural development in general and cotton development in particular, the majority of the LGAs in the districts where cotton is a major cash crop do not quite score highly with regard to how they undertake to promote the crop. To date, in spite of the huge amounts of revenue which they collect on an annual basis in the form of district crop levy, only a small percentage of them tend to plough back for supporting either cotton production through extension related activities or the enforcement and monitoring of compliance to rules and regulations of the Cotton Industry Act No. 2 of 2001.

The dismal failure by most LGAs to collaborate with TCB in the enforcement of the Cotton Industry Act and its regulations is explained by the fact that some employees of the LGA hierarchy tend to engage in cotton related businesses as agents of some of the officially licensed cotton buyers cum ginners in activities relating to seed cotton buying; the distribution of seeds for planting as well as pesticides and their applicators. Under such circumstances, TCB quite often finds itself on a collision course with the very people and institutions that should be helping it to regulate the industry. Thus, each time a cotton buying post or a ginnery is closed by TCB staff for breach of regulations misunderstandings quite often tend to erupt between TCB and their owners.

An even worse scenario often arises each year at the commencement of the cotton season. In their quest to maximize revenue collection from cotton, some LGAs tend to engage in activities that are quite clearly inimical to the emergence of a true and strong PPP in two ways. First, while most levies, taxes and fees relating to cotton buying, ginning, exporting, education and the like were scrapped off by central government way back in 2006, a plethora of other taxes tends to just emerge suddenly during the cotton buying season.

The taxes tend to come in the form of voluntary payments for the Uhuru torch and seating allowances. In some districts, the education levy has been reinstated under the guise of a by-law. This brings us to a second issue, namely, the ambiguity of the law on the taxation of cotton; with each LGA capable of enacting a by-law that contradicts the main law on cotton, how can TCB, farmers and ginners hope to bring a unified enforcement of such law? Under normal circumstances one would tend to expect that LGAs would enact by-laws that complement rather than contradict the main law applicable to the commodity. This is currently not the case for cotton.

Regarding the implementation of rural and agricultural development with regard to cotton as envisaged under the agricultural sector development strategy (ASDP), the role of LGA has become increasingly doubtful in many parts of the country primarily because of the lack of adequate human resource capacity in project formulation, design and management at all district levels.

10.11 State Agencies

There are a number of quasi-government institutions within and outside the agricultural sector, whose public roles are critical in the proper functioning of the cotton sub-sector. Some such institutions include the Tanzania Official Seed Certification Institute (TOSCI) which collaborates with the Cotton Board and cotton R & D stations in ensuring that appropriate cotton varieties are released to farmers after proper testing, registration and certification; Tropical Pesticides Research Institute (TPRI) which serves to register all pesticides destined for cotton and other crops as well as participating in the monitoring the quality of such products both upon entry in Tanzania as well as their performance at field level; Tanzania Bureau of Standards (TBS) which collaborates with the Cotton Board in managing the southern, central and eastern African Regional Testing Centre for promotion of the instrument testing of cotton fibre quality under the umbrella of the Commercial Standardization of Instrument Testing for Cotton (CSITC); and National Environmental Management Council (NEMC) which collaborates with the Cotton Board in the monitoring of the safe handling and disposal of old and expired toxic agrochemicals relating to cotton. Unfortunately, because these quasi-government institutions quite often operate independently and report to different authorities, coordination of their activities has tended to be difficult at times.

10.12 Stakeholders' Meetings

One of the lessons learnt from the liberalization not only of cotton marketing but also of other commodities in Tanzania, has been the fact that the liberalization process did not immediately result in the emergence of well-developed marketing systems where all the appropriate institutions such as functioning credit markets, adequate contract enforcement, and good marketing information exist i.e. where "the invisible hand" of the market supplies all the critical functions as has been the case in the more developed economies.

Thus, in spite of increased private sector participation between 1994 and 1999, the provision of some key goods and services most notably the upkeep of lint quality, the financing of cotton R & D, market information and seasonal inputs became extremely problematic largely due to coordination related challenges. The inability by the market to provide for such essential services and goods in the case of cotton became further exacerbated by the failure of TCLSB initially and later TCB as *de facto* regulatory arms of the government to actively and efficiently engage in their new roles after the reforms due to emerging financial, structural and legal problems which came to greatly plague both institutions between 1994 and 2006.

Similarly, for quite a long time, most cotton stakeholders remained largely unaware of the new functions of crop boards and so continued to look at them as providers of everything as was the case in the past. Inevitably, the performance of the cotton industry became affected as reflected by annual output declining to one of the lowest levels in production history by the 1999/00 marketing season as described earlier. Because the impacts of the decline in the fortunes of the cotton value started to affect directly or indirectly the welfare of its stakeholders, there arose a necessity for all concerned parties to deliberate on how to halt a further deterioration in the performance of the cotton industry. Such imperative went on to form the basis for the emergence after market reforms of a formalized forum for all the stakeholders to meet, consult and deliberate on all aspects and issues relating to the development of the industry.

Prior to 1994 stakeholders' meetings were being called on a rather ad hoc basis by the cotton marketing parastatals at the instigation of the government in the aftermath of some major crises primarily in order to chart out how to deal with them. For example, one such meeting was held between 16th and 19th of May 1984 in Mwanza under the chairmanship of President Julius Nyerere to discuss on why the industry was up until then not performing well enough. It may be recalled that the economy in general and the cotton industry in particular were in very bad shape after having been hurt by the effects of the war with Uganda and the oil crisis of 1983. Moreover, it was also revealed at that point in time the government was embroiled in negotiations with the IFI for possible aid assistance.

214

At that meeting, some of the factors that were identified to be contributing to the stagnation of cotton production included the declining of soil fertility in the WCGA; cotton facing stiff competition from food crops in the ECGA; inadequate mechanization of agriculture; farmer's lack of incentives to increase production and productivity; inadequate extension services; effects of frequent incidences of famine and a general deterioration in the discipline of farmers on one hand and government leaders on the other. One major outcome of that particular stakeholders' meeting was with regard to the need to implement the resolve by government to reform TCMB and the Regional Cooperative Unions. Nevertheless, on account of the rather ad hoc nature of that particular meeting, there were no planned follow up meetings for monitoring the extent to which the resolutions had been implemented.

Between 1995 and 1998, a series of other meetings were held which for the first time also involved the new private ginners apart from the regular participants, namely, the cooperative unions, cotton research, TCLSB and officials from the Ministry of Agriculture. Such meetings again met on an ad hoc basis to deliberate on issues that arose within the sector from time to time. During that period one of the emerging issues was with regard to the urgent need for the industry to form an industry-wide body that would unite incoming members of the private sector and other incumbent stakeholders for purposes of articulating their interests as well as the need to find out how the cotton sub-sector would deal with the procurement and distribution of seasonal inputs and the financing of cotton R & D under the new liberalized market regime. Two major and quite historic outcomes of those particular meetings were with regard to the formation of TCA and CDF in 1998 and 1999 respectively.

In Shinyanga region the ruling party CCM on its own initiative summoned an ad hoc cotton stakeholders' meeting on 24th November 1998 involving a select group of people comprising of party pundits and activists, the RCUs, cotton R & D scientists, TCLSB and government officials to deliberate on the declining fortunes of the cotton industry in the country as a whole and in that region in particular and how the situation could best be halted and reversed. Rather surprisingly private buyers cum ginners were deliberately not invited to the meeting. Nonetheless, the significance of CCM's initiative could not be overstated suffice to say that the ruling party had become quite concerned with the wider implications of cotton's future in the country's largest cotton producing region.

The holding of stakeholders' meetings as well the consultations concerning the overall fate of the cotton industry took an increasingly more structured and objective approach with effect from the start of the 21st century. Between 25th and 26th March 2000, the government convened a meeting which was chaired by President Benjamin Mkapa to ponder on why the cooperatives in general and cotton cooperatives in particular had not been performing well after crop marketing liberalization. In the case of cotton, their market share had plummeted from 100% by 1994 to less than 10% by 2000.

Such scenario was quite clearly not to the liking of the government that had for many years looked upon the cooperatives as the cornerstone of grass-root support for cotton production and marketing by smallholder farmers. The meeting was truly historic in the sense that unlike the previous highly powered meetings which ended up being just big talk shops, its discussions and resolutions went on to form the basis for the establishment of the Ministry of Cooperatives and marketing (MCM). The latter, in spite of having lasted for just five years, namely, between 2000 and 2005, it is credited for having passionately articulated and pushed for the establishment of the blue print for a new cooperative era in Tanzania.

Between 27th and 28th March 2000, just after the stakeholders' meeting on cooperatives, another big and equally highly powered meeting involving mainly key cotton stakeholders, was held in Mwanza. The objective of that meeting was primarily to review the status of the cotton industry in the aftermath crop marketing liberalization. The meeting attracted the attendance of some 300 cotton stakeholders comprising of representatives from all agricultural sector-ministries, ginners, cotton farmers, cooperatives, banks, textile and apparel mills, agrochemical dealers and collateral firms.

Under the chairmanship of the Vice President Omar Juma the meeting provided an exhaustive review of the performance of the cotton industry for the period between 1994 and 1999. That meeting became largely credited for coming up with two crucial blue-prints for the revival of the cotton industry; the so-called Mwanza Resolution and the industry's first ever Cotton Sector Development Strategy (CSDS-1). The two interventions went on to form the basis for the eventual recovery of cotton production as well as the emergence of a renewed spirit amongst stakeholders of cooperating and collaborating for the sustainable development of the cotton industry.

One prominent outcome of the cotton stakeholders' meeting held in 2000 was the emerging need by all the stakeholders to meet more frequently and in a more structured manner than in the past. As a result, from 2000 onwards, stakeholders met in Mwanza on annual basis with TCB increasingly taking the responsibility to organize and convene them. During the 2003/04 cropping season an attempt was made to have the stakeholders meetings organized in both the ECGA and WCGA on some kind of a rotational basis. However, after just one meeting in the ECGA during the 2003/04 cropping season, the initiative had to be abandoned largely due to the declining importance of cotton in the ECGA.

A compromise was reached whereby stakeholders' meetings took place on a biennial basis in a bid to improve cost-effectiveness as well as give an opportunity for stakeholders to follow up on many of the resolutions that were passed at preceding meetings. From 2010 onwards, the holding of annual stakeholders' meetings became a mandatory obligation for all commodity stakeholders. Under the new system, all commodity boards are now required by law to organize and convene commodity specific stakeholders' meetings on an annual basis.

The adoption of stakeholders' meetings as part and parcel of a new corporate responsibility has not been without reason. Within the cotton industry, for example, stakeholders found out that without the much needed coordination and consultation between them, especially for the period between 1994 and 1999, their cotton-based livelihoods were teetering towards the brink of an abyss. Thus, there has now emerged a new spirit whereby stakeholders increasingly believe that inclusion and shared values promise trust and cooperative behaviour and the ready exchange of information without which the industry would cease to exist. The emergence of such spirit has been reflected by increased stakeholders attendance and participation during the meetings and perhaps more importantly by the fact that they are also increasingly demanding for the meetings to be convened if and when the convener does not seem to abide by the time schedules.

Partly as a consequence of such industry-wide consultative meetings between members of both the public and private sectors on issues and challenges relating to the overall development of the cotton industry, there has emerged an excellent rapport between the major categories of stakeholders and due to cotton's huge diversity of stakeholders and interests, the meetings have also tended to bring about a sense of tolerance and understanding to a diversity of thoughts, perspectives and opinions on many of the issues such as declining production, productivity and quality of cotton which apparently became of great concern in the aftermath of crop marketing liberalization.

Among the many proposals put for discussion before the stakeholders' meetings on how to address the issues of declining production, productivity and quality, two are worth citing here, namely; the use of "pass books" and the introduction of "contract farming" for cotton. In view of their novelty and apparent newness to the Tanzanian cotton sub-sector it was deemed critical that the proposals to introduce the two initiatives should first get the blessings of all the stakeholders without whose active support they would be doomed to fail. What was badly needed at that time was stakeholders' grasp of what was at stake as well as their approval and support during the implementation phase.

The logic behind the introduction of the "pass book system" was quite simple. In the aftermath of crop marketing liberalization farmers could no longer access their seasonal inputs on credit as was the case during the single marketing channel system because the incoming private buyers could not hazard losing their cash for fear of farmers to whom they had given their credit defaulting on payment and instead selling it to some other buyer – a practice which notoriously came to be referred to side-selling.

To circumvent such malpractice a new system was proposed which required each farmer to serve part of his current season's revenue which would then be used to procure the much needed seasonal inputs at the start of the cropping season. Because such system had never been tried before and it was deemed important to have it piloted prior to its roll out throughout the country. Piloting of the "pass book system" was done in the two districts of Bukombe and Geita during the 2003/04 cropping season. Results of the pilot study were then presented to a stakeholders' meeting which then endorsed it for adoption throughout the country during the 2003/04 season.

The introduction of contract farming for conventional cotton in the country was approached in much the same way as the "pass book system". The logic behind contract farming was quite simply to solve the interlinked problems of low production, low productivity and contamination of cotton by contractually tying each cotton farmer to a buyer cum ginner who would provide the seasonal inputs to such farmers on credit on the understanding that the farmers would repay by selling their cotton only to the designated buyer cum ginner so that he would recoup his investment.

In essence CF was being introduced to mimic the previous single channel marketing system for the provision of inputs and credit under a competitive market setting. Thus, prior to its endorsement and subsequent passage for adoption during the May 2010 stakeholders' meeting, contract farming for conventional cotton had undergone a successful piloting in Bunda and Musoma districts of Mara region during the 2008/09 season.

A point to note is that prior to the piloting of both the pass book system and contract farming for conventional cotton production the stakeholders had been called upon to critically study, understand and debate on the two innovations and how they were expected to work and hence contribute to solving the problems then facing the cotton industry. During the deliberations that took place prior to the piloting of both the "pass- book" and contract farming, it had become quite apparent that unless and until there was a consensus on the modalities for the adoption of both innovations, they would be doomed to fail in the long run.

And so the idea of piloting them in designated locations served to greatly array fears on the possible failure of such schemes in addition to providing the stakeholders with the opportunity for studying them in greater detail. Such collective approaches to dealing with apparently contentious issues within the industry went on to become one of milestones for the cotton subsector.

Unfortunately, by adopting a hypocritical rather than critical approach to dealing with some of the challenges associated with the "pass-book", some stakeholders resorted to killing the "pass-book" outside the cotton stakeholder's forum. As discussed earlier, the use of the "pass-book" system was not foolproof and even its beneficiaries were well aware of such fact. Nevertheless, the few politicians who had earlier failed to kill the "pass-book" during the 2006 cotton stakeholders meeting in Mwanza campaigned and ultimately succeeded to have it disbanded by government in Dodoma during the 2007/08 parliamentary budget session. During the 2006 stakeholders' meeting in Mwanza farmers as well as other people had strongly opposed the disbandment of the "pass-book" for fear that without a better alternative or viable fallback position cotton output was bound to fall again as most farmers would end up losing their crop to the insects.

The fears voiced by stakeholders in general, and farmers in particular, became vindicated during the 2009/10 season when annual cotton output and insecticide use on cotton dropped by 28% and 52% respectively due to a majority farmers failing to buy their insecticides on a cash basis in spite of a 30% government subsidization of prices for such insecticides in the aftermath of the abolition of the pass book by government. On a brighter note, the furor arising out of such an apparent "crisis" was that it seemed to have re-ignited the need for more sustainable approaches to the resolution of the seasonal input puzzle for cotton and the possible adoption of contract farming for conventional cotton became one option. TCB had earlier tried to advocate for the adoption of CF but for reasons cited earlier, the timing was probably just not right.

The increased role of cotton stakeholders' meetings to find solutions to operational challenges and crises arising within the subsector was vividly illustrated when another saga dubbed the "non-germinating acid delinted seeds" occurred during the 2005/06 cropping season. In that season, an unfortunate event occurred during which attempts to introduce the use of acid delinted seed resulted in batches of acid delinted seed that had been sown in Bunda, Magu, Sengerema and Geita failing to germinate properly. In the other districts such as Meatu and Igunga in the WCGA as well as Kilosa, Bagamoyo and Morogoro in the ECGA where acid delinted seed had also been distributed no complaints on seeds failing to germinate were received from farmers. What proved to be particularly paradoxical with this issue at that point in time was the fact that in spite of TCB trying very hard to explain to the public on what had actually happened and the steps which it had taken to resolve the issue including replacing all the acid delinted seed by the good and trusted fuzzy seed free of charge, a few very influential people sought to politicize the issue.

TCB had sought to introduce the use of acid delinted seed out of the increasing need to transform the seed industry. Unfortunately, the delinting process was carried out incompetently at two out of four ginneries resulting in some non-viable seed being passed on to the farmers. That fact was publicly acknowledged by TCB because as a professional body one of the great strengths of science is admitting that one is wrong. When a scientist proposes a hypothesis that fails to be confirmed by the data, there may be disappointment but there is no dishonour so long as the scientist accepts the evidence and moves on.

The same, unfortunately, is not often true in politics. Politicians who make mistakes too often stand by their bad decisions fearing the humiliation of a u-turn than the damage they cause by ploughing ahead. Interestingly, in spite of politicians attempting to use the seed saga to create a mountain out of a mole hill, the industry went on to attain yet another milestone by raising annual cotton output to 126, 229 tons of lint in that fateful season. Such, output was even higher than 114,573 tons obtained during the preceding season of 2004/05. Thus, in two successive seasons, cotton output in the country went up and beyond the 100,000 tons of lint which could not be reached for the entire twentieth century.

Coincidentally, the saga on "undelinted seed" just like the one on the "pass book" went on to prove to be a blessing in disguise. In its aftermath, there emerged an even stronger resolve by the industry to overhaul the existing system of recycling seed for planting by adopting a separate system for the multiplication and processing of certified seed. The motivation behind the need for a new system was the imperative to circumvent some of the constraints relating to the poor germination of fuzzy seeds as a result of adulteration of seed cotton prior to its sale and ginning; poor packaging and labeling as well as the rather rampant abuse and misuse of planting seed. Hence the introduction and subsequent adoption of certified acid delinted seed was widely being seen as an answer to the prevailing mess in seed industry for cotton.

The difficulties experienced in trying to use stakeholders' meetings to deliberate on some major and occasionally contentious issues relating to the industry as a whole such as the "pass book" system; the issue of "non-germinating acid delinted seeds" and the institutionalization of contract farming, among others, helped to show that while the institutionalization of stakeholders' meetings was a fantastic approach to bringing the different interest groups into one arena where issues of mutual interest would be discussed, getting the diverse interest groups or stakeholders to agree on a *modus operandi* for the success of such meetings proved to be a tough nut to crack.

For example, on account of vested interests, and in cotton there are plenty of them, the issue of representation became quite problematic indeed. For example, in an obvious attempt to ensure the inclusion of all the core stakeholders, problems arose on how to optimize the representation of the different categories and hence the size of the meetings given the huge diversity of stakeholders along the cotton value chain. Farmer's representation, for example, became quite a bone of contention given their big numbers but without any credible organization from the grass roots.

TCB sought to deal with farmer's representation problem by picking farmers' representatives on the basis of a list of those that had participated in the on-going annual competition on best farming practices at district, regional and zonal levels. Such an approach became criticized for being biased against the majority of farmers who did not participate in the competitions, although, in principle, each farmer is by default a participant in the national competition. Nevertheless, with the formation of TACOGA in 2006 farmers' representation and hence participation during stakeholders' meetings became considerably easier although, as expected, some quarters within the stakeholders' meeting had their reservations on TACOGA's legitimacy to represent farmers. To them, the cooperatives were probably the more befitting representatives.

The inclusion, and hence participation of farmers in the stakeholders' meetings, began to take effect during the 2006 meeting at which time the issue of the pass book was being hotly debated. In that year, some politicians brought up a proposal demanding for the "pass book" to be disbanded in the wake of a series of complaints against it. Their seemingly authoritative approach to the pass book issue would seem to have been guided by a common assumption amongst most members of parliament that simply because they represent the electorate in their designated political constituencies it automatically follows that they are the de facto representatives of everybody there including the farmers in those areas. Thus, they saw it right to speak on behalf of the farmers who were also present at the meeting.

It was therefore quite baffling to them when the farmers present at the meeting stood up under the banner of their organization and out-rightly objected to the proposal on the disbandment of the "pass-book" being spearheaded by the legislators. Farmers had apparently been disappointed because the politicians had not consulted their organization on the issue of the "passbook" and hence their views on the "passbook" were quite biased against it.

Thus, in the opinion of the farmers, the politicians present at the meeting were just not qualified to speak on their behalf about the pros and cons of the pass book. Secondly, and perhaps more importantly, farmers have recently realized that their so-called parliamentary representatives tend to stay in cities and towns and have the tendency to stay waiting to pounce only on issues with potential political capital.

During the meeting, farmers' general stance on the pass book, and in particular against the motion proposed by the politicians to have it disbanded, greatly irritated the politicians. One popular legislator from Bariadi district was so disgusted by the event that he went on to publicly denounce the farmers as TCB's mercenaries who had been brought to the stakeholder's meeting merely to insult the lawmakers present.

Farmers have recently realized that through their association they stand a better chance of being heard and to have an impact because it is their association and not the politicians that is quite often in regular contact with them regarding their constraints and challenges. That politicians are irrelevant because they tend to prefer urban to rural lifestyles became quite evident during the proceedings of the seed saga when they were bluntly asked and I quote "when seeds could not germinate and TCB/TCA were running around to replace the bad seeds you fellows merely stayed in Dar es Salaam without coming to help out" end of quote.

It would, therefore, appear that simply because the majority of cotton farmers in the country are largely semi-literate, a few individuals, and mostly politicians, for that matter have quite often sought to capitalize on such fact by profanely purporting to be better positioned to speak on behalf of the cotton farmers and their problems than either the government or any other institution or association for that matter. Partly as a result of one category of stakeholders considering themselves more important than the others there emerged a major operational difficulty with regard to how to make the stakeholders' meetings both effective and meaningful as discussions quite often became polarized between the "warring groups". Such scenario became quite vivid during the discussions on the "non-germinating acid delinted seeds" saga as discussions nearly became polarized between politicians on one hand and other groups, particularly government officials, on the other. Interestingly, in spite of the discussions never really getting out of hand and resulting say in brawls as such, the heat generated by the war of words between the opposing groups was evidently quite perceptible.

As is often the case at meetings involving people from diverse backgrounds and interests, a few stakeholders, most notably the high ranking government officials in general, and politicians in particular, sought to dominate the discussions. Thus, rather than airing out their viewpoints in a concise manner, they often became engaged in long monologues in an attempt to depict themselves as being more knowledgeable about agricultural development issues than the other meeting participants.

As a result, other key stakeholders particularly the technocrats resorted to keeping mum lest they get into unnecessary confrontation with the self-styled political agriculturists. Such attitudes tended to risk the stakeholder meetings becoming lecture theatres rather than avenues where de facto interested parties met to discuss issues on equal footing.

On other occasions, some relatively half–cooked policy

initiatives and decisions were brought up before the stakeholders' meetings for the purpose of seeking an endorsement. Ironically, some of these were quite clearly controversial in nature and the attempt was merely to use the stakeholders' meetings as rubber stamps. Three incidents relating to such controversial initiatives and decisions are worth citing here.

During the 2008/09 marketing season, an attempt was made to forcefully introduce the WRS and toll ginning all over the WCGA. It ended up being a total fiasco as will be discussed in greater detail later. Similarly, during the 2010/11season there was a futile attempt to switch from the use of steel yard weighing balances to Salter balances without prior stakeholders' consultation and hence agreement. Again the initiative collapsed for the main reason that the cotton buyers cum ginners who own and use several thousands of such weighing scales vehemently opposed it because their views and concerns on the intended switch were not taken into any consideration by the government.

Finally, during the 2009/10 marketing season quite an interesting episode happened. For reasons that were not yet unknown to most cotton stakeholders, a move was hatched within the agricultural ministry that sought to sideline CDTF from its major statutory task of procuring agrochemicals for the industry. The intention was apparently to circumvent the existing system whereby pesticides are procured centrally by way of a tender. And so pesticides were in a sense allowed to get to smallholders without any regulatory controls whatsoever. It all happened under the guise of the so-called voucher scheme that was to be introduced in that season.

The outcome was a disaster because the industry became a dump yard not only for products that are neither registered nor recommended for use on cotton but also sub-standard and fake products. Perhaps, more importantly, the resource-poor smallholders became forced to "buy", so to speak, such materials at exorbitant prices that were in excess of 4000 shillings per acre pack. Through voucher coupons given to them farmers became forced to buy such expensive pesticides for no reason at all.

As a result, the bulk of the cotton crop in that season ended up being lost to insects because of the ineffectiveness of the pesticides provided under the voucher scheme as discussed earlier. Thus, in spite of inputs worth up to nine billion shillings having been provided under the so-called voucher scheme the cotton output during the 2009/10 cropping season reached 163,518 tons of seed cotton as compared to 267,004 tons in the preceding season when the voucher scheme was not used.

It may be recalled that in April 2006 CDTF became institutionalized partly under the instigation of the government. The latter had at that point in time wanted to completely disengage itself from its involvement in all commodity development trust funds so that they would be owned and managed by stakeholders themselves. CDF as a predecessor of CDTF had in 2001 been formed as part of the statute that also formed TCB and so it was a de facto government institution rather than a stakeholders' instrument. Thus, by denying CDTF from carrying out one of its core functions relating to pesticide procurement by tender was quite clearly a case of policy incoherence on the part of government.

Later, it became known that the decision by government to circumvent the well established tender system in ordering agrochemicals for cotton in that fateful cropping season was influenced by the greed of some agrochemical companies whose products had previously failed to enter the market through normal competitive bidding, apparently for not complying with regulatory requirements. At a cotton stakeholders' meeting held in May 2010, the previous tender system for procuring cotton agrochemicals and other inputs became reinstated with effect from the 2011/12 cropping season. It may also be recalled that ever since CDF and CDTF started using such system, the unit cost of pesticides used on cotton had at no time gone beyond 3,000 shillings per acre pack as opposed to prices of over 4,000 shillings charged during the 2009/10 cropping season.

Finally, a major challenge facing the stakeholders' meetings has been their inability to closely follow up on some of the key resolutions that tend to be passed from time to time. For example, whereas the need for LGAs to spend up to 10% of their revenues from cotton levies to prop their up districtcotton related extension services has been said time and again, this resolution has only been implemented by a handful of the LGAs. Similarly, in spite of LGAs being frequently reminded of their obligation to collaborate with TCB in the enforcement of a series of cotton related regulations and with the Agency for Weights and Measures Agency in the monitoring of buying malpractices involving tempered weighing scales and the like, their involvement has, to say the least, tended to be rather perfunctory in nature. The failure by stakeholders to be accountable to the forum has tended to undermine the credibility of the meetings being held.

In conclusion, it may well be said that in spite of some of the difficulties that continue to be experienced in organizing, financing and managing the stakeholder meetings, the return of the industry to centre stage as evidenced by three bumper harvests within a period of less than five years during the 2004/05, 2005/06 and 2008/09 markcting scasons owes much to the collaborative work which has evolved within the sub-sector in recent years. Stakeholders' meetings have become an extremely important vehicle not only for assuring meaningful consultation on many critical issues relating to the cotton industry but also for enhancing efficient and effective coordination between the government and the ever growing private sector.

Chapter 11

COTTON AND POLITICS IN TANZANIA

"Politics: The conduct of public affairs for private advantage"
Ambrose Bierce; US Author & Satirist (1842 – 1914)

11.1 Politics of cotton

One of the legacies of the late President Julius Nyerere was his obsession with the "war" against the triumvirate of ignorance, diseases and poverty. During his lifetime he fervently spoke about the need to eliminate the three "enemies" as he used to refer to them. In his attempts to fight poverty, for example, Nyerere quite logically focused on the need for increased agricultural output because he was keenly aware that for the vast majority of the rural population their livelihoods were almost inextricably linked to agriculture.

However, in trying to push for increased agricultural output, Nyerere realized that he needed all kinds of resources at his disposal by resorting to the use of three major instruments, namely, policies, politics and coercion. The villagization policy, for example, was extremely well intentioned in its bid to improve the accessibility of critical social services, such as health care, education and clean drinking water as well as the scarce agricultural extension services to the vast majority of the rural population.

Nevertheless, the villagization process could not live up to its objectives, primarily because it was poorly planned and implemented. The wider ramifications of such failure as manifested by stagnating or declining agricultural output, became quite evident during the 1970s and early 1980s. The launching of slogans such as; *"Siasa ni Kilimo"* or "Agriculture is Politics" as well as *"Kilimo cha Kufa na Kupona"* or "Agriculture as a matter of life or death" during that particular period was thus seen as a strategy to get agricultural output back on track again.

In the late 1970s, Nyerere's frustration with the continued underperformance of the agricultural sector culminated in one of his most notable pronouncements during which he threatened to sack all agricultural extension staff in the country. He had apparently become so disillusioned with them that he became convinced that agricultural development could probably still flourish without them on board. To date, more than fifty years after independence, agricultural development has still not yet delivered in spite of a spate of policy and institutional reforms and no doubt we are now witnessing the emergence of yet another slogan dubbed "Kilimo Kwanza" or "Agriculture First".

One area in the agricultural sector that has perhaps been always looked at as some kind of a litmus test for the general performance and health of the sector, has been the level of annual outputs of the so-called cash crops, especially, the likes of coffee, cotton, cashew, tobacco, tea, sugar cane, sisal and pyrethrum. It is perhaps a truism that because these crops account for a significant portion of the much needed foreign exchange earnings for the country, year in and year out, the government has quite naturally tended to be extremely wary of any negative change in the fortunes of any of these commodities. In the case of cotton, the situation is even more precarious because of its huge political and socioeconomic importance given the fact that in the chain from seed to fibre cotton related activities support directly or indirectly the livelihoods of an estimated 40% of the population and thence the electorate for that matter.

Unfortunately, in many of the attempts used to assure a healthy and sustainable development of the agricultural sector in general, and the cotton industry in particular, the utility of the principle of "sound science as a foundation of good public policy" has tended to falter all the time due to increased politicization. As a result, professionals have tended to find it extremely difficult to advise and inform the government and politicians on how to steer the industry to growth. It is, therefore, not hard to see why professionalism and pragmatism have so far not been the major drivers of the ultimate destiny of the industry. In this chapter an attempt is made to explain how a relentless politicization of cotton and hence the trivialization of science and technology has contributed to the rather prolonged under-development of the cotton industry in the country.

Contemporary thinking has it that citizens of any country can affect the policy choices of their governments and hence their destiny through either lobbying or voting. In the US, Japan and Korea cotton and rice have respectively remained as extremely protected and politically very significant crops in spite of their being produced by just a minority group of farmers. Paradoxically, such scenario has persisted over time in spite of the immense worldwide pressure being put to bear on respective governments to have the support and protection being channeled to such crops to be removed.

In the USA, Japan and Korea, the persistence of such protected crops owes very much to the efforts of pressure and lobbying groups that have been very active in defending such crops in their respective countries. On the other hand, farmers in Africa have been finding it very difficult to influence policy on matters affecting their livelihoods largely due to organizational difficulties which tend to make their greater numbers unable to influence policy as is the case with, say, business communities. Nevertheless, because numbers are quite often useful in gaining political mileage during an electoral competition, all politicians do, as a rule, resort to doing all kinds of things in a bid to woo farmers and hence their votes on any occasion.

Unfortunately, the "politicians" whom President Nyerere had agitated to go out and about to preach about agricultural transformation, resorted to politicizing agricultural science

232

instead. They quickly capitalized on the prevailing scarcity of "change agents" in the country to establish their own legitimacy as a new breed of "home grown agricultural experts". Such legitimacy would seem to emanate from the mere fact that most, if not all politicians, were born to the peasant farmers of Tanzania and so they are more than adequately qualified to talk about agriculture. Over the years, such innately groomed agriculturalists have been turning tables against the *de facto* college trained agricultural professionals by assuming all kinds of roles on matters relating to TDT and increasingly on policy formulation as well. As a result, the thin line distinguishing agriculture as a science and a profession from a game has become increasingly blurred over time.

Cotton is one crop that perhaps best illustrates the extent to which politics can negatively affect the growth of an industry in an era of rapid technological growth. It is perhaps a truism that wherever it is grown, and particularly in the tropics, cotton is immensely beloved of insect pests and politicians. In both the ECGA and WCGA politicians just love cotton because its endless catalogue of woes coupled with the numerous farmers associated with it tend to provide the politicians with virtually anything worth talking about at any time.

Perhaps more importantly, politicians just love cotton because it is the major lifeline of the poorest of the poor in the harsh semi-arid environments of the country where it tends to be grown. Moreover, because of its role in supporting the livelihoods of almost 40% of the country's population the cotton industry has quite often become the most ideal vehicle for achieving certain objectives and no doubt most politicians tend to evaluate it in terms of political capital to be had. Such an assessment was recently underscored by a "civil servant" who has transformed himself into a politician when he had this to say, and I quote, "to a businessman money is all that matters; but to a politician, like me, it is the number of votes that count" end of quote.

Unfortunately, in their quest to woo potential voters and thence stay on in office, politicians have been engaging in a variety of tactics and strategies without pondering on whether or not some of their actions are in the best long term interests of the cotton industry. For example, there has been a growing tendency whereby politicians resort to either keeping mum or condoning some of the infringements made by farmers with regard to cotton related best farming practices.

In so doing, politicians have rather unknowingly been drawing those farmers into an unnecessary collision course with researchers and extension officers. Such standoff between farmers on one side and the proponents of the TDT process on the other, has not been in the best interests of cotton development because just as it is the grass that suffers when elephants either fight or make love, the current low level of cotton production and productivity in Tanzania has by and large been due to both direct and indirect effects of clashes between politics and science as the rest of this chapter will try to show.

11.2 Politicization of extension services

The primary objective in cotton production is of course profitability. However, for that to happen farmers have got to optimize yield levels by adopting certain prescribed best farming practices. In both the tropical and sub-tropical regions where cotton is grown, there are some fairly standard preconditions for the realization of economic yields such as the need for cotton to be sown in time and on properly spaced lines as well as the need to control weeds and insect pests. For some pests, such as the pink bollworm, control tends to be most effective and quite cheap if farmers cooperate in implementing an area-wide destruction of crop residues after harvest followed by the observance of a closed season during which no cotton is to be grown.

Unfortunately, most farmers in Tanzania have been unable

234

to obtain economic cotton yields largely because they do not comply with the critical requirements for cotton farming. In both the ECGA and WCGA, farmers are required to grow cotton in accordance with the packages of the so-called "ten-commandments" which tend to prescribe how and when cotton should be planted, spaced, thinned, weeded, fertilized, sprayed for control of pests, harvested and crop residues disposed with. In spite of such preconditions for optimizing cotton yields farmers only rarely comply with the full package of recommendations and in the case of those complied with, they tend to be carried out to varying degrees of efficiency and accuracy. Two areas of the package are worth discussing here as they relate to the politicization of extension services.

Up until the mid-1970s, there was a continued and quite often a rigorous enforcement of the area-wide destruction of crop residues as well as a strict observance of a three-month closed season after cotton harvest. As a result, populations of the pink bollworm (PBW), as well as their damage on cotton, in both the ECGA and WCGA remained quite low indeed. Such state of affairs owed to the fact that both before and after independence acts of non-compliance with the end of season destruction of crop residues were not tolerated at all and all defaulters were being punished by caning using the agricultural department (AD) stick.

Such kind of forceful enforcement of cotton regulations by extension service staff no longer exists these days. One of the reasons for the slackened enforcement of the regulation is that politicians belonging to opposition parties have been speaking against punishments that are being meted by extension staff to defaulting farmers. Such politicians have argued, rather publicly, that because agriculture is a private business it should not be subject to any regulatory control whatsoever.

As a result of the majority of farmers failing to observe

the end of season uprooting and burning of crop residues, there have been increased incidences of ratoon cotton or simply old cotton plants that have been left to re-grow in the field. Consequently, there has also been an increased upsurge of the PBW and other pests notably stainer bugs, *Dysdercus spp.* The practice of ratooning of cotton has now become quite common in the districts of Bariadi, Maswa and Meatu in Shinyanga region as well as in the Igunga district of Tabora region. The fear now is that the practice will spread to other districts in spite of the dangers associated with it. Such practice was quite uncommon during the colonial period because the enforcement of the concept of a "closed season" i.e. a period of three or more months during which no plant remains of the previous cropping season were allowed to co-exist with the next season's cotton crop was strictly monitored.

One other aspect of cotton farming that has been a major source of friction between politicians and technology development and transfer (TDT) institutions is with regard to the intercropping of cotton with other crops. For many years cotton farmers in Tanzania have been required to refrain from intercropping cotton with other crops in general, and maize in particular. Reasons for the objection to such practices were discussed earlier and relate to the need to minimize damage to cotton from its major pest called the American bollworm or *H. armigera* as well as to encourage farmers to optimize their cotton plant populations per ha by planting their cotton in properly spaced rows.

Unfortunately, inspite of repeated calls for cotton not to be intercropped with maize the practice does seem to have become fully institutionalized these days, particularly, in some parts of the WCGA. Such intransigence on the part of cotton farmers owes quite a lot to the direct support and encouragement that they have been getting from some influential politicians. After the re-entry of multi-party politics in Tanzania and continued government disengagement from direct productive and marketing functions, some opportunistic politicians ventured to fill the void by agitating for farmers to be left alone on grounds that agriculture is an entirely private business matter.

In one of the parliamentary sessions in 2008, one prominent politician from Bariadi complained about farmers in his constituency being harassed by agricultural extension agents for intercropping their cotton with maize. The issue became even more protracted when another parliamentarian from the same district went on to incite cotton farmers to beat up any extension officer who dared to take punitive action against those that had defied the intercropping ban.

The Bariadi district in the WCGA is not only home to one of the major opposition political parties in the country but it is also the leading cotton producing district in the country. On average, the district accounts for well over 20% of total annual national cotton output. Given its present potential, Bariadi could quite easily double or even treble its current annual cotton output if and when cotton farmers were to fully adopt the recommended production package as advocated by TDT institutions. Unfortunately, such production prospects may not be realized in the short-term due to political influences currently prevailing in the district.

There are other implications arising out of the failure by TDT institutions and the LGAs to have any impact on the enforcement of best farming practices for cotton, particularly, those relating to the ban on cotton and maize intercropping as well as the observance of the "closed season" after crop harvest. There has recently developed within the cotton industry a perceived sense of fear amongst civil servants that if they were to pragmatically enforce the rules and regulations as per book farmers would most probably shift their present allegiance with the ruling CCM party to any of the fast emerging opposition as some kind of reflection of their frustration with government. Such sentiments were apparently exemplified during the campaigns for the 2005 general election.

In Maswa district, where the intercropping of cotton with maize is quite well established, the Civic United Front (CUF) or more popularly CUF which is one of the major opposition political parties in the country, in its desperate attempt to woo voters in the district, vowed to scrape off the by-law on the intercropping of cotton with maize, if it won the general elections in 2005. To counter such initiative, pro-CCM pundits likewise joined the bandwagon in support of the illegal practice lest they lose the election to their underdogs in a district where maize-cotton intercropping is quite firmly entrenched. In the end a pro-CCM candidate went on to win the parliamentary seat for Maswa on the premise of a false promise because the intercropping ban is still very much in force.

The corollary then, is that in an attempt to hang on in power, politicians broke the very law that battalions of expensively trained agricultural advisors have been trying so hard to defend on behalf of their government for ages. One rightfully wonders, therefore, if extension officers and research scientists can morally stand up to defend the by-law on intercropping before any group of cotton farmers in Maswa or elsewhere in the country. Such an abuse of science to direct the political and social life of a society is quite clearly bad for politics and for science. It has perhaps been for interventions like this one that in spite of over sixty years of preaching on aspects of cotton farming by TDT institutions Tanzanian average cotton yields have remained amongst some of the very lowest in the world.

As a result of its increased politicization over the years, the agricultural profession has similarly become increasingly trivialized both as a science and a profession. Consequently, agriculture has tended to lose considerable relevance and respect and no doubt up until 2007 Tanzania was still facing a conspicuous mismatch between the numbers of extension staff actually needed to work for the sector vis-a-vis those physically present on the ground as discussed earlier. Recruitment of more extension staff has become increasingly difficult over the years not that there are no qualified candidates on the job market, but because the newly trained ones coming out of the agricultural university and related training institutions prefer to join other more reputable but not necessarily more remunerative jobs. Such outlook from the new graduates is further being compounded by the working atmosphere under the LGAs where in spite of their training in agriculture, they tend to be assigned to duties largely unrelated to agriculture.

The scenario for TDT in relation to cotton is no longer tenable. To date a group of self-styled politician cum-agriculturists does seem to have taken control. During stakeholders' meetings or even in public gatherings, conference halls or even in parliament they tend to speak with the loudest voice on virtually all issues even controversial ones such as the GMO debate and the red bollworm (RBW)issue among others. The bona fide agricultural professionals tend to resign to mere silence knowing that "to be right, you do not need to have the loudest voice" as the famous Chinese proverb goes.

11.3 Politicization of prices

Apart from the obvious squabbling between technocrats and politicians on technical issues, the tendency by government to regularly intervene into the workings of the cotton market much more so than in markets for other crops, has quite inadvertently created an impression to the effect that cotton unlike most other crops, is a de facto "government crop" rather than theirs. During the 2005 marketing season farmers used this fact coupled with its enormous socioeconomic clout to influence political outcomes. In that season farmers sought to use the economic importance of cotton as well as its association with perhaps more farmers than any other cash crop in the country to pressure the government into doing things that it would not do under normal circumstances.

Due to purely unforeseen circumstances on the global market for cotton producers prices dropped from 300 shillings per kg at the start of the buying season in July to 250 shillings per kg of seed cotton and below that after just two weeks. Such news was not well received by cotton farmers and being an election year they threatened to vote for the opposition rather than the incumbent CCM government if the latter did not intervene to get the prices right. Rather unexpectedly the government acquiesced to farmers' demands by scrapping off the unpopular education levy as well as scaling down TCB, CDTF and district crop levies in a desperate attempt to boost prices. And so by exploiting the crop's huge economic importance as well as their own numerical advantage to influence political outcomes, farmers were able to realize their economic objectives.

Cotton farming in the country has been going on for just over one hundred years now. Nevertheless, when compared to cotton farming in other countries, both in Africa and elsewhere in the world, where farming has increasingly become commercial in outlook, cotton farmers in Tanzania would seem to lack the motivation for a paradigm shift. While the difficulties associated with the provision of seasonal inputs and credit markets are well known, it is also true that the promotion of wrong price policies especially for inputs is to blame.

For many years politicians have sought to appease cotton farmers by trying to keep the cost of cotton production as low as possible mainly through subsidies. For example, with regard to seed for planting the policy has tended to advocate for the unit price for seed to be kept very low in order to allow more and more resource poor farmers to access such seed because most of them are considered unable to pay market

240

based prices for cottonseed. Thus, at unit prices of only up to 15 shillings per kg prior to liberalization up to 30,000 tons of seed were being used for planting on an annual basis.

Unfortunately, most of such seed ended up being grossly misused by farmers, for example, by being broadcasted rather than sown in properly spaced rows and for being used as cattle feed. Between 1999 and 2006 the unit cost of fuzzy seed for planting remained in the order of just 15 to 120 shillings per kg or 375 to 3000 shillings for the 25 kg of seed needed per ha. During the 2007/08 cropping season, the price of cottonseed for planting was raised to 250 shillings per kg.

The price rise was apparently necessitated by increases in the cost of most oil seeds in the country in the wake of tariffs being imposed by the government in an attempt to regulate imports of semi-refined palm oil from the Far East. Had the cost of cotton seed been maintained at 120 shillings per kg, most if not all of it, would have been diverted to oil production as millers were well positioned to offer a much higher price due the high demand for the oil seeds. Had that happened, two things would have happened; a big outcry for lack of seeds for planting and increased health related risks due to fungicide treated seeds being crushed for edible oil.

Nevertheless, due to many stakeholders not being aware of the prevailing imbalance in the supply and demand of oilseeds in the country, both TCA and TCB became blamed for apparently "letting cotton farmers down" by hiking the price for seed, blames which later proved to be quite unfounded. In the end, farmers bought all the seed at the market price of 250 shillings per kg after realizing that even retail prices for locally produced cottonseed oil had also increased substantially. A similar episode was noted during the 1997/98 cropping season when a rise in the price of seed for planting from 30 to 90 shillings per kg caused quite a pandemonium during a meeting that had been called by CCM on 24th November 1998.

To date, less than 20,000 tons of seed are distributed to farmers annually in spite of the area under cotton production remaining basically the same. Using a seed rate of 25 kg/ha for an area under cotton estimated to be 500,000 ha, Tanzania would be expected to use only about 12,500 tons of seed on an annual basis. That up to 20,000 tons tend to be used annually would seem to suggest that either the area under cotton on an annual basis is grossly underestimated or that the broadcasting of cotton seed continues to be the norm in spite of repeated calls for the adoption of line planting. Thus, unless and until these two factors are addressed quickly, the reliability of present statistics on input use as well as trends on the production, productivity and profitability of cotton would leave quite a lot be desired.

The issue of seed broadcasting remains quite puzzling. Apart from Tanzania, the only other countries where the broadcasting of seed during planting is still the norm are Ethiopia and Iran. Unfortunately, Shinyanga region (recently split into Simiyu and Shinyanga regions) that accounts for nearly 60% of Tanzania's annual output is also the stronghold of the practice of broadcasting cottonseed during planting. This fact, unless changed quickly, tends to significantly limit the chances of that region becoming the *de facto* "cotton belt" of Tanzania. Ironically, the continued broadcasting of cottonseed during sowing as is also the case for sorghum, bulrush and finger millet, is by and large being partly perpetuated by the current politicization of cotton in general and price policies in particular.

In most of the maize growing areas of the country, and especially, in the southern and southern highland regions of Tanzania, farmers often buy certified maize seed at the equivalent of 2.0 US dollars or more per kg and are quite willing to pay that price or a higher one because the seed used gives them value for their money if and when used properly according to recommended best farming practices for maize. For the same reason cotton farmers should be able to pay a higher price for good quality cottonseed if by adopting the best farming practices they become assured of obtaining economic yields.

Unfortunately, in most of the cotton producing areas, cotton farming is not treated as a business like any other business and this may be the reason why in spite of the low prices for their seed, they have not yet adopted the recommended best farming practices as is the case for food cum cash crops such as maize in the southern regions of Tanzania. Cotton farmers can perhaps hope to improve their cotton yields drastically if for example efforts by government can be made to facilitate for the introduction of acid delinted seed. Such seed that costs more but promises increased yield and profitability would make good economic and practical sense as well.

During the 2009 cropping season the prices for acid and brush delinted seed in Zimbabwe were in the order of 0.95 and 0.90 USA dollars per kg. Unfortunately the fact that there is already a budding opposition to the introduction of such seed in Tanzania goes a long way to confirming both the backwardness of cotton farming and the extent of its politicization in Tanzania.

Rather surprisingly, in spite of their awareness of cotton farmers' plight in relation to low productivity, high production costs and proneness to volatile global cotton prices, politicians have only been paying lip service to the socioeconomic importance of cotton in the country. Maize, unlike cotton, has for a long time been a major beneficiary of government input subsidies. While its importance for food security is undeniable, the fertilizers and other imported inputs destined for maize have tended to be imported using the hard cash earned from exports of cotton and other cash crops.

Nevertheless, cash crops remained without any support until the 2007/08 farming season when for the first time ever in a post liberalization era, the government was pressured to subsidize cotton insecticide price by 30 percent. Since then the government has continued to offer such support although the modalities for doing so have tended to benefit third parties rather than the farmers.

In the USA the government spends up to 4 billion dollars in subsidies annually just for its 25, 000 cotton farmers as well as several other billions merely to project a good image of its cotton industry. In the case of Tanzania, where cotton supports the livelihoods of 40% of the population, such support by way of subsidized seasonal inputs had to come after a lot of lobbying by law makers from the two major cotton growing areas who apparently constitute quite a big majority in parliament. In Francophone Africa, the cotton industry is apparently being treated like a king because of its significance to the economies of most countries there. The situation in WCGA where cotton is seen in similar light could also be significantly improved if politicians stopped their rhetoric and half-hearted commitment to cotton farmers' welfare.

11.4 Politicization of the red bollworm
Within the cotton industry the subject concerning the red bollworm is perhaps one of the classic examples on how cotton has become increasingly utilized as an important vehicle for fulfilling the political ambitions of certain people. The ban on cotton growing in the southern and southern highland regions of Tanzania as argued earlier was imposed merely as a precautionary measure to ensure that both the ECGA and WCGA remain entirely free of the red bollworm which in the context of the entire East African region is a *de facto* quarantine pest. Such scientific reasoning would seem to have been understood by the majority of stakeholders up until the mid 1980s when a few politicians started to query on why the ban had continued to be in force.

The agricultural sector in Tanzania has on many occasions witnessed outbreaks of pests and diseases the majority of which could have been prevented if government leaders and politicians had bothered to heed scientific advice. Between 1970 and 2000, Tanzania witnessed very devastating outbreaks of several quarantine pests and diseases for example; the Banana Weevil in the late 1970s; the Larger Grain Borer (Dumuzi) in 1981; the Cassava Mealy Bug *(Kidung'ata wa muhogo)* in 1987 and the Cassava Mosaic; Banana and Coffee Wilts in LZ between 1990 and 2000. In the mid-1970s the country also witnessed the devastating outbreak of Cholera in many parts of the country. The outbreak of such disease which was previously unknown in the country could have been very easily contained at source when it first occurred but due to laxity and politics it managed to spread all over the country and it has since then become endemic in Tanzania.

In spite of the loss of several thousand human lives to Cholera as well as immense crop losses brought about by outbreaks of plant pests and diseases, some politicians have still continued to doubt the significance of the ban on cotton farming in the southern and southern highland regions of Tanzania and hence the relevance of the quarantine zone that was put in place by colonialists in a bid to prevent the further spread of the red bollworm into Tanzania and the East African region as a whole.

Partly as a result of politicians and other stakeholders not heeding to the warnings by R & D, encroachment into the quarantine zone inevitably culminated in the red bollworm making an incursion into commercially grown cotton in the district of Chunya for the very first time in early 1999. Thus, the earlier forecast that the red bollworm had not yet found its way into the cotton growing areas of Tanzania due to a lack of opportunity went on to prove correct. Since then, its further spread in Tanzania was arrested, thanks to prompt action taken by the government to ban cotton farming in Mbeya region with effect from 2000.

Surprisingly, in spite of the gravity of the implications of the historic occurrence of the red bollworm on commercial cotton in Mbeya region in 1999 as well as the revelation in 2009 about the red bollworm having been found on wild cottons growing areas that are even closer to both the ECGA and WCGA than Chunya, politicians have still continued to belittle the increased danger of its entry into those areas now rather than at any other time in the history of cotton cultivation.

Most of the politicians have tended to remain either indifferent or just totally insensitive to the wider ramifications of red bollworm entry into both the ECGA and WCGA. Such politicians when in parliament have continued to publicly advocate and demand for the lifting of the existing cotton ban on cotton cultivation, particularly, in Mbeya region with immediate effect. Paradoxically, in what may be judged as either lack of an informed opinion on the issue or just sheer partisanship, politicians in the WCGA have been totally supportive of the idea to lift the ban on cotton farming in the south in spite of the grave implications on the fate of cotton growing there.

The debate on the red bollworm has been going on since the mid-1970s when lawmakers from the southern regions of Lindi and Mtwara agitated for the introduction of cotton in those regions in their bid to diversify from a largely cashew based economy. The debate became more protracted in the aftermath of the banning of cotton farming all over Mbeya region in 2000 the repercussions of which were discussed earlier.

In what appeared to be an attempt to discredit the evidence provided by cotton R & D scientists on the sighting of the red bollworm on cotton in Chunya district, one of the legislators from Mbeya had argued in parliament that the samples of the red bollworms purported to have come from Chunya did not in fact originate there, but were collected

246

from some other place. Because the larval specimens were contained in what he erroneously referred to as "test tubes" they could have come from elsewhere and not necessarily Chunya.

The irony of his argument though was that rather than checking up with the Uyole Agricultural Research Centre that lies well within the Mbeya constituency, on the authenticity of the samples and the claim, the politician resorted to bringing up a largely scientific issue for debate in a forum dominated by politicians instead. What needed to be proven beyond reasonable doubt was not whether the larval specimens were carried in test tubes or more correctly in glass vials but rather whether the correctness of the information provided and the specimens shown could be authenticated independently via well established scientific approaches or protocols.

Nevertheless, because of the prevailing perception that the issue of the red bollworm is largely fictional and that the scientists who advise government policy from an entirely neutral perspective are to be distrusted, the apparent credibility problem currently facing the agricultural profession becomes even more serious. What the learned lawmaker needed to understand is the fact that whether it is right or wrong, true or junk, science should never be prostituted for political ends.

In an apparent attempt to trivialize the red bollworm threat in Mbeya region, another prominent politician cum lawmaker had this to say in mid-2005 before a highly powered consultative meeting on cotton development held in Dodoma; "you do not tell people not to have sex in order to prevent HIV-Aids, you give them condoms instead. So if killing the red bollworm means spraying the cotton crop more times than is currently the case, then for heaven's sake give the farmers the insecticides they need" end of quote.

Such were the words coming from the mouth of a lawmaker who had, for quite sometime, been advocating for the lifting of the quarantine zone over the entire southern and southern highland regions of Tanzania. Nevertheless, he intimated to me after the meeting that while he was aware of the scientific and economic reasons behind the ban, he needed to be seen by the electorate in his constituency that he was fighting for the lifting the ban as his chances of re-election during the 2005 general elections depended quite heavily on the ban being lifted. He had apparently been warned that unless and until cotton farming was re-introduced in his constituency lying deep inside the quarantine zone, he stood no chance of being re-elected.

One obvious corollary to the assertion made by the legislator was that farmers in his constituency had been growing cotton without being aware either of their infringement of the quarantine law or being uninformed on the economic implications of a potential red bollworm incursion into their cotton farms. Because the quarantine law has been around since the late 1940s, it is pretty unlikely that farmers have not been aware of its existence and the reasons behind it.

Cotton farming in Mbeya region was initially confined to the district of Chunya. However, due to poor monitoring and poor enforcement of the quarantine order, it eventually spread into other areas deep in the quarantine zone. For lack of legal action and farmers' infringement of the law being largely condoned by politicians, the red bollworm whose populations have repeatedly been found throughout the zone was able to expand its range under the circumstances.

The red bollworm saga in Tanzania has greatly helped bring to light how some politicians, like some bad religious preachers, can toy with peoples' psychology for their own interests. In politics as in religious matters, what one talks about or preaches about need not be what one really believes in. In the case of the red bollworm problem, some of the ex-ministers of the agricultural portfolio who had vehemently defended the ban on cotton farming in the southern and southern highland regions of Tanzania turned into being the staunchest supporters of the crusade seeking to lift such ban after they had left office.

In other words, the cotton ban was justified while they were in office but not after they got out of the government's payroll. Such behavior is reminiscent of what some members of the religious clergy tend to say to their congregations; "follow what I say to you but not what I do". On a similar note, during the campaigns for the 2010 elections one incumbent legislator was asked to indicate how he would respond if he were asked to comment about the on-going war against an illicit brew dubbed *"gongo"*. This is what he promised to say "get on with it but do not get apprehended" unquote. To the scientists who advise on policy, such behaviour of not calling a spade a spade does spell grave danger because it means that politicians are not to be entirely trusted for all what they say.

11.5 Politicization of co-operatives

Cooperatives are known the world over for their roles in providing marketing as well as credit related services to their bona fide members. It is widely acknowledged that most cooperatives have tended to emerge in the aftermath of some kind of market failure; either markets being absent or because a few profit maximizing firms use their monopoly power to exploit single farmers as was the case for cotton in Tanganyika where marketing injustices and malpractices then being perpetrated by a few cotton buyers of Asian origin were instrumental for the formation of the AMCs.

As a result of their growing economic power, the colonial administration in Tanganyika became increasingly wary of them because they had started to wield considerable political influence as well and at a time when the on-going struggle for independence was fast gaining momentum. Thus, it tried to advise the cooperative leadership against engaging in politics as that would have gravely undermined the developmental goals that they were seeking to accomplish.

After independence, the new government similarly became concerned with the increasing economic and political influence of the cooperatives. Such concerns became reflected by the cooperatives becoming accused of mismanagement and corruption. A Presidential Committee of Enquiry formed in 1966 to probe into such allegations found out among other things that the cooperatives had also become susceptible to political interference. The latter became well manifested by some of the events that occurred between 1976 and 1984 and between 1984 and 1999 because since then cotton AMCs became quite weakened to be able to continue with cotton business as was the case in the past.

During the first decade of the 21st century, a series of politically motivated interventions in the workings of cooperatives and other government institutions prompted Kitwana Kondo, the former chairman of the Cashew Board of Tanzania (CBT) and a long time veteran in public service, to say "when an elderly person breaks wind, it is the children who often get punished for the act". He was in fact referring to a couple of incidents during which CBT was apparently being blamed for some costly outcomes within the cashew industry due politically motivated interventions made by the agricultural ministry officials.

Similarly, many of the operational ills that are currently facing the cotton cooperatives in Tanzania are by and large an outcome of politically motivated interventions that began during the era of compulsory villagization in the early 1970s. Since then, a series of other policy and institutional reforms went on to completely curtail the identity, structure and functionality of the AMCs. After liberalization, the state had to come in and write off bad debts, provide management staff as well as offer "export guarantee schemes" just to keep them afloat. In the run up to the 2010 general elections, additional pledges were made to help keep them liquid.

Such support has recently come under fire both within government and by the general public. The big debate is not about why the cooperatives should be supported and promoted by government but rather on how such support should best be administered, accounted for and sustained. There have been concerns amongst the cotton stakeholders that continued inflows of tax-payer's money to many of the cotton cooperatives coupled with increased government involvement in the daily management of their affairs is not sustainable in the long term. Such support has, rather unfortunately, tended to inculcate a false feeling amongst the RCUs that they are de facto public rather than private institutions. Thus, rather than looking at their working relations with TCB along the lines of a regulator and the "regulated", they have instead tended to look at the relationship as one of two sister institutions under the MAFC. As a result, the day to day workings between them and TCB as well as TCA on matters relating to licensing and payment of statutory levies have tended to become unnecessarily constrained.

Unfortunately, apart from the material support which has been flowing to the RCUs from government, some of the public utterances by politicians and government officials such as praising the cooperatives while castigating private companies on allegations of profiteering and stealing from cotton farmers have tended to make the private buyers cum ginners increasingly doubtful of government's sincerity on PPP.

Such utterances are not perceived as being in line with the need for government to provide a level playing field to all cotton actors for the main reason that RCUs have them-selves been guilty of documented pilferage and grand scale thefts. Furthermore, because the government is on record for having given highly profiled announcements regarding its intentions to prosecute members of the RCUs who had engaged in the pilferage, looting and misappropriation of tax payers' money and yet doing absolutely nothing about it until now, other stakeholders have resigned to thinking that unlike the AMCs of the past, the RCUs are mere instruments for achieving certain political objectives more than anything else.

During the 2008/09 marketing season, for example, an attempt was made by the Mwanza regional government to prop up the NCU by conferring upon it a cotton buying monopoly in Mwanza region. In that season, all private cotton buyers cum ginners were warned against buying seed cotton directly from cotton farmers as currently provided for under the Cotton Industry Act No. 2 of 2001. They were instead directed to procure such cotton only through designated primary societies (PS).

The move was initially seen as a deliberate attempt by government to curb some of the prevailing buying malpractices by confining cotton buying to just a few designated posts owned by PS. Earlier, during the 2004/05 season ginners had proposed to the government the need to make cotton buying more transparent by centralizing it at a few designated PS where cotton would be bought under some kind of an auction system.

However, such initiative could not take off at that point in time and no feedback on the matter was ever given to the ginners. It was, therefore, quite flabbergasting to note that it resurfaced just a week prior to the start of the season and without other stakeholders including TCB as regulator being duly informed or consulted on the issue. Consequently, all sorts of questions started being asked on why just Mwanza region; why at that point in time and not in 2004/05 and why in a hushed up manner among other questions. Quite surely, there were more questions than answers on that intervention and no doubt it could not take off.

In the final analysis, it became evident to most stakeholders that such initiative had apparently been taken by the Mwanza regional, authorities in an attempt to confer a competitive advantage to NCU that had since 1994 failed to meaningfully engage in cotton buying and ginning due to numerous operational problems as discussed earlier in connection with all cooperatives in general. In the Igunga district of Tabora region, cotton buyers have been buying their cotton through designated PSs for many seasons. They became compelled to do so by an executive order from the LGA that was seeking to improve its crop cess collection from cotton. The system has since then failed to attract the interests of other districts in the WCGA primarily because it is being seen as unable to engender the much needed price competition between cotton buyers among other operational problems.

During the 2008/09 marketing season, the Shinyanga and Mwanza regional authorities similarly sought to introduce the warehouse receipt system (WRS) in their respective regions in what later became known to be a carefully calculated move to grant seed cotton buying monopolies to their two ailing giant RCUs, namely, SHIRECU and NCU respectively. The regional authorities had apparently wanted to achieve that object under the guise of an imperative to showcase the intentions of the government to resuscitate the two RCUs that had failed to make any impact on the cotton market under the prevailing competitive conditions.

The attempt to introduce the WRS had apparently not taken into consideration a number of key factors and so it too ended up being a fiasco. The authorities had apparently forgotten that as of that point in time, private buyers cum ginners were at liberty, under the cotton statute, to procure their seed cotton directly from individual farmers and not through a third party as the regional authorities had wanted them to do.

Thus, had cotton buyers been compelled to engage in toll ginning, they would have had the onus to seek for legal redress. Secondly, for lack of any prior stakeholders' consultation and hence requisite preparations, the initiative to introduce the WRS lacked the necessary good will and tacit support. Consequently, most stakeholders interpreted the initiatives as veiled attempts by the government to return the seed cotton buying monopolies to the RCUs. Finally, the

RCUs on their own free will publicly acknowledged that even if the buying monopolies had indeed been granted to them they would still not be in a position to undertake the WRS with toll ginning due to inadequate organizational, financial and infrastructural readiness.

With regard to cotton, the WRS with toll ginning has only been successful in the Babati district of Manyara region in the ECGA where the Oridoyi PS has since 2003 been using it for cotton marketing. Attempts to introduce such system to the WCGA where more than 98% of the cotton crop is produced have since 2003 proven quite futile. Reasons for such failure are discussed later. In the aftermath of the WRS episode, one question that remained unanswered in the minds of most stakeholders was on whether the intervention had been made in good faith as a result of a growing impatience regarding the slow diffusion of the WRS as well as perhaps the imperative to speed up the revival of the cooperative movement or it was just one of those pre-election initiatives that seek to show that the government is doing something about cooperatives. In the end, it became amply clear that neither the efforts to help the cooperatives nor to foster the PPP spirit were helped by the intervention.

On the basis of the abortive interventions cited above, there has emerged a rather strong feeling amongst the majority of the common people and especially the politicians that unless and until the CCM-led government is seen to help out the RCUs it may not be able to attract the votes particularly from the WCGA which are deemed crucial to stay on in power. Unfortunately, such feelings have tended to push the government into propping up the mere survivorship of present state-sponsored and state-maintained RCUs rather than helping the emergence of new and genuinely independent cooperatives akin to those formed during the era of the late Paul Bomani. Fortunately, such short sighted politicking was put to rest when the Prime Minister, Mizengo Pinda boldly and categorically called for concrete and resolute action against wrong doings that are being perpetrated by a few persons within the RCUs without fearing whether or not the CCM government would lose electoral votes.

The promotion of strong, viable and independent cooperatives has long been one of the pillars of government policy. Following the demise of independent cooperatives way back in 1976, the state has increasingly found itself obliged to help bring about new and healthy cooperatives that will no longer depend on government handouts for their economic well being and competitiveness by creating a more favourable legal and policy environment. Some progress to that end was made when the government formed the Ministry for Cooperatives and Marketing (MCM) in 2000; passed the Cooperative Act No. 20 of 2003 and launched the Cooperative Reform and Modernization Program (CRMP) in 2005. In 2009 the government took a very significant step when it undertook to decouple cooperative development from government ministries by creating a semi-autonomous Cooperative Development Commission. Such extremely commendable actions seem to have a genuine will to facilitate the formation of such voluntary and democratically functioning structures with self-regulatory powers as is the case with most other private business.

11.6 Conclusion

The slogans *"Kilimo ni Siasa"* or "Agriculture is Politics" and recently *"Kilimo Kwanza"* were well intentioned to highlight the need to get agriculture moving again after periods of stagnation. Unfortunately, after a period of two or more decades the slogan *"Kilimo ni Siasa"* only proved to be a political slogan being used to profile agriculture without doing anything tangible about its advancement. Similarly, *"Kilimo Kwanza"* which is a 2009 government initiative that aspires, through a ten pillar, multi-stakeholders' strategy, to launch a "green revolution" in Tanzanian agriculture may be positioned to suffer a similar fate unless and until the gap between rhetoric and reality is bridged.

Most manifestations of vested interests by politicians have had something to do with the need to stay on in power indefinitely by striving to be seen by the electorate as doing something about agriculture. Such trend if unchecked or unregulated will continue to be the primary driver for the emergence of most kinds of placatory overtures that are being perpetrated by politicians even if by doing so it will mean farmers in their constituencies remaining stuck to peasantry.

Thus, unless and until there is a heartfelt appreciation of agriculture as a science and a profession like medicine, engineering and the like, Tanzania cannot hope to make much headway in agricultural development so long as some highly placed politicians use their offices and positions to interfere with the professional workings of the commodity industries. For many years, there has existed some erroneous feeling amongst some of our politicians that because they are bona fide sons and daughters of the rural Tanzanians, they automatically qualify to assume the roles of the agriculturally trained professionals without question.

Such a misconception may very well be one of the main reasons why most cotton farmers in the greater part of the WCGA continue to grow cotton in exactly the same way that their great grandfathers did several decades ago. To date, under a very rapidly globalizing agriculture, such self-styled politicians cum agriculturists may be unknowingly hurrying up the destiny of our smallholders into the dustbin of history. In spite of such attitudes and challenges, agriculturalists and other scientists as a whole, must soldier on because as Kennedy, the former president of the Entomological Society of America (ESA) once said, and I quote; "in the public policy arena, it is vital that we do not compromise the special position of science as a provider of objective information. And it is equally vital that we do not compromise the role of scientists as honest brokers of that information" unquote.

Chapter **12**

THE FUTURE OF COTTON IN TANZANIA

"Once we accept our limits, we go beyond them" Anonymous.

12.1 The Tanzania cotton industry is by no means jinxed

During the first decade of the 21st century Tanzania's annual cotton output exceeded the threshold of 100,000 tons for the first time ever since cotton farming was introduced in 1906. During the 2004/05, 2005/06 and 2008/09 marketing seasons cotton output reached 114,540; 126,229 and 123,080 tons of lint respectively. For the entire period between 1906 when the German colonial administration introduced cotton farming in Tanzania and 1999, annual cotton output had remained well below 100,000 tons of lint and only managing to reach a peak of 96, 372 tons of lint during the 1992/93 marketing season.

The attainment of a peak output of 126,229 tons of lint at the time of the first centenary of cotton farming in the country was of some significance to the cotton industry in at least two major aspects. Firstly, the achievement went on to prove that the Tanzanian cotton industry is by no means jinxed as some stakeholders had tended to believe because throughout the twentieth century annual cotton output remained well below 100,000 tons in contrast to other countries where for the same or even smaller acreage under cotton significantly higher annual outputs were being obtained.

Secondly, after falling rather disastrously from an all time high of 96,374 tons of lint prior to liberalization to a mere 35,476 tons of lint by the close of the twentieth century, it took the industry six years for output to rise from that level during the 1999/00 marketing season to a new peak record of 126, 229 tons by the 2005/06 marketing season. Such facts tend to show that, in spite of its relatively huge comparative advantage in cotton, Tanzania still faces formidable constraints and challenges in trying to boost cotton production, productivity and profitability.

During the colonial period both the Germans and the British used coercion and invariably force in their bid to get the indigenous people to produce a lot of cotton both quickly and cheaply. Unfortunately, such approaches failed. After independence, other approaches, such as the compulsory villagization programme as well as the institutionalization of crop authorities and regional cooperative unions were adopted but still agricultural output stagnated. Starting from the mid-1980s the government embarked on an economic reform programme that came to a head during the early 1990s when commodity markets were liberalized. It was generally hoped that the introduction of price and other incentives would motivate and thence stimulate farmers to increase agricultural output in general and cotton output in particular. However, what happened between 1994 and 1999 was quite a big anticlimax because rather than going up, annual cotton output went on to fall in the aftermath of liberalization.

And so, when cotton output started to recover during the first decade of the 21st century, some people began asking whether or not the realization of 126,229 tons of lint wasn't a fluke? Yet, others enquired whether the feat could ever be sustained? Thus, in contemplating for an increase in cotton output beyond 126,229 tons of lint stakeholders must carefully ponder on the saying that "experience is recognizing a mistake when you are about to make it again". Furthermore, apart from raising annual cotton output, time has come when perhaps Tanzania has got to rethink the issue on the continued export of lint rather than textile and apparel. Unless such problem is solved, Tanzania may not expect to fully exploit its vast comparative advantage in cotton if increased annual output will entail the country continuing to export up to 70% of its cotton as lint as has been the case over the past fifty years or so.

12.2 New initiatives for boosting production, productivity and quality

The need for Tanzania to raise its average cotton yields cannot be over-emphasized. Raising yields is critical for boosting farmers' income as well as generating the surpluses for agro-processing industries most of which only need to be revitalized. Increased cotton production for domestic processing into textiles and apparel will also most certainly reduce Tanzania's current proneness to phenomena such as declining terms of trade, price volatility and other ills often associated with commodity trade.

Tanzania has the potential to increase its annual cotton output by a factor of three or four. For example, while annual cotton output in Burkina Faso increased by over a hundred times from 3,000 to 298,000 tons of lint between 1965 and 2005, in Tanzania cotton output only increased twofold from 67,000 to just 126,229 tons of lint for about the same area of 500,000 ha under cultivation. A critical examination of facts, tends to show that cotton increased more rapidly in B. Faso than in Tanzania for two major reasons. Firstly, under the single channel marketing systems built around public monopolies, cotton companies in Francophone countries in general, and B. Faso in particular, have actively been emphasizing the need for cotton farmers to fully comply with the requirements for best farming practices coupled with the appropriate use of seasonal inputs. The adoption and commercialization of biotech cotton during the 2008/09 cropping season is anticipated to further boost cotton production in that country.

Secondly, in spite of both B. Faso and Tanzania having similarly embarked on the bandwagon of market reforms in 1994, the performance of the cotton industry in B. Faso has been much better than the Tanzanian one for the main reason that B. Faso and most other Francophone countries opted for a more gradual approach to the liberalization and privatization of its cotton industry. In Tanzania and other Anglophone countries, the two processes were undertaken using fire-brigade type of approaches and hence their industries very nearly collapsed and no doubt they have long struggled to recover from the adverse effects brought about by the reforms.

Between 1999/00 and 2008/09 cotton output in Tanzania rose nearly four times from 35,476 to 126,229 tons of lint. During that period the total area sown to cotton annually ranged between 350,000 and 500,000 ha. For the same cotton area Burkina Faso has been producing an average of 300,000 tons of lint per year, nearly three times of Tanzania's output. Rather interestingly, during the annual nation-wide cotton competitions carried out between 2004 and 2009 farmers who had meticulously complied with the recommended best farming practices obtained seed cotton yields of up to 3,875 kg/ha which are five times higher than the current national average of 750 kg of seed cotton per ha. The corollary here is that the current annual cotton output in Tanzania can in fact be doubled or even trebled without increasing the acreage under cultivation as corroborated by such yield data of course subject to more and more farmers adopting the recommended best farming practices.

261

Table No. 30: **A comparison of the annual cotton production trends for Burkina Faso and Tanzania**

Burkina Faso	3	8	18	23	46	77	69	64	114	257	298	147	207
Tanzania	67	71	42	53	31	48	96	82	41	114	126	67	123

Source: **Technical Centre for Agricultural and Rural Cooperation ACP-EU (CTA)**

Table No. 31: **A comparison of the area under cotton cultivation between Burkina Faso and Tanzania for the period from 1965 to 2008**

Country	Cropping season												
	1965	1970	1975	1980	1985	1990	1992	1995	2000	2004	2005	2007	2008
Burkina Faso	3	8	18	23	46	176	177	210	260	585	630	400	500
Tanzania	283	283	380	387	370	320	430	344	182	500	510	450	510

Source: **Technical Centre for Agricultural and Rural Cooperation ACP-EU (CTA), December 2008**

Nevertheless, the need to raise productivity must be accompanied by efforts seeking to improve quality too. After liberalization, its reputation as "white gold" became lost due to contamination related problems and thence Tanzanian lint became less preferred on the global market as reflected by the loss of the premiums that it used to enjoy prior to liberalization. Unfortunately, under the prevailing price competition model, tackling the productivity and quality issues has proven very difficult because of the large number of ginners and hence vastly contrasting attitudes towards the sustainability of the industry. Thus, in seeking to simultaneously address the twin issues of productivity and quality other approaches are needed, three of which are discussed here:

12.2.1 Contract farming

All over the world, farming is a business just like any other and for which reason cotton farmers too must make money or go out of business. However, because most smallholders are unable to attain economic yields, they often tend to combine farming with other income generating work. One way by which farmers can hope to realize economical cotton yields is by engaging in contract farming. Contract farming offers possibilities for motivating farmers to increase production, productivity and the quality of their seed cotton by taking some of the risks away from cotton farming for example by providing some upfront financing, something which smallholders have increasingly found very difficult to achieve on their own, especially after liberalization. All over the world, conventionally produced cotton has proven to be an extremely input intensive crop. In Tanzania and most other countries in SSA that have tried it, the failure of the competitive market structure to adequately and effectively deal with input credit as well as input supply has been one of the major factors limiting increased production and productivity. Contract farming (CF) offers great prospects for simultaneously increasing cotton productivity and quality by tying smallholders to individual ginners with regard to the provision of critical seasonal inputs, such as certified seed, fertilizers, insecticides and picking bags as well as extension, marketing and other related support services on condition that farmers would in turn sell their seed cotton to the respective ginners with whom they entered into a negotiated and legally binding contract. Furthermore, by linking smallholders directly to investors with the requisite managerial, technological and other critical resources, CF has the potential to bring about the much desired transformation in farm operations from the present peasant/subsistence oriented farming to farming which is more enlightened, increasingly knowledge intensive and market oriented in scope.

In Zambia, Zimbabwe and South Africa (and a lesser extent Mozambique) where cotton production has since the early 1990s been undertaken under CF arrangements, these countries have managed to maintain reasonably high average yields as well as high levels of lint quality primarily as a result of farmers' increased compliance to good farming practices, optimized use of inputs such as fertilizers and insecticides; rigorous grading and routine use of picking bags. As a result, lint exported from Zambia and Zimbabwe has tended to be eligible for premiums on the global market.

Tanzania has been rather cautious with regard to the adoption and institutionalization of CF for conventional cotton production in spite of it being already in use for the production of organic cotton, tobacco and sugar cane. In the cotton growing countries of Zambia and Zimbabwe, CF was until recently being faulted for its lack of a legal and regulatory framework. As a result, both farmers and ginners found the loopholes for engaging in "side selling" and "side buying" respectively whereby farmers deliberately default on paying their credit by selling their seed cotton to some else who was not in contract with them and likewise the ginners buying cotton from farmers who had registered with some other ginners.

Thus, if it is to succeed, contract farming quite often needs an enabling government policy, or even requires that government insist on it. This will ensure buyers cum ginners the controlled competition they need to make contract farming to work. To that end Tanzania resolved to amend the current Cotton Industry Act No. 2 of 2001 with a view to accommodating CF as well as the rules and regulations necessary to make it work efficiently and effectively.

Similarly, to gauge the extent to which farmers and other stakeholders can partake in conventional cotton production under CF arrangements, a pilot study was conducted during the 2008/09 cropping season in the Bunda and Musoma districts of Mara region. It was on the basis of the results from the pilot study as well as the inclusion of a legal-regulatory framework for guiding CF that cotton stakeholders at their biennial meeting held on 12th May 2010 unanimously resolved to have contract farming formally adopted and institutionalized. Basically, the legal-regulatory framework will seek to deal with two potential and critical challenges besetting CF.

On the part of the commercial partner, the framework would like to ensure that the commercial partner, often with monopsony powers, does not renege on the contractual arrangements when the crop is ready, say by offering lower prices or imposing higher quality standards. In the case of farmers, it will seek to ensure discipline in collective action for the producer organization to meet the terms of the contract and especially to ensure that members resist the temptation of side sales. In spite of its unanimous adoption at the stakeholders' meeting held in 2010 as well as the massive moral and material support which contract farming has been getting from the Gatsby Charitable Foundation, getting it to work all over the cotton growing areas is likely to become a major challenge.

The adoption of CF for conventional cotton production is likely to be problematic albeit initially in view lessons gained from the organic cotton experience. The major huddle would seem to be with regard to the failure on the part of farmers to grasp the logic behind CF and especially the significance of abiding to the contractual obligations. Under organic cotton farming farmers outside the project area often tended to channel their seed cotton to their neighbours in the contract area due to higher prices being paid for organically grown cotton. Similarly, when pest pressure was high, farmers in the project area took to their neighbours growing conventional cotton for provision of insecticides. Thus, where adjacent ginners offer differing incentives under CF problems are likely to emerge by way of side selling or side buying.

The Swiss supported project on organic cotton production under the company called biORE started in the early 1990s in the Meatu district of Shinyanga region. By 2009 the number of participating farmers had risen to 1,626 from 722. The area under organic cotton production also expanded from 3,318 ha in the early 1990s to 9,580 ha by 2009. Annual lint output rose from 750 tons in the 1990s to 1634 tons by 2009 making Tanzania the third leading producer of organic cotton in the world after Turkey and Syria. Other producers include China, USA, Uganda, Egypt and Burkina Faso. Nevertheless, the amount of organic cotton produced in the country amounts to just less than 1.5% of the total annual cotton output. During the 2008/09 marketing season a total of 175,113 tons of organic cotton was produced worldwide from an area of about 250,000 ha in 22 countries accounting for 0.76% of global cotton output.

While the statistics look quite impressive, attempts to have the production of organic cotton extended to other areas have proven futile. Considerations, such as a niche market, certification huddles, practical problems of growing organic cotton under tropical conditions, economics of producing organic cotton, among other factors, have tended to limit production. Nonetheless, difficulties experienced while monitoring to ensure that only organic cotton is bought as well as ensuring that pesticides are not smuggled and then used on organic cotton have also contributed to limiting its expansion.

To date, CF has become accepted as a norm in only a few crops such as tobacco, sugar cane and cut flowers all of which share some common features, such as being linked to a relatively small number of buying companies and where there are some special marketing requirements relating to product quality. In spite of its well known potential for increasing productivity and improving quality, the introduction of CF to the cotton industry has tended to be passively resisted and mainly by certain segments of the stakeholder community.

Opportunistic buyers cum ginners tend to come in two categories; companies or individual persons engaging in one or more cotton related businesses. Both categories have tended to oppose the institutionalization of CF for the main reason that its requirement for upfront payment of sizeable amounts of cash for facilitating the provision of designated public goods is being seen as a barrier to market entry. Individual persons who oppose CF do it on grounds that CF is seeking to put an end to activities of middlemen also famously known as "marching guys", agents or unlicensed cotton buyers by linking farmers through either their farmer business groups (FBGs) or primary societies directly with the ginners. Private companies and people opposed to CF seek to behave like typical opportunistic hunters, namely, coming in only when market conditions are favourable for big profits and not when risks are high. Such companies and individuals have tended to frequent the cotton market largely on account of its history of easy entry and exit.

The institutionalization of CF has also been facing opposition from some politicians who have the erroneous view that the institutionalization of CF will inevitably culminate in the demise of RCUs. Because the proper functioning of CF largely depends on a good working relationship between a ginner cum cotton buyer and a network of the so-called farmer business groups (FBGs), it is being alleged that the FBGs will bring about the demise of primary societies (PSs) without which the RCUs cannot operate. Such misconception seems to be premised on the prevailing poor state of most PSs in both the WCGA and ECGA. Such views are quite clearly a case of deliberate disinformation or misconception because both the FBGs and PSs are entirely free to enter into contract with any prospective ginner cum buyer in any of the designated area of operation of CF. In conclusion, it may be said that the introduction of CF is being objected to primarily because it seeks to put the more sustainable controls for the operation of the Tanzanian cotton market than has previously been the case.

12.2.2 Village Auction system

In an attempt to deal more specifically with the contamination problem, TCA in the early 2000s, put up before the government a proposal that would have necessitated the use of a centralized village auction system (VAS). The latter was to be used as an instrument for curbing some of the malpractices commonly occurring in cotton marketing in relation to the contamination as well as adulteration of cotton. Up until that point in time the more serious ginners had become genuinely disenchanted with some of the guerrilla tactics that were being deployed by their competitors during the procurement of seed cotton from farmers such as buying before the start of the official season, buying at night and using mobile trucks rather than official buying posts as designated places for all official transactions.

Under the VAS it was envisaged that all seed cotton in the country would be bought at a few designated buying posts within both the WCGA and ECGA on an auction basis. The logic behind the proposal was that mere peer pressure would greatly help in ensuring that each farmer grades his or her cotton prior to its delivery at the designated buying or auction post. The overriding objective behind the auction system was thus to curb contamination and adulteration of seed cotton as well as a series of buying and marketing malpractices such as rampant tax evasion; under-reporting/ or falsification of seed cotton procurement data by some ginners. Perhaps more importantly, the VAS was being seen as a credible post liberalization era policy instrument for the strengthening of primary societies as well as institutionalization of credit lending to primary societies or farmers associations.

In spite of its apparent appeal and potential benefits that it would confer to the cotton industry as a whole as well as broadening the possibilities of rebuilding many of the PS in cotton areas, the VAS initiative ended up being a non-starter. From purely a legal and regulatory perspective, the deployment of the VAS would have necessitated the amendment of the existing cotton statute that still provides for seed cotton to be bought from virtually any buying post provided that it has been duly inspected and passed by TCB. Secondly, there exists on a countrywide basis a huge shortage of suitable warehouses that would constitute suitable auction posts.

To date, most of the warehouses that were constructed by TLSMB several decades back and which are currently under the ownership of PS are totally inadequate and woefully dilapidated. It is precisely for this reason that most private cotton buyers tend to lease privately owned houses and warehouses for the storage of their seed cotton. Thirdly, implementation of the VAS could not take off presumably because of the potential risks that would arise such as collusion amongst the buyers; increased operational costs and in particular security risks arising due to the movement of substantial amounts of money over vast distances given the poor rural road infrastructure.

12.2.3 The Warehouse Receipt System

Like the VAS and CF, the potential of the WRS to significantly contribute to the reduction of the level of seed cotton contamination prior to its sale or ginning was premised on the assumption that through peer pressure being exerted during cotton buying, there will be little incentive for one individual to engage in the non-grading of seed cotton as well as its adulteration before sale if the chances of being detected or exposed remain very high throughout the marketing chain.

However, unlike CF and VAS, the WRS also has the added advantage of utilizing farm produce as collateral for bank credit, something which allows the owners to sell their lint and cotton seed directly to either an overseas buyer or a local ginner without having to sell through a third party as is the currently the case in Tanzania. Perhaps more importantly, although CF, VAS and WRS have the potential to foster and strengthen the emergence of a true cooperative spirit amongst farmers, in the case of the WRS success is entirely dependent on the existence of strong primary societies without which it cannot hope to be implemented successfully.

The WRS was introduced under the aegis of the Common Fund for Commodities (CFC) funded project on the Coffee and Cotton Market Development and Promotion in Eastern and Southern Africa and has since then become quite successful with regard to coffee but not cotton marketing. Its extension to cashew marketing in Mtwara region during the 2007/08 marketing season aroused so much interest and publicity that some political pundits became convinced that the WRS is the new panacea for all crop marketing related problems arising after crop marketing liberalization.

The use of the WRS with respect to cotton marketing began during the 2003/04 marketing season in the ECGA where due to the lack of a reliable market outlet for farmer's cotton after crop marketing liberalization, farmers found it difficult to sell their relatively small quantities of cotton that they had produced. To solve their marketing problems they opted for toll ginning coupled with use of the WRS an idea that was pioneered by cotton farmers of the Oridoyi Primary Society in Babati district in Manyara region. Under the leadership of their primary cooperative society, they secured a bank loan from CRDB bank using their seed cotton as collateral. The loan was then used to pay for transport of their seed cotton and subsequent ginning at the KNCU ginnery in Moshi as well as a first partial payment to all members. Both the lint and seed were subsequently sold off and the proceeds thus obtained used to repay the bank loan and accrued interest. The remainder of the cash was then given back to the members of the PS as a second payment. Farmers of the Oridoyi Primary Society have since the 2003/04 marketing season managed to raise cotton output from 19,462 kg of seed cotton produced during the 1999/00 marketing season to 916,925 kg by 2005/06.

Attempts to introduce toll ginning coupled with the WRS in the WCGA where several cotton buyers were already competing among themselves and against several cooperative unions for the purchase of seed cotton from farmers proved quite difficult. During the 2005/06 marketing season, an attempt to introduce toll ginning with WRS at the Manawa ginnery in Misungwi district of Mwanza region crumbled to dust, simply because NCU which owns the ginnery thwarted the initiative apparently for fear that its most reliable PS nearest to the ginnery would have become cut off, thus, rendering NCU redundant. In other words, by marketing its cotton directly to overseas buyers, the PS would have essentially by-passed NCU that has for many years been acting as its de facto third party in cotton trade.

Similarly, during the 2007/08 marketing season, the WRS with toll ginning was first introduced at the SHIRECU ginnery of Uzogore by a local firm called Sibuka FM. In that season less than 50 tons of seed cotton were obtained through the WRS. In the following season, the company tried to extend the system to two more PSs within Meatu district, but such attempts proved futile because farmers preferred to get paid for their seed cotton at the prevailing market price and in one installment rather in two or three installments that is typical of the WRS. Mara region has tended to offer far better prospects for the establishment of the WRS coupled with toll ginning because its PSs were recently re-established and which for lack of a RCU as in other regions would tend to operate without any managerial restraints capable of being imposed by it. However, because all the ginneries that were previously under the defunct Mara Region Cooperative Union are still under liquidation, attempts by some of the PSs to introduce the WRS using privately owned ginneries have so far proven unsuccessful.

On the basis of experiences so far gained in coffee, cashew and cotton marketing involving the WRS, it is evident that the quality of management as well as membership of cooperative PS or any collective group of farmers, is critical for its success. This is exemplified by the continued utilization of the WRS with toll ginning in the ECGA, but, not in the WCGA. In the latter, cotton cooperatives are extremely beleaguered by a multitude of structural, managerial, operational and financial problems that tend to greatly constrain the adoption of WRS with toll ginning. Because the WRS works quite well with either a cooperative PS or where a group of 30 or more people have voluntarily agreed to collectively market their commodity by the WRS, some people and especially politicians from the opposition political parties, have tended to instill a sense of fear towards the WRS by alleging that the push by government to introduce the WRS is in fact a veiled attempt to resuscitate the cooperatives of the late 1980s and early 1990s. Unfortunately, the public still looks at cooperatives with a great sense of suspicion because of their actions during the 1980s.

The success of the WRS is not only dependent on the quality of leadership of a PS or a voluntary group of people but also on some unique features of the commodity being marketed. One of the false assumptions made regarding the WRS has been that because it has worked well for some crops, it can similarly be applied to all other crops including cotton. Considerations such as the need for cotton to be ginned prior to export, the need for Tanzanian lint to be exported during a particular period of the trading calendar as well as who owns the ginning facilities, may determine whether or not WRS works or does not work for cotton. Tanzania and other cotton producing countries of the southern hemisphere account for only 10% of global cotton output annually. Such cotton has to be sold to the global market cotton between September and November each year if it is to benefit from cotton trade because after that window the global cotton market becomes flooded by the much bigger crop coming from the northern hemisphere. Thus it can be seen that Tanzania cannot afford to delay the sales of its cotton beyond that window of opportunity because it is a price taker with regard to cotton whose prices are volatile and on a long-term downward trend.

On the other hand, cashew, unlike cotton can be sold internationally either as raw or processed nuts and Tanzania with a global market share of 8% for cashew can influence world market prices by withholding its unsold cashew stocks as it did during the 2007/08. The same is not feasible with cotton where Tanzania has a 0.5% share of global output and it is perhaps for this reason that most ginners often seek to sell their cotton during the July to September trading window. During the 2004/05 marketing season, for example, farmers at the Gula Primary Society in Bunda district could not engage in toll ginning at the Virian ginnery simply because the ginnery owner was under pressure to gin his seed cotton in a bid to comply with contractual obligations abroad. The corollary here is that because the bulk of the operational ginning capacity in WCGA is no longer in the hands of the RCUs but in private hands, the WRS and toll ginning cannot be expected to take off smoothly unless and until either private ginners are compelled e.g. by law to engage in toll ginning only or RCUs have succeeded in recapitalizing their ginning capacity.

12.3 Fostering a value chain perspective to cotton development

Tanzania, like most SSA cotton producing and exporting countries, has been trying to address some of the challenges that are associated with its continued dependency on the development paradigm based on exports of primary commodities. To date, not much progress has been made primarily because stakeholders within the cotton industry have for a long been mainly focused on producing two key products for sale; lint and cottonseed oil. Had a value chain or supply chain perspective been adopted to critically analyze the cotton industry, more emphasis would have probably been directed on the production of a series of value added products such as textiles, garments, vegetable oil and cotton seed cake.

In a generic cotton value chain there are only two primary industries, namely, textile manufacturing and vegetable oil milling from which two final products are obtained: textiles and vegetable oil. Unfortunately, in dealing with the constraints and challenges relating to the two primary industries, the adoption of a sectoral rather than a GVC approach, Tanzania has not been able to highlight the major constraints and hence the likely investment opportunities. For example, the vegetable oil industry as discussed earlier, remains largely undeveloped.

Thus, in spite of increased cotton output in recent years, there hasn't been a concomitant increase in the amount of edible oil derived from cotton seed to help minimize the importation of palm oil from the Far East. Similarly, as a result of limited extraction of cottonseed oil from cottonseed, businesses that would have been based on the use of other by-products of the oil milling industry such as hulls, meal and cake remain relatively undeveloped in spite of the existing potentials. Given Tanzania's huge livestock sector, it is amazing that the needs for its rapidly diversifying industries have remained largely un-factored in the cotton development strategy using the value chain approach.

Two recent global market developments have greatly helped to reinforce the need for cotton development to be approached from a value chain perspective. During the 2003/04 cotton-marketing season for example, some unforeseen market developments in China mainland resulted in local producer prices for cotton dropping from the declared indicative price of 300 shillings per kg of seed cotton to 250 and below. Up until that season, China as the largest cotton producing country on earth was regarded as a "swing factor" for its ability to influence global prices for cotton by acting as a net exporter of cotton in one season and just the opposite in the subsequent season. The abrupt drop in producer price occurred just prior to the 2005 general elections and so the government was compelled to buoy up the producer price by scrapping of some levies as well as reducing the applicable rates for the others lest it face a political backlash due to farmers' furore arising after the price drop. The major lessons learnt were that the continued export of cotton in raw form as well as the inability of our ginners to use price risk management tools had become our Achilles heel in global cotton trade.

During the financial and economic crisis of 2008/09, Tanzania was again rudely reminded of the folly or futility of the development paradigm based on exports of commodities as producer prices for its three major cash crops, namely, coffee, cotton and cashew tumbled on the global market. In the case of cotton, 22,504 out of 123,080 tons of lint (18.3% of the crop) produced in the country during the 2008/09 marketing season, remained unsold by December 2008 due to cotton prices falling from 72 cents per pound FOT in mid-September to 45 by December 30th.

By mid-April 2009, prices had further dipped to 40 cents per pound FOT as a consequence of a rapidly unfolding global financial meltdown and economic slowdown in the USA. Such a deteriorating economic situation occurred barely two months prior to the start of a subsequent marketing season and just one year prior to the next general elections in 2010. Inevitably, the government found itself compelled to provide a rescue and stimulus package lest the commodity industry collapse entirely.

The lesson learnt in the aftermath of the crisis has been that the impacts on the cotton industry would have been far less damaging politically and economically if Tanzania had been exporting textiles and apparel rather cotton lint. In trying to shift from a dependency on exports of raw cotton to exports of textiles and apparel, TCB is increasingly being called to link lint production with its utilization by local mills. To that end three issues have become quite critical and must be addressed soon rather than later, namely, the need to upgrade most of the present infrastructure, the imperative to push for the establishment of garment industries and the need to attract new investments in the textile and apparel industries as a whole.

12.4 Walking the talk on Public-Private Partnership

Prior to liberalization, crop boards and cooperatives were the main players with regard to overseeing the production, processing and marketing of cotton. Due to the monopolies enjoyed by these institutions during the era of the single channel marketing system, they became blamed for many of the inefficiencies associated with the production, processing and marketing of cotton at that point in time. Thus, when evaluated on the basis of the quality of service delivery, cost-effectiveness or degree of reaching the farmer with regard to services such as the provision of input supply, rural finance and marketing services, these institutions tended to score quite low marks.

The introduction of liberalization was thus seen as a strategy for ensuring that the provision of such services would be improved significantly. Liberalization was envisaged to bring that about by delineating the key public, private and shared functions and in the case of shared ones deciding and agreeing on how best they can be shared and funded by members of the private and public sectors. Unfortunately, such demarcation of functions came about in 2006 long after the industry had gone into turmoil.

Box No. 4: **Public, private and shared functions within the cotton subsector**

Public functions:
- Licensing of market entrants at all levels of the value chain
- Setting and enforcing of quality standards
- Provision and dissemination of market information Shared functions:-
  - Provision of seasonal inputs
  - Financing of cotton R & D
  - Development and promotion of the industry
  - Advising on policy and legal matters
  - Coordination of the industry

Private functions – the rest relating to production, processing and marketing

12.5 Enhancing the legal-regulatory framework

Most SSA countries acquiesced to market reforms in general and crop marketing liberalization in particular in anticipation of renewed growth for their economies in general and the agricultural sectors in particular. Nevertheless, the transition from a single channel marketing system dominated by marketing boards and cooperatives to a competitive market was not entirely a smooth one.

In Tanzania and other Anglophone countries, notably Kenya, Uganda and Malawi, their approaches to liberalization nearly culminated in the demise of their commodity sub-sectors that not too long ago were booming. A key factor for the unanticipated results is apparently the fact that the institutional and policy reforms were conceived and implemented without any clear "road map" on how the envisaged new market structure with or without either the crop boards or agricultural marketing cooperatives would operate and take care of things.

In the case of Tanzania, the period between 1994 and 2001 witnessed burgeoning malpractices relating to buying, ginning and export, mainly due to the lack of a legal and regulatory framework, defined as the set of rules, regulations and other legal instruments that are imposed on participants in the sector to enable it to operate efficiently and limit conflicts. The rather fluid market situation came about as a result of an unregulated entry of new and often uninitiated market participants as TCLSB merely acted as a paper tiger in spite of being a de facto regulatory institution.

Rather sadly for the industry, in spite of the Cotton Industry Act No. 2 of 2001 eventually being put in place in 2001 and TCLSB being replaced by TCB, such legal and regulatory framework came just too late for the comfort of the industry. A lot of damage had already been done and correcting for the mistakes as well as the tarnished image of the cotton industry became quite an uphill task indeed. Under the new statute the newly instituted TCB became empowered to improve the efficiency and functioning of the cotton market by licensing of market entrants at each level of the system; setting and enforcing quality standards as well as collating and disseminating market information-tasks which it ought to have taken up on day one after liberalization.

Unfortunately, the change of roles for commodity boards from being instruments for substituting private traders in commodity marketing to institutions for improving the efficiency and functioning of commodity markets was not well received let alone understood by some key cotton stakeholders most notably the farmers as well as politicians. To most such people, the transfer of marketing functions from TCMB to private traders who only operate with a profit motive in their minds was quite unsettling to say the least.

For the same reason, they have become uncertain whether TCB in its new regulatory roles after the demise of TCMB and TCLSB can deliver in stamping its authority on behalf of government over the cotton market. Such uncertainty has subsequently brought about a feeling amongst some people that the government should not in any way let go its grip on cotton and other commodities whose marketing has become liberalized. In other words, the functions of commodity boards should be more and more inclined towards safe guarding and fostering the interests of the numerous resource-poor farmers against the better organized and well to do businessmen.

To reinforce its support to such thinking, the government, with effect from July 2006, decided that commodity bodies as *de facto* state-led institutions operating within the constraints determined by wider government policies and regulations should have their regulatory functions funded directly by government. In the case of TCB, its regulatory functions were up until June 2006 being funded by the cotton industry via a statutory levy charged on cotton exports. The apparent change of policy does seem to have been necessitated by the fact that although TCB's board of directors had representatives from the major cotton stakeholders, TCB tended to be managed more and more as a *de facto* government institution or department rather than as a truly industry owned body which is strictly accountable to the stakeholders.

Policy analysts and IMIs interpreted the new policy decision by government as both positive and well intentioned.

Politically, the government was seen as doing the right thing for easing the tax burden on smallholders by scrapping off the statutory levies. Because market regulation is a core function of the state and crop boards undertake it on its behalf, the decision to finance the functions of crop boards directly from the treasury rather than the levies was therefore quite logical. TCB and other crop boards warmly welcomed the policy initiative on a perceived understanding that it would help them circumvent the problems commonly associated with levy collection such as under-collection due to rampant evasion, under-declaration of crop purchases by crop buyers as well as the annual seasonality of revenue inflows occasioned by vagaries of weather and other calamities that tend to have a bearing on crop size.

However, after just a season of implementation, crop boards became quite disillusioned with the new financing mechanism. Contrary to their expectations, disbursements from government not only declined by fifty percent or more, but were also made way out of phase with the peak periods of demand in their working calendars. By 2010 all crop boards found out to their dismay that they had become significantly worse off financially than they were prior to 2006. Such declines in funding have spelt disaster for commodities such as cotton and tobacco. In view of their annual cropping cycles and their association with numerous poor farmers in semi-arid areas of the country, they often tend to require more frequent monitoring and supervision. So, if one wanted to disband these entities, as well as curtail the production of key commodities in the country, the most effective way would be to cut off funding.

Another unanticipated outcome associated with the commodity sub-sector becoming funded centrally from the treasury was the issue of commodity boards becoming increasingly subject to regulatory capture and politicization. In a nutshell, while crop boards as state regulatory agencies were created to act in the public interest, they instead act in favour of the commercial or special interests that dominate in the industry or sector for which they have been charged to regulate.

Consequently, commodity boards have become prone to frequent and unwarranted interventions in the functioning of the markets that they regulate. As can be seen most such interventions are motivated by vested rather than public interests. Although each commodity sub-sector has had its own share of such interventions, the cotton sub-sector is rife with such episodes; the abolition of the "pass book system" in 2008/09; the *ad hoc* launching of the voucher scheme; the targeted liberalization of pesticide use on cotton during the 2009/10 seasons and the abortive introduction of the WRS constitute a good testimony.

Partly as a result of such ad hoc intervetions, the widely anticipated recovery of the cotton subsector has so far failed to materialize. In the end stakeholders have tended to become extremely wary of most government initiatives. So, while markets are not perfect because they are run by humans who also make mistakes, it becomes even more dangerous if the same humans run government where they make different and often more costly mistakes largely for political and economic gain because in the end it is the taxpayer who pays.

Paradoxically, challenges such as those cited above tend to be associated with the so-called "regulatory boards" rather than the other so-called "regulatory authorities". The latter, such as the Energy and Water Utilities Regulatory Authority (EWURA), the Surface and Marine Transport Regulatory Authority (SUMATRA), the Tanzania Communications Regulatory Authority (TCRA), the Social Security Regulatory Authority (SSRA) and quite exceptionally the Bank of Tanzania (BOT) seem to operate more smoothly and predictably. One point is quite clear though. With perhaps the exception of BOT, these regulatory authorities tend to operate with financing from sources other than government coffers and perhaps for this reason they are fairly independent and with a lot of clout in their areas of jurisdiction.

On the other hand, in spite of overseeing a very dominant subsector that accounts for up to 65% of Tanzania's total merchandize exports, commodity boards are neither well respected nor as effective as is the case with the "regulatory authorities". Thus in spite of these bodies also having their own boards of directors, they still lack the clout and the independence being enjoyed by the "regulatory authorities". Because crop boards tend to oversee the development of a major and critical sector in the economy, their status, at least in the past, was well recognized when up until the early 1980s they were referred to as "crop authorities".

Their status became downgraded after market reforms presumably on the assumption that agriculture would become less important. Amazingly, in the USA, the EU, South Korea and Japan their governments tend to strongly protect their relatively small groups of very rich farmers. In Tanzania, the institutions purporting to help and protect several millions of very poor smallholders have become just as weak as the farmers they seek to protect.

Problems being faced by crop boards in the enforcement of the legal and regulatory frameworks of their respective sub-sectors tend to be exacerbated by the weak collaboration from the LGAs. The latter, in the case of cotton, apart from being an overseer of rural development, they are also expected to facilitate the enforcement of statutes such as the Cotton Industry Act No. 2 of 2001 and its regulations as enacted by central government. Nevertheless, in spite of the vast sums of money collected by way of district crop levies charged on cotton on an annual basis, the LGAs have quite often been reluctant to collaborate with TCB in the enforcement of the cotton statute and its regulations and in promoting the welfare of the industry in general.

On the other hand, because LGAs are also mandated to make by-laws, some of their by-laws have tended to conflict with some of the main laws issued by central government. Some of the examples to this effect were discussed earlier in connection with levies and taxes. Similarly, because some of the staff under the LGAs tend to engage in one or more of the cotton related businesses such as seed cotton buying, selling of and distribution of seasonal inputs on behalf of the ginners, they tend to be formidable accomplices to the malpractices committed by some cotton buyers cum-ginners and so quite naturally they will not support TCB during the enforcement of rules and regulations of the cotton statutes. Thus, unless and until the issue of conflict of interests is resolved institutionally, TCB will continue to find it very difficult to provide the level playing field that is badly needed for a truly competitive market.

12.6 The need for a reform of the global trade regime

The financial and macroeconomic reform programme that was undertaken by DE between the mid-1980s and early 1990s, was largely aimed at bringing about the integration of their economies into the globalization process through trade. Because the bulk of the 30 percent of the cotton lint that annually crosses international borders before it is consumed by the textile and apparel industries comes from the commodity dependent countries of SSA, the importance of international trade for their overall economic development cannot be over-emphasized. International trade is also of particular significance to cotton because much of the world's cotton that crosses international borders at least once more before getting to its final consumers in the form of yarn, fabric and clothing, comes from SSA.

Nevertheless, Tanzania and other cotton exporting countries have yet to fully benefit from agricultural trade in general and cotton trade in particular. Largely on account of the OECD countries imposing barriers to agricultural merchandise from DE and depressing global prices for cotton by way of trade distorting subsidies, the share of agricultural exports destined for the industrial world has stagnated over the years. It follows, therefore, that due to their vast comparative advantage in agriculture, developing countries have quite naturally been pushing for agricultural trade reform in order to better integrate this sector into global markets.

Discussions to reform the global trading regime have been going on for ages and under the ongoing discussions agriculture has tended to dominate the agenda primarily because of its interest to both the DE and AE and in particular due to its controversial nature. Nevertheless, because it commands the highest levels of trade distortions, agriculture offers, perhaps the greatest potential for gains from trade reform.

To date the major objective of on-going discussions on agriculture is simply to lower trade barriers around the world that would allow countries to increase trade globally. At a meeting held in Qatar in 2001, the Doha Development Round (also referred to as Doha Development Agenda or simply DDA) negotiated on a number of issues relating to market access and on the need to reduce and ultimately eliminate all forms of export subsidies as well as bring about substantial reductions in trade distorting support. During the meeting a group of SSA countries, the so-called C4 countries comprising of Benin, Burkina Faso, Mali and Chad came up with the famous Cotton Initiative as a battle cry for all cotton producing and exporting SSA countries to have all distortions caused by domestic and border policies of the industrial countries eliminated quickly.

In their submission, the C4 countries reiterated the plight being suffered by cotton farmers in SSA due to their countries failing to benefit from the international trade due to distortions caused by export subsidies as well as tariffs imposed on raw cotton, textiles and clothing imports into the OECD countries. It is widely being acknowledged that a global deal that curtails trade distorting subsidies, removes all merchandise trade barriers and raises global prices, would be extremely beneficial for cotton as it will go on to directly benefit incomes of millions of the world's poorest farmers. It has been estimated that if all trade barriers in agriculture, services and manufactures were reduced as a result of the conclusion of the Doha Development Agenda say by 2015 there would be an increase in global welfare of between100 and 300 billion USA dollars.

Nevertheless, international trade is still facing many restrictions in spite of some progress having been made to reduce some of the rules and regulations that have governed such trade for ages. The issue of cotton subsidies is one case in mind.

Stiglitz has summed up the wider ramifications of protectionism as follows:

Box No.5: **Stiglitz summarization of the implications of protectionism**

----- "In the most recent trade talks, for example, enormous attention has focused on developed countries' protection of their agricultural sectors – protection that exist because of the power of vested agricultural interests there. Such protectionism has become emblematic of the hypocrisy of the West in preaching free trade yet practicing something quite different. Some 25,000 rich American cotton farmers, reliant on government subsidies for cotton, divide among themselves some US dollars 3 billion US dollars 4 billion dollars a year, leading to higher production and lower prices. The damage that these subsidies wreak on some 10 million cotton farmers eking a subsistence living in SSA is enormous. Yet the USA seems willing to put the interests of 25,000 American cotton farmers above that of the global trading system and the well-being of millions in the developing world. If those in the developing world respond with anger, it is understandable".

As a result of commodity prices remaining artificially low due to subsidies and trade barriers being imposed by a few rich industrial countries, DE countries, in spite of their comparative advantage in agricultural goods, have tended to be unable to exploit their comparative advantage in cotton production. Such measures have tended to undermine quite severely the opportunity of millions of the people still working on the land to trade their way out of poverty. Thus, unless and until the global trading regime is reformed, there will be no hope for cotton prices to become more remunerative in both the short and long run.

WTO meetings on the Doha Development Agenda (DDA) have tended to frequently end up in a stalemate before collapsing eventually. At the Cancun Ministerial Meeting in 2003, the north–south divide was most prominent as a result of issues of farm subsidies in agriculture becoming the major sticking point. The meeting ended without agreement on a negotiating framework as some developing countries walked out because of lack of movement on agriculture. In 2005 the Hong Kong Ministerial Meeting similarly ended with very limited agreement, the most significant accomplishment being the setting of a 2013 deadline for ending agricultural export subsidies. Recently, talks at the WTO stalled thus forcing it to call a de facto suspension of the Round ostensibly over the failure of members to agree on the next steps in the agricultural negotiations.

The repeated failure of the talks on the Doha Round as well as the lack of progress over most of the key issues is increasingly being attributed to the emergence of a new architecture of power politics in the international community with Brazil, China and India increasingly being pitted against the USA. Such trend does seem to have also undermined the credibility of the WTO as a multilateral trade governance body. The world is now increasingly marked by trading blocks thus raising concerns that trade is no longer multilaterally oriented but rather regionally or even bilaterally oriented as a result of the WTO becoming increasingly unable to govern trade.

The EU and USA have since March 2001 and May 2000 been respectively offering preferential market access to exports of a group of African countries through the EBA and AGOA arrangements. Under such non-reciprocal preferential trade agreements (PTA) the EU and the USA have been extending market access to developing countries in order to promote their integration into the world trade system and thereby contribute to their economic development as well. Among the many sectors eligible under the trade agreements, the textile sector is obviously a key one for the DE. Because in the process of making clothing, apparel assembly is the most intensive in low skilled labour, and because this factor is relatively abundant in DE, they have a comparative advantage in engaging in low-wage cost operations.

Nevertheless, EBA and AGOA have different product specific rules of origin (PSRO) that determine the criteria for apparel to be entitled for duty-free access under these preferences. Under EBA production from yarn entails that a double transformation process must take place in the beneficiary country with the yarn being woven into fabric and then the fabric cut and made-up into clothing. Restrictive rules of origin (RoO) have apparently contributed to an under-utilization of the EBA regime in Tanzania and most DEs. The compulsion for clothing products to be made from domestically produced fabrics or fabric from EU countries has become a major supply-side constraint for countries such as Tanzania that do not yet have the capacity, either to produce quality fabrics locally, or to provide competitive fabrics that can be used as inputs to exports. As a result, most apparel exports from Tanzania do not yet qualify for preferential treatment in the EU market. Similarly, because Tanzania has not quite diversified its export structure or even invested in new industries with the aim of promoting industrialization, it has instead concentrated on primary commodities and low skilled, labour intensive manufactures – in other words, preferential market access on its own is not sufficient to solve supply-side constraints of Tanzania and other DE countries.

On the other hand, AGOA which confers duty-free access to apparel regardless of the origin of fabric used to produce it, tends to allow lesser developed countries to use third-country fabric and still meet the criteria for AGOA preferences, meaning that African producers can purchase fabric from cheaper sources. Thus, under the special rule "SR", the PSRO for apparel under AGOA consists of a "single transformation" requirement. This means that a specific apparel product produced in a qualifying African country using third country fabric can gain preferential access in the USA but not to the EU. In a nutshell, the AGOA SR has altered the relative incentives of SSA producers selling to the USA and EU market by removing any restrictions on the origin of fabric used to produce clothing. The relaxation of RoO by allowing the use of fabric from any origin tends to allow for increased exports of apparel and broadens the range of apparel exported by DE to the USA. Not surprisingly, Tanzania and other SSA countries would seem to have benefited more from AGOA than from EBA.

12.7 Concluding comments
The first decade of the 21st century showed that some of the constraints and challenges that may have been holding back the development of the cotton industry in Tanzania for much of the 20th century are not totally insurmountable. Thus, between 2004 and 2009 the country witnessed cotton output exceeding 100,000 tons of lint on three occasions for the first time in over one hundred years. Partly due to such

increased output and thence exports of cotton, the country did not quite significantly feel the impact of the global economic and financial crisis of 2008/09. A bumper harvest obtained in that season greatly helped to cushion the economy in spite of the prevailing low cotton prices. It is, therefore, in Tanzania's own interest to boost commodity output and thence exports.

As a result of new production technology, average global yields for cotton rose to a biological peak of 790 kg of lint per ha (approximately 2000 kg of seed cotton per ha) in 2007.The adoption and utilization of currently available best farming practices in Tanzania has the potential to enable most cotton farmers to work towards bridging the huge yield gap of up to four times that currently exists between Tanzanian average yields and the global average. Cooperation between the private sector and the government can help bring this about by facilitating farmers to adopt new technology that not only raises yield but also reduces the unit cost of producing cotton.

Cotton farmers have increasingly demonstrated the willingness to transform their peasant and subsistence farming to farming with a business and profit motive in mind. Thus, during the ongoing CDTF sponsored annual nationwide cotton farming competitions, the awards being provided to regional and zonal winners have acted to catalyze more farmers to increasingly adopt better farming practices and thereby raise seed cotton yields in excess of 2000 kg/ha. Thus, efforts by government to similarly support farmers growing cash crops to boost output by way of subsidized inputs and facilitation on the uptake of new technologies as has been the case for food crops are to be commended.

Because the biggest constraints to increased cotton output in Tanzania relate to limited seasonal input use as well as non-compliance with best farming practices, attempts being taken by government to boost seasonal input use are not likely to bear fruit unless and until there is a requisite institutional arrangement for that. One model that offers such possibility is CF. Paradoxically, in spite of its utility for the production of a series of other key cash crops such as tea, tobacco, sugar cane, cut flowers as well as seed production for designated food crops, CF has been facing significant opposition with regard to its institutionalization for the production of conventional but not organic cotton. Reasons for such opposition were discussed earlier. It is quite gratifying to note, therefore, that the government has finally put its full weight behind the institutionalization of CF just as this book goes into publication.

In most cotton growing areas, the youth population is increasingly flocking to the cities because of the prospects that urbanization and city life seem to offer. Nevertheless, incentives provided at farm level can help to stem such tide and CF would seem to be an appropriate vehicle to do so because it addresses some of the requisite incentives for farming that are currently missing in conventional cotton production. Government investment in improved infrastructure in the rural areas and its commitment to genuine institutional changes coupled with the provision of new technologies and market structures (to facilitate access to markets, assets and finance) under CF may go a long way to providing the necessary incentives to farmers and the youth to adopt farming as a viable business.

Tanzania has a considerable comparative advantage in cotton but its participation in cotton related global trade is being constrained by both the low volumes as well as low quality of the lint that it produces. Unfortunately, the price competition model that Tanzania has been following in the aftermath of the epic market reforms of the 1990s has so far failed to address the twin problem of low volumes and low quality and no doubt the resolution taken in 2006 to raise output to 270,000 tons of lint by 2015 may not materialize. The major lesson learnt points to the need for the government, ginners, farmers and other stakeholders to work more closely together than in the past. Perhaps more importantly, unless and until they earnestly walk the talk on most of their pronouncements about cotton development, history is likely to haunt them. To date sisal shares with cotton a unique place on the Tanzania coat of arms for very good historical, political and economic considerations. This book will have served a useful purpose if cotton does not live to succumb to the same fate that befell sisal.

Chapter 13

POLICY RECOMMENDATIONS

The major thrust of this book has been to review the performance of the Tanzanian cotton industry and how some of the policy and institutional reforms undertaken from time to time have tended to affect its overall outlook. To date, the future of the industry still looks bleak in spite of its enormous potential as well as unsurpassed comparative advantages.

One distinguishing feature of the Tanzanian cotton industry has been its rather chronic underperformance all along the value chain. As a result, there still continues to exist a huge and conspicuous mismatch between what the seed to fibre value chain currently delivers in terms of annual outputs vis-a-vis what it is quite capable of delivering if it were operating optimally.

The underlying factors behind such an undesirable state of affairs are by and large quite well known to most stakeholders. And so what would seem to be missing is perhaps the lack of requisite motivation and collective good will. In this chapter, I seek to re-emphasize some of the priority issues that, in the context of recent developments at local and global levels would seem, at least in my opinion, to be of some critical importance in helping to steer the cotton industry to the pathway of sustainable development.

Chapter 1.0 **Introduction**
- Review the reforms so far undertaken within the commodity subsector to gauge the extent to which public and private partnership can help improve policy formulation as well as governance in light of new developments.

Chapter 2.0 **Cotton: A Global Overview**

- Tanzania should seek to urgently reclaim the unique features of its global position in cotton, namely, its former position of being leader in the production of roller-ginned lint, in the provision of clean and hand picked cotton as well as its capability and reliability in timely delivering its lint to the global market during the critical period between September and December each year.

Chapter 3.0 **Historical Overview of Cotton in Tanzania**

- Antiquated policies relating to the use of force, coercion and intimidation as well as ad hoc government intervention as instruments and tools to boost production of designated food and cash crops should be disbanded forthwith.

Chapter 4.0 **Cotton R & D in Tanzania**

- Rationalize as quickly as possible the structure, functioning, coordination and financing of cotton R & D in a bid to enhance efficiency, effectiveness and delivery of outputs in order to keep pace with current global market trends for the cotton fibre.

- Urgently review the status of variety cum ginnery zone system with a view to advising on more appropriate adjustments that are needed to mainstream the drive for privatization of the production, processing and marketing of certified acid delinted seed.

- Existing best farming practices for cotton in both the ECGA and WCGA need to be urgently reviewed in the wake of new developments particularly climate change and newly emerging technologies that tend to enhance yields and lower production costs.

- Initiate R & D programmes that will allow for mechanized and irrigated cotton farming as well as the introduction and institutionalization of GMO technology.

- Initiate pilot IPM and Insecticide Resistance Monitoring

and Management Programmes with a view to optimizing pesticide use on cotton.

Chapter **5.0 The Saga of the Red Bollworm**

- Urgently update the status of the spread of the red bollworm in the quarantine zone as well as its implications on the future of cotton farming in both the ECGA and WCGA.

- Establish a network of traps both pheromone and light traps (where feasible) to act as a monitoring system for the red bollworm both near and within the existing quarantine zone.

Chapter 6.0 **Cotton Production Trends in Tanzania**

- Quantify by way of a baseline survey the number of farmers actually involved in cotton farming as well as why this changes over time.

- Formalize the use of acid delinted seed for planting.

- Institutionalize the newly established Public-Private-Partnership for seed multiplication, processing and distribution system for cotton.

- Enforce a code for Best Cotton Farming Practices.

- Carefully consider and repackage the incentives necessary to attract farmers to grow cotton as well as maintain their allegiance to cotton farming.

Chapter **7.0 Cotton Marketing in Tanzania**

- Resolve the constraints that result in the commencement of the cotton season being unduly delayed each year and decide on whether or not the start of the cotton season should begin on a designated date.

- Review the need and relevance of the WRS for cotton in the WCGA.

- Put in place modalities that will allow producer prices for cotton to be determined by the laws of supply and demand as is the case for other crops and goods in general.

- Review the storage needs for cotton given the fact that society level storage is awfully inadequate and too badly run down to be able to meet increased cotton output.

Chapter 8.0 **The Ginning Industry in Tanzania**

- Establish policy and regulatory guidelines that will govern the type of ginning equipment that is best suited to serve the Tanzanian cotton market needs

- Provide a framework for the optimized use of ginnery equipment by regulating importation as well as use of existing ones on the basis of age, technology and location.

- Tanzania to urgently build the capacity to have all its cotton tested for quality parameters by adopting the instrument based testing system using HVIs.

Chapter 9.0 **The Textile and Apparel Industries in Tanzania**

- Reverse the policies geared at "production of lint for export to those promoting lint for the domestic textile and apparel industry" instead.

- Revive and strengthen TEXMAT for self-regulation of the textile and apparel industries.

- Urgently rehabilitate and capitalize the textile and apparel mills in the country.

- Promote quality yarn production and knitting in order to boost garment production and thence the increased use of Tanzanian lint domestically; and.

- Invest in the requisite technical and managerial skills development that will allow the textile and apparel industries to take off smoothly again.

Chapter 10.0 **The Cotton Stakeholders in Tanzania**

- Reorganize TCA into an umbrella organization that oversees the interests of associations representing ginners, shippers, farmers, textile manufacturers and the rest.

- Constituent associations of TCA to have codes of service or conduct.

- Review the structure, representation and functioning of stakeholders' meetings.

Chapter 11.0 **Cotton and Politics in Tanzania**
- The government should seek to facilitate the formation of strong and independent agricultural marketing cooperatives or associations that will stand on their own.

- The government, through TCB and other agencies, should urgently establish a robust and functional market information system that will help to keep all cotton stakeholders fully informed on what is going on within the cotton value chain.

- Cotton stakeholders' meetings should be carefully structured and managed so as to help depoliticize them.

Chapter 12.0 **The Future of Cotton in Tanzania**
- Contract farming should be institutionalized as a first step in revamping production, productivity and the promotion of high quality lint in the country.

- The status, functioning, management and financing of crop or commodity boards to be reviewed with a view to building up on their strengths rather than the weaknesses as was exemplified prior to market reforms when they were de facto "authorities" as is the case now for the likes of SUMATRA, EWURA, TCRA, BOT.

- The textile and apparel industries have to date failed to make any significant inroads into either AGOA or EBA. Tanzania should join hands with other SSA countries in negotiating for better deals in relation to the two facilities.

BIBLIOGRAPHY

1. AgCLIR Assessment Tanzania: Tanzania, 2010. URL: http://bizclir.com/galleries/country-assessment-AgCLIR pdf.

2. Ajieh, P. C., A. E. Agwu and A. C. Anyanwu.2008. "Constraints to privatization and commercialization of agricultural extension services as perceived by extension professionals and farmers". *African Journal of Agricultural Research. Vol. 3* (5), pp 343 – 347.

3. Akiyama, T., J. Baffes, D. Larson and P. Varangis.2001. "Commodity Market Reforms - Lessons of Two Decades". *The World Bank,* Washington D. C.

4. Anderson, K., and V. Ernesto. 2006. "The WTO's Doha Cotton Initiative: A Tale of two issues". World Bank Policy Research Working Paper 3918.

5. Anderson, K., and W. A. Masters. Editors. 2009. "Distortions to Agricultural Incentives in Africa". Pp 656. *The World Bank,* Washington D.C.

6. Andrews, D. J.; and A. H. Kassam. 1976. "Importance of multiple cropping in increasing world food supplies". In R.I. Papendick, A. Sanchez and G.B. Triplett, Eds., *Multiple Cropping,* pg 1–10. ASA Special Publication 27, Madison, WI, USA.

7. Baffes, J. 2002. "Tanzania's Cotton Sector: Constraints and Challenges in a Global Environment". *Development Prospects Group and African Region Working Paper Series No.42.* World Bank, Washington D.C.

8. Baffes, J. 2004. "Tanzania's Cotton Sector: Reforms, Constraints and Challenges". *Development Policy Review 22, No.1:* 75 – 96.

9. Bargawi, H. 2008. "Tanzania's Agricultural Institutions in Flux.Lessons from Coffee and Cotton Producing

Villages".NCCR Trade Regulation.Swiss National Centre of Competence in Research. Working Paper No. 2009/20.

10. Bates, R., H. 2005. *States and Markets in Tropical Africa (2nd Edition)*, Berkeley: University of California Press.

11. Beintema, N. M., T. M. Ngaihura and T. N. Kirway. 2003. *Tanzania: ASTI Country Brief No. 3:* 1 – 9.

12. Bell, A. A. 1999. "Diseases of Cotton". In W. C Smith, J.T. Cothren, Eds, *Cotton: Origin, History, Technology and Production.* John Wiley & Sons, Inc., N.Y. USA, pp 553 – 593.

13. Braun, Von Joachim., P. Hazel., C. Poulton., S. Wiggins and A. R. Dorward. 2007. The Future of Small Farms for Poverty Reduction and Growth. *2020 Discussion Paper No. 42.* Washington, DC. International Food Policy Research Institute.

14. Bremmer, I. 2010. "The end of The Free Market". Portfolio/ Penguin.

15. Brubaker, C. L., F. M. Bourland and J. E. Wendel. 1999. "The Origin and Domestication of Cotton". In C. W. Smith and J. T. Cothren, eds., *Cotton: Origin, History, Technology and Production.* John Wiley & Sons, Inc., N.Y. USA, pp 3 – 31.

16. Buckman, G. 2005. *Global Trade: Past Mistakes, Future Choices.* Fernwood Publishing Ltd, Halifax, Nova Scotia.

17. Chambo, S. A. 2009. Agricultural Cooperatives: Roles in Food Security and Rural Development; Paper presented to Expert Group Meeting on Cooperatives; 28 – 30 April 2009, New York.

18. Chaudhry, M. Rafiq and A. Guitchounts. 2003. Cotton Facts. Technical Paper No. 25 of the Common Fund for Commodities, International Cotton Advisory Committee.

19. Christopher, B. B. and E. Matambatsere. 2005. Marketing Boards. *The New Palgrave Dictionary of Economics, 2nd Edition,* (London: Palgrave MacMillan)

20. Coleman, W., W. Gilliam and T. Josling. 2004. *Agriculture in the New Global Economy*. Edward Elgar Publishing Ltd.Corti, C. W. (2005).

21. What is a white gold? Progress on the issues! www.gold.org/assts/files.

22. Cotton Contamination Surveys: 1999-2001-2003-2005-2007. ITMF (International Textile Manufacturers Federation).

23. Cotton: Futures and Options. *New York Board of Trade:* URL-www.nybot.com

24. Coughlin, P. and P. Mworia. 2001. SADC Study of the Textile and Garment Industries: *Tanzania.*

25. Dorward, A. R., J. G. Kydd and C. D. Poulton. Eds 1998. *Smallholder Cash Crop Production under Market Liberalization: A Perspective.* Willingford. CAB International.

26. Ellis, F. 1992. *Agricultural Policies in Developing Countries.* Cambridge Univeristy Press, Cambridge.

27. Estur, G. 2005. "The Competitiveness of African Cotton in the World Market". *Introduction to Special Edition of Cotton Outlook on Cotton in Africa*, March 2005.

28. Estur, G. 2008. "Quality and Marketing of Cotton in Africa". Background paper for Comparative Analysis of Organization and Performance of African Cotton Sectors: Learning from Reform Experience, World Bank, Washington, DC.

29. Estur, G and N. Gergely. 2009. "The Economics of Roller Ginning Technology and Implications for African Cotton Sectors ". Background paper for Comparative Analysis of Organization and Performance of African Cotton Sectors: Learning from Reform Experience, World Bank, and Washington, DC.

30. Fitt, G. P. 1989. The Ecology of *Heliothis* species in relation to agroecosystems. Ann. Rev. Ent. 34: 17 – 52.

31. Gibbon, P. 1998. "King Cotton under Market Sovereignty: The Private Marketing Chain for Cotton in Western Tanzania, 1997/98". CDR Working Paper Sub-series No. ii. 98.17. pp 1- 66.

32. Gibbon, P. 1999. "Free Competition without Sustainable Development? Tanzania Cotton Sector Liberalization, 1994/95 to 1997/98." Journal of Development Studies 36 (1): 128 – 150.

33. Gilbert, C. L. 2006. "Trends and Volatility in Agricultural Commodity Prices". In A. Sarris and D. Hallam, Eds., *Agricultural Commodity Markets and Trade:* pp. 31 – 60. Northampton, MA: Food and Agriculture Organization of the United Nations and Edward Elgar.

34. Gilham, F., T. Bell, T. Arin, G. A. Matthews, C le Rumeur and A. Hearn 1995. "Cotton Production Prospects for the Next Decade".World Bank Technical Paper No. 287.

35. Gilson, I., Colin Poulton, Kelvin Balcombe and Sheila Page. 2004. "Understanding the impact of Cotton Subsidies on developing countries". www.odi.uk/ resources/3608.pdf Goreux, L. and J. Macrae. 2003. "Reforming the Cotton Sector in Sub-Saharan Africa". World Bank African Region Working Paper Series No. 47: 1-67

36. Hildebrand, P. E. 1976. Generating technology for traditional farmers: a multidisciplinary methodology. Conference on developing economies in agrarian regions: a search for methodology. Rockefeller Foundation Conference Centre, Bellaio, Italy, 4-6 August 1976.

37. Hillocks, R. J. 2005. Is there a role for Bt cotton in IPM for smallholders in Africa? *International Journal of Pest Management 51* (2) 131 – 141.

38. Integrated Value Chain Analyses and Implications for Public Private Partnerships: Cases of Maize, Cotton and

Textiles and Tourism. Global Development Solutions; www.GDS.LLC.com.

39. International Cotton Advisory Committee. *Review of the World Situation. Vol. 62* No. 5 May – June 2009.

40. International Service for the Acquisition of Agricultural biotech Applications. Global Status of Commercialized Biotech and GM crops: 2008. ISAAA Brief 39, 2008.

41. Jones, G. B and P. M. Kapingu 1982. "Breeding". In Ukiriguru 50 Years of Research.Tanzania Agricultural Research Organization.

42. Kabissa, J. C. B. 1989.Evaluation of damage thresholds for insecticidal control of *Helicoverpa armigera* (Hubner) (Lepidoptera: Noctuidae) on cotton in eastern Tanzania. Bull. Ent. Res. 79: 95 – 98.

43. Kabissa, J. C. B. 1990. Seasonal Occurrence and damage by *Pectinophora gossypiella* (Saunders) (Lepidoptera: *Gelechiidae). Tropical Pest Management 36:* 356-358.

44. Kabissa, J. C. B. 2004. Pest Control and Sustainable Smallholder Cotton Production: Progress and Prospects. *In Proceedings of the World Cotton Research Conference 3:* Cape Town, South Africa, 9 - 13 March 2003. Edited by Annette Swanepoel. Pp 1261 – 1270.

45. Kabissa, J. C. B. 2005. Cotton Production in Tanzania: Present Status and Future Prospects. Cotton in Africa: Special Feature. Cotton Outlook, March 2005. P 30 – 36.

46. Kabissa, J. C. B. and B. T. Nyambo. 1989. The Red Bollworm Worm *Diparopsis castanea* (Hamps) (Lepidoptera: Noctuidae) and cotton in Tanzania. *Tropical Pest Management 35:* 190-192.

47. Kabissa, J. C. B., E. Temu, M. Ng'homa and F. Mrosso. 1997. Control of Cotton Pests in Tanzania: Progress and

prospects. In: *African Crop Science Conference Proceedings, Vol. 3:* 1159 3: 1159-1166.

48. Kabissa, J. C. B., W. Heemskerk, E. E. Temu and J. Anania. 1998. Effect of Structural Adjustment Programmes on Pest Control in Tanzania: Case Study of *Helicoverpa armigera* (Hubner) on Cotton. In *Proceedings of the World Cotton Research Conference.* Athens, Greece, September 6 – 12. Chief Editor: Fred M. Gilham, pg 818 – 822.

49. Kennedy, G. G and D. C. Margolies 1985. Mobile Arthropod Pests: Management in Diversified Agroecosystems. *Bulletin of the Entomological Society of America. 31:* (3) 21-35.

50. Kherallah, M., C. Delgado, E. Gabre – Madhin, N. Minot and M. Johnson 2002. *"Reforming Agricultural Markets in Africa",* Baltimore: Johns Hopkins University Press.

51. Larsen, N.M. 2003. "Re-regulating a Failed Market: The Tanzania Cotton Sector 1999 – 2002". Working Paper Sub-series on Globalization and Economic Restructuring in Africa. No. XX 111. IIS/GI Kongevej Working Paper 03.2

52. Larsen, N.M. 2003. "Quality Standard Setting in the Global Cotton Chain and Cotton Sector Reforms in SSA. Working Paper Sub-series on Globalization and Economic Restructuring in Africa". No. XX1V IIS/GI/ Kongevej Working Paper Series 03.7. Institute for International Studies, Copen Hagen.

53. Latha, H. 2000. "Profile of Tanzanian Textile Sector". Paper prepared for UNIDO.

54. Lele, U and R. E. Christiansen 1989. "Markets, Marketing Boards, and Cooperatives in Africa. Issues in Adjustment Policy". MADIA Discussion Paper 11, World Bank, Washington, D.C.

55. Lele, U., Nicholas Van de Walle and Mathurin Gbetiobouo

1989. "Cotton in Africa: An Analysis of Differences in Performance" MADIA Discussion Paper No. 7, World Bank, Washington, DC.

56. Linde, Van der M., W. C. S. Heemskerk, E. G. Kaitaba and L. J. Law 1995. "Ginnery Location Study in Tanzania". The Royal Netherlands Embassy, Tanzania.

57. Lundberg, M. "Agricultural Market Reforms". URL: http://Error! Hyperlink reference not valid.

58. Maghimbi, S. 2010. "Cooperatives in Tanzania Mainland: Revival and Growth". Coop Africa working Paper No. 14.

59. Maro, W., and C. Poulton. 2005. "Tanzania Country Report: 2003/04 Production Season". Report produced for the Competition and Coordination in Cotton Market Systems of Southern and Eastern Africa Project, Wye, Imperial College, London.

60. Matthews, G. A and J. P. Turnstall 1968. Scouting for pests and the timing of spray applications. Cotton Growing Review. 45: 115 – 126.

61. Matthews, G. A., and J. P. Tunstall. 2006. "Smallholder cotton production in sub-Saharan Africa: An Assessment of the way forward". International Journal of Pest Management, 52: 149 – 153.

62. Mayfield D. M., W. S. Anthony, Sidney E. Hughs, William F. Lalor and Roy V. Baker. 1999. "Ginning". In C. Wayne Smith and J. Cothren, eds., *Cotton: Origin, History, Technology, and Production*. Wiley Series in Crop Science.

63. Mitchell, D and J. Baffes. 2002. "Tanzania Agricultural Exports: Challenges and Constraints in a Global Environment". *The World Bank*, Washington, D.C.

64. Mueller, S. D. 2006. "Rural Development, Environmental Sustainability, and Poverty Alleviation: A Critique of Current Paradigms". DESA Working Paper No. 11.

65. Murphy, S. 2006. "Concentrated Market Power and Agricultural Trade". Ecofair trade Dialogue Discussion Papers. No. 1/August 2006.

66. Narayan, S., and A. Gulati. 2002. "Globalization and the smallholder: a review of issues and implications". Markets and Structural Studies Division Discussion Paper N. 50. Washington, D.C. International Food Policy Research Institute.

67. Netherlands Development Corporation. 1994. Evaluation of the Netherlands Development Programme with Tanzania.

68. Norman, D.W., Hayward J.A. & Hallam H. R. (1974). An assessment of cotton growing recommendations as applied by Nigerian farmers. Cotton Growers Review. 51, 266 – 280.

69. Nyambo, B. T. 1989.The use of scouting in the control of *Heliothis armigera* in the Western Cotton Growing Area of Tanzania. *Crop Protection 8:* 310 -317.

70. Onumah, G., and R. Butterworth. 2005. Coffee and Cotton Marketing Development and Trade Promotion in Eastern and Southern Africa. *Monthly Report: April 2005: NRI.*

71. Oplas, N. 2008.When Governments Politicize Agriculture. URL: http://www.minimalgovernment.net

72. Osakwe, P.N. 2007. Emerging Issues and Concerns of African Countries in the WTO negotiations on Agriculture and the Doha Round. In Jamie Morrison and Alexander Sarris, eds., WTO Rules for Agriculture Compatible with Development. Trade and Markets Division, FAO, Rome. Pp 335 – 360.

73. Pan, S., M. Welch, S. Mohanty and Mohamadou Fadiga 2006.The Impact of India's Cotton Yield on U.S and World Cotton Markets.Briefing Paper CERI – BP06-03. Cotton Economics Research Institute, Texas Tech University.

74. Pearson E. O. and R. C. Maxwell-Darling 1958. The Insect Pests of Cotton in tropical Africa. Empire Cotton Growing Corporation and Commonwealth Institute of Entomology.

75. Poulton, C., P. Gibbon, B. Hanyani-Mlambo, J. Kydd, W. Maro, M. Nylandsted Larsen, A. Osorio, D. Tschirley and B. Zulu. 2004. "Competition and Coordination in Liberalized African Cotton Market Systems". *World development 32* (3): 519 – 36.

76. Prakash, D. 2000.Development of Agricultural Cooperatives – Relevance of Japanese Experiences to Developing Countries. Paper presented at the 14th ICA ¬Japan International Training Course on "Strengthening Management of Agricultural Cooperatives in Asia" held at IDACA, Tokyo, Japan April 18, 2000.

77. Reed, W. 1965.*Heliothis armigera* (Hubner) Noctuidae in western Tanganyika: II. Ecology and natural and chemical control, *Bull. Ent. Res. 56:* 127- 56:

78. Ruh, A. P. 2005. "The Functions of a Cotton Merchant". Paper Presented to ACSA International Cotton Institute at Rhodes College Memphis TN.

79. Sam, A., Dinsdale, P., MacDonald, D., Martelli, C., Hill, K. and J.C.B Kabissa. 2011. Tanzania Textiles and Garment Development Strategy. Interim Report for the Ministry of Industry and Trade: A study funded by the Tanzania Gatsby Trust.

80. Sarris, A., Sara Salvastano and Luc Christiansen 2006. "Agriculture and Poverty in Commodity Dependent African Countries. A Rural Household Perspective from the United Republic of Tanzania". *FAO Commodities and Trade Technical Paper No. 9*

81. Shepherd, A., and S. Farolfi. 1999. "Export Crop Liberalization in Africa: A Review". *FAO Agricultural Services Bulletin No. 135.*

82. Stiglitz, J. E. 2003. "The Roaring Nineties". Penguin books.

83. Stiglitz, J. E. 2001. *"Globalization and Its Discontents"*. Penguin books

84. Stiglitz, J. E. 2006. *"Making Globalization Work"*. Penguin books

85. Swaine, G., A. C. Evans and J. B. Ward. 1955. The Cotton Red bollworm Problem in Southern Tanganyika. *The E. A. Agric. Journal (1955) 20.*

86. Tanganyika. 1946. "The cotton (Quarantine Area: Sothern Province) Order". *Government Notice 265 of 1946.*

87. Tanzania. 1965. "The cotton (Quarantine Area) Order, 1965". *Government Notice 1965, No. 306. Supplement 60 Cap. 362, pp 19 – 20.*

88. Temu, E. F., and F.P. Mrosso. 1999. "The Red bollworm *(Diparopsis castanea,* (Hamps) (Lepidoptera) and the Quarantine Area in Southern Tanzania". *Ministry of Agriculture Internal Report, Tanzania.*

89. TCB Corporate Strategic Plan, 2007.

90. The Cotton (QUARANTINE AREA) ORDER, 1965 G.N 1965 No. 306.

91. Tschirley, D., Colin Poulton & Patrick Labaste. Eds. 2009. "Organization and Performance of Cotton Sectors in Africa: Learning from Reform Experience". *The World Bank,* Washington D.C.

92. United Nations Conference on Trade and Development: *"The Least Developed Countries Report 2004"* p. 19.

93. United Nations Conference on Trade and Development: *"The Least Developed Countries Report 2004"* p. 27.

94. United Republic of Tanzania.1994. "Guidelines on buying and selling procedures of traditional agricultural export crops".

95. United Republic of Tanzania.2006. "Agricultural Sector Development Programme (ASDP).Government Programme Document".

96. Varangis, P., T. Akiyama and E. Thigpen. 1990. "Recent Developments and Pricing Systems for Agricultural Export Commodities in Sub – Saharan Africa". *World Bank Working papers No. 431.*

97. Wiggins, S., and L. Cabral 2007. "Politics and the Future of Ministries of Agriculture: Rethinking Roles and Transforming Agendas". URL: www.future-agriculture. org.

98. Wiley, R. W. 1979. "Intercropping-its importance and research needs. Part 1. Competition and yield advantages". *Field Crops Abstracts 32:* 1 – 10.

99. Williams, S. 2003. Pesticide Provision in Liberalized Africa: Out of Control? *Agricultural Research and Extension Network. Paper No. 126.*

ABOUT THE AUTHOR

1.0 PERSONAL PARTICULARS
1.1 *Surname:*   Kabissa
1.2 *First name:*   Joe
1.3 *Other names:*   Barry Cheguevara
1.4 *Date of birth:* 22nd April, 1949
1.5 *Nationality:*   Tanzanian
1.6 *Sex:*   Male
1.7 *Marital status:* Married
1.8 *Telephones:*   +255 022 2124511; +255754375898
1.9 *Email addresses:* joekabissa@yahoo.co.uk
                      joekabissa@gmail.com

2.0 EDUCATIONAL BACKGROUND
2.1 PhD (University of Dar es Salaam) 1993
2.2 MSc (Colorado State University) 1983
2.3 BSc (University of Dar es Salaam) 1975

3.0 WORK EXPERIENCE
3.1 Executive Director at the Kamal Group of Companies from July 15, 2010 to date;
3.2 Director General, Tanzania Cotton Board from May 1999 to April 2010;
3.3 Zonal Director of Research and Training, Lake Zone from Sept. 1993 to May 1999;
3.4 Head of Cotton Research at Ilonga Agricultural Research & Training Institute; 1977 - 1993;
3.5 Head of General Entomology Section at Ilonga Agricultural Research & Training Institute, 1975 - 1977

4.0 AFFILIATIONS
4.1 Member of the Entomological Society of America, 1984 to date
4.2 Member of the National Plant Protection Advisory Committee; from 1989 to 1992;

4.3   Team Leader of the National Crop Loss Assessment Survey Team; from 1992 to 1995;

4.4   Member of the International Editorial Group for the World Cotton Research Conference 3;

4.5   Member of the Board of Directors; Quton Tanzania from 2012 to date;

4.6   Member of the Board of Directors; SeedCO Tanzania, from 2013 to date;

4.7   Member of the Board of Trustees; Textile and Garment Association of Tanzania; from 2013 to date;

5.0   HONOURS AND AWARDS

5.1   Recipient of the Best Worker's Award for 1989; Ilonga Agricultural Research & Training Institute;

5.2   Recipient of the Best Worker's Award for 1990; Ilonga Agricultural Research & Training Institute; and

5.3   Recipient of the Best Workers Award for 2003; Tanzania Cotton Board.

6.0 PROFESSIONAL DEVELOPMENT

6.1 Participated at 7, 5 and 2 international conferences, workshops and seminars as well as 10 plenary meetings of the International Cotton Advisory Committee.

6.2 Took part in two consultancy assignments; a Textile and Garment Development Strategy and a Mid-Term Review of the Cotton Sector Development Program.

7.0 SCHOLARLY CONTRIBUTIONS

7.1 A book chapter in the Encyclopedia of Entomology; The African Armyworm, *Spodoptera exempta:*

7.2 10 refereed journal publications;

7.3 5 refereed international conference papers;

7.4 4 non-refereed papers.